BEYOND
ATHEISM,
BEYOND
GOD

BEYOND ATHEISM, BEYOND GOD

THE QUEST FOR TRANSCENDENT BEING

PHILIP A. STAHL

iUniverse LLC
Bloomington

Beyond Atheism, Beyond God
The Quest for Transcendent Being

iUniverse books may be ordered through booksellers or by contacting:

iUniverse LLC
1663 Liberty Drive
Bloomington, IN 47403
www.iuniverse.com
1-800-Authors (1-800-288-4677)

ISBN: 978-1-4759-9824-5 (sc)
ISBN: 978-1-4759-9828-3 (hc)
ISBN: 978-1-4759-9829-0 (ebk)

Library of Congress Control Number: 2013912930

Printed in the United States of America

iUniverse rev. date: 08/14/2013

CONTENTS

INTRODUCTION

Beyond Atheism: Beyond God is intended as a book—end to my series of three earlier atheist books, beginning with *The Atheist's Handbook to Modern Materialism* (2000). What uniquely qualifies me to write this book? Start with my Catholic beginnings as an altar boy and the intensive exposure to standard theology courses at Loyola University in the 1960s. Add to that the fact that I have been an atheist for more than 35 years, during which time I engaged in numerous debates with religious opponents, mainly in Barbados where I lived for twenty years. I have also had atheist essays and letters published in *The Barbados Nation* and *Barbados Advocate News*, as well as in *The Baltimore Evening Sun*.

Beyond my atheist credentials, I hold a Bachelors degree in Astronomy and have been a member of the American Astronomical Society for more than thirty years. I have a Master of Philosophy degree in Physics and have also been a member of the American Geophysical Union for more than twenty five years and the American Mathematical Society for more than twenty years. In other words, I am well qualified to discuss the scientific and mathematical aspects of the theories put forward in this book.

When I included quantum mechanics in my first book, I'd already sown the seeds to advance beyond a reductionist-oriented atheism. If scientific Materialism is ever to ascend beyond the trite atomistic Materialism of the ancient Greek Epicureans, quantum mechanics had to be integrated within it, but most hard core atheists rejected its inclusion. For them, it left too many indeterminate spooks running loose, which were interpreted as metaphysical mind traps.

In the wake of the book's publication and release, I delivered a well-received lecture at the American Atheist Convention in Orlando, Florida, in April of 2001. This basically detailed my path to Atheism, and what provoked me to follow that route out of Catholicism.

Some years beyond that speech, I began more and more to tone down my rhetoric and seek a more nuanced argument format and content. One such point I kept hammering home was that no atheist in his right mind *denies* a deity or god, any more than he'd deny the tooth fairy, the Easter Bunny or Santa. Apart from the fact that denial is an implicit, indirect acknowledgement of validation of the entity, one cannot deny a hypothetical entity for which no empirical evidence exists in the first place.

After completing *Dialectical Atheism,* my previous atheist book, I began to re-examine the premise that atheism needs to be isolated as a separate, skeptical domain. The more I explored this possibility, the more convinced I became that isolating atheism from the matrix of skepticism was unnecessary. It increasingly seemed to me that calling attention to oneself as an atheist was redundant and rational skepticism subsumed atheism as a special subset.

Beyond Atheism Beyond God starts from that original premise, then explores what this means in a world in which we lack absolute knowledge. To fix ideas, I am reminded of the bead analogy of the great cosmologist E.A. Milne. He created the concept of a bead sliding on a string, with its ends defined as 1 and 0, as shown below:

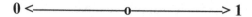

0 <──────────o──────────> 1

Milne argued that this was a useful device by which to gauge one's acceptance of assorted claims, from unicorns, to Martians to God. The 1 end of the string defined absolute certainty, or a probability of 1.0, meaning there could be no doubt at all. The 0 end meant absolute impossibility or an associated probability of zero of occurrence. No truly serious person then could write off God as having probability 0, or putting his bead at the 0 end.

My problems with atheism emerged over the last few years, including:

1- The inability of any two atheists to agree on even basic principles for their positions

2- The tendency of many atheists to abandon the strict position of *absence of belief* and instead attacking others' beliefs outright, hence veering into *anti-theism* as opposed to atheism (the simple withholding of belief in a claim already made).

3- The corruption of epistemological atheism by interjection of irrelevant economic-political overtones, especially libertarianism, which I believe demeaned the atheists asserting it and atheism overall.

4- The inability to forge a rational bridge between weak or implicit atheism and strong or explicit atheism.

5- The self-assured position that one could definitely know that a transcendent or ultimate power did not exist.

6- The ultra-reductionist stance that consciousness is simply reducible to Newtonian classical interactions, and that since the human brain operates by hindsight-based dynamics only, no real time interpretative reality is feasible.

The last especially grated on me and I became more and more aware of it as I argued with believers in assorted groups. As my mindset softened from the strong to the weak atheist position (based on simply withholding belief in a claim for given deity) I appreciated that a component of agnosticism factored strongly into such withholding, and hence I began to describe myself more as an *agnostic atheist*.

The latter avers that all supernatural propositions or claims *are inherently unknowable* by the human mind, because they are untestable, and so not worth discussing, any more than six-inch elves, polka dotted unicorns or fairies. In this sense, unbelief (and even withholding of belief) is not even necessary, since who would actually believe in a pink elf or unicorn enough to warrant defending the opposite position? On this basis, there'd be even less merit to arguing over an invisible Being. Thus, without any capacity for knowledge about it, it is redundant.

It was at this point that I ended my membership in American Atheists because I felt their stance was based more on strong or explicit atheism, and hence incompatible with my own much weaker (implicit) stance. Let me note that this didn't amount to any formal rejection or anything like that, but merely a formal recognition that the American Atheists organization had goals and priorities no longer shared by me. As with a couple in an amicable divorce, the parting implied separate growth directions and emphases, nothing more.

Given this, many may be surprised to learn that I remain a dedicated Scientific Materialist. There is no reason I see to give up that philosophy, and certainly notwithstanding anything I've written earlier. If then Materialism, as I noted in my book, *The Atheist's Handbook to Materialism*, is now really a *physicalism*, then it follows that it must be compatible with Scientific Materialism, including the moral—ethical aspects of:

1- Provisionalism: That is, seeing all ethical judgments as provisional and not absolute or permanent. Because the world and human minds are rapidly changing, so also must ethics.

2- Rejection of all supernatural influences or abodes: In other words, there can be no credible morality or ethics contingent upon fantastical entities such as demons, wights, Satan or abodes such as hell, purgatory and limbo.

3- The replacement of the supernatural concept of soul with the more apt physicalist concept of consciousness which also embraces quantum features.

The effect of these changes has been to pave the way for a more realistic, cogent and effective ethics and morality less likely to be exploited by the power mongers or sacred source apologists. The primary aim of this book then is to arrive at a transcendent concept of Being that also surpasses absolutism and naïve or dogmatic deity templates.

If skeptics then charge that no such entity is feasible, they will also have to admit that all hope for humanity to come together is lost. They will also need to concede they are removing a fundamental foundation of meaning for billions. If, on the other hand, religious believers declare that their particular God must prevail and is not subject to questioning by any "infidels", then they have to see they are worshipping a projection of their own minds and not an absolute at all.

This is basically the motivation for Part One. Thus, Chapters I-IV expand further on why simplistic or naïve versions of deity must be rejected, at least by all rational and mature adults. I attend to the U.S.A. especially, since it stands alone among western, industrialized nations in its devotion to childish concepts of deity which keep too many citizens at a backward level of thought Socio-economic data have shown how this form of god-obsession is directly connected to economic inequality.

Basically, as people fall behind in their economic station, they tend to latch onto anything which delivers respite or comfort. The naïve, loving God-as-parent concept fits this need to a tee. But it does so at great cost, preventing the affected populace from seeing how the plutocrats and oligarchs that created the economic inequality are just fine with people clinging to invisible daddies in the sky. Those affected would do much better to rid themselves of such mental shackles, but much of this depends on having an ethical structure in place to justify the change.

There follows Chapter V, which goes far beyond the minimalist ethical structure in my first book, *The Atheist's Handbook to Modern Materialism*. In the current work, I show that a kind of subjective morality already exists which believers claim comes from God, or emerges from their scriptures, special doctrines and dogmas. Hence, they have much more leeway than they think to move forward to truly rationalist ethics and morality.

Part Two (Chapters VI-XII) is mainly concerned with developments in stochastic quantum mechanics and why and how they encouraged me to change my reductionist mindset. This part is directed more at hard core atheists with a scientific-mathematical background. However, much information can still be plumbed from the more descriptive sections. As I show, many of the quantum concepts (e.g. nonlocality) support emergence and possibly holistic transcendence.

This broadened perspective, away from hard core mechanistic reductionism, led me to examine David Bohm's version of modern quantum mechanics. In effect, Bohmian quantum mechanics will figure into much of the content, and this presumes some mathematical background. Quantum mechanics ultimately is a mathematical theory that doesn't lend itself to facile analogies or descriptive language. Nevertheless, I have tried to keep the majority of equations confined to the Appendices.

The Appendices embody mathematical details that I believe will overtax even the mathematically-savvy if incorporated into the main text. So there I look more closely at Bohm's pilot wave thesis and the evidence for it. I show more applications of the quantum mechanics mentioned in the main text, and then expand on how one might engage a higher unitary Being by exploration of several esoteric aspects. These include: the holomovement of David Bohm, John Cramer's offer and echo waves, retarded time potentials and parallel universes as embodied in the Multiverse conjecture.

PART ONE

BASICS & REFERENCE MARKERS

I: OF GOD AND GOD-CONCEPTS

According to a number of surveys, including those sponsored by the Pew Forum on Religion and a June 3, 2011 Gallup poll, more than 9 in 10 Americans believe in God. Ah, but what specific kind of God? Parsing the same surveys, roughly 55 percent of Americans believe in a God who is capable of counting every hair in each human's nose, and on his or her head. Meanwhile 40 percent believe in a deity far more remote, and often to the extent it barely qualifies as a divinity. Among these are the Deists, whose beliefs I summarized in Chapter 1 of my second book.

The fact is that when Americans' beliefs are micro-analyzed, they're found to adhere to more gods than for which they're capable of articulating attributes! More astounding, detailed religious test-form surveys show that they don't even know that much about their own 'good Books' or religions! Many others attribute the concept *Do unto others as you would have them do unto you* to Jesus, when this principle underscores all cultures and religions dating back into antiquity to the time of Hammurabi, Confucius and perhaps beyond[1].

---

[1]   Epstein: *Good Without God*, 113.

Susan Jacoby documents further gross deficiencies in Americans' religious knowledge[2]:

A majority of adults, in which is supposed to be the most religious nation in the developed world, cannot name the four Gospels or identify Genesis as the first book of the Bible.

What this shows is that if Americans can't even parse their own revelatory sources, they also can't have a serious grasp of anything supernatural and transcendent. They would certainly be challenged to properly parse and separate supernatural concepts according to the rigorous criteria set out by Pascal Boyer who notes[3]:

The information contained in key tags of the statement or concept must contradict information provided by the ontological category.

Therefore all terms set out in supernaturalist contexts, i.e. force, thought, knowledge, acts etc. *must contradict the tag in a known (physical) ontological category*. For example, *supernatural force* must be shown to contradict physical force, say given by Newton's 2nd law of motion ($F = ma$) and be explained in depth to show its workability in a supernatural domain. This extends to supernatural ethics and why it contradicts normative human ethical expectations. Apart from this, almost four-fifths of Americans believe in miracles but associate them with everything from nature's beauty or order and serendipitous coincidences to hearing God's voice in terms of evidence for supernatural intrusion

---

[2]   Jacoby: *The Age of American Unreason*, 25.
[3]   Boyer: *Religion Explained: The Evolutionary Origins of Religious Thought'*, 51

into human lives. This is according to a 2008 Pew Forum on Religion & Public Life survey[4].

On further questioning, few Americans who accept miracles appreciate that an agent which so interjects itself in the temporal world, thereby using finite energy to effect a miracle or miraculous coincidence, *cannot be infinite or eternal*. But this should not come as a surprise, since Americans often posit contradictory divine attributes that disclose considerable ambiguity about what they think they know, or believe[5].

Consider the assertion that *God is Omnipresent and transcendent*

As indicated by the diagram of Fig. 1 this results in a direct contradiction. For if the circle C defines creation (according to most orthodox religionists) and beyond (gray area) is creator = God, then the two are separate. In this case, God may be said to *transcend* creation, since no simple identification is allowed. However, God is then no longer *omnipresent* which means present *everywhere*: birds, rocks, trees, oceans, lions . . . . even dog poop.

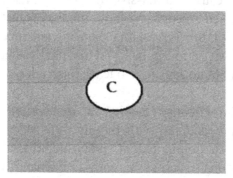

Fig. 1: If creation is denoted by the subset C– and a transcendent creator-God by the external gray then omnipresence cannot apply, since there is no divine presence in C.

---

4   See, e.g. www.religions.pewforum.org/reports
5   Stenger.: 2007, *God—The Failed Hypothesis*, 30.

Thus, a contradiction arises between the attributes *transcendent* and *omnipresent*. A priest of my acquaintance once argued that there can be such a thing as *differentially quantified omnipresence* so the divine presence in humans must always vastly exceed that in dog poop. However, as I pointed out to him, if you differentially quantify the attribute you essentially limit it in specific domains, so in those domains, since there is less of it, the attribute can be said to be diminished.

Given this confusion, it's no surprise that orthodox theists vary greatly in terms of the extent to which they believe their God interacts with the world. After analyzing in-depth surveys for Baylor's Institute for Studies of Religion in 2005 and 2007, Paul Froese and Christopher Bader concluded[6]:

• Most Americans who believe God is highly involved in the details of this life embrace an Authoritative God (31 percent). This entity can be loving but also extremely judgmental and punishing. Perhaps to the extent of directing a tornado into a porn store, or causing a massive disaster in a nation presumed full of "unsaved" people. (Many fundamentalist Christians, in the wake of the Fukushima tsunami and nuclear reactor disaster in Japan, seriously believed that God visited it upon the Buddhist and Shinto Japanese to teach them a lesson or two.)

• 24% of Americans envision a Benevolent God. This entity isn't preoccupied with meting out justice but always involved like a doting parent: inspiring, directing or even physically saving his children, with divine handiwork evident everywhere. Their God doesn't cause disasters but perhaps allows some and prevents others for good reason.

---

[6]   Froese and Bader:2010, *America's Four Gods: What We Say About God—and What That Says About Us*, 4.

In each of these cases, a myopic and self-referential perspective is at work which translates into an arrogant deity that works wonders on behalf of some, but not all people. The latter benevolent deity is especially fascinating in the aftermath of the horrific 2012 Aurora Colorado theater massacre, when 12 were shot dead by an assault weapon wielding murderer, but 58 survived. Among the survivors, all kinds of personal special dispensation stories were narrated afterwards.

One of the surviving victims, Bonnie Kate Pourciau, actually claimed "God was holding us in His hands" as the shooting unfolded, and hence she and her friend Elizabeth managed to walk out of the Century 16 cinema with Bonnie having only one gunshot in her leg[7]. (One wonders, of course, if God really was holding her in His hands, how in His infinite power he could have allowed even that stray bullet to hit her.)

A question arises here for Bonnie Kate and other Personal Divine Exceptionalists: How is it that your God's power did not extend to the others under fire or running for their lives? How is it that He could have allowed little 6-year old Veronica Moser-Sullivan to die? Didn't that child deserve life and survival as much as you did? Why didn't that umbrella of presumably infinite divine power and protection cover all and sundry, instead of just you and your friend?

In the end it really matters not, except again, that The Denver Post gave credence and legitimacy to such shallow views and beliefs by publishing them. The truth is that those like Bonnie Kate and her friend simply lucked out. There was no real divinity clasping her hand except in her mind. It was a case of pure dumb luck that her seat wasn't more directly in the gunman's line of fire.

In this case of pure chance governing one's life events, we find no more than twenty-four percent of the population in agreement, according to the Froese and Bader Baylor

---

[7]   Bartels,, Lynn.: *The Denver Post*, July 26, 2012, 1A

study. These are distinguished by their belief in a distant, unconcerned and unconnected God not dissimilar to that of Deism.

More telling than the previous examples, an online questionnaire posed by Boston University Religious Studies scholar Stephen Prothero. He had the audacity to ask CNN's Belief Blog readers: *Where was God in Aurora?* He found ambiguous results, but with seven basic responses:

1- There is no God.

2- Don't blame God, blame Satan.

3- Don't blame God, blame us (free will).

4- God was behind the massacre, and it was just.

5- God was present at the massacre, but with the victims, not the perpetrator.

6- Which God? (a personal, human-like God is a myth).

7- Who knows? It's a mystery."

These responses reminded me of a telephone poll I took while living in Barbados in 1978, in preparation for an article on God concepts. I'd asked: *What is God?* The answers I received included[8]:

Jesus is God

Jehovah is God

God is love

---

[8]   Stahl, *The Barbados Nation*, Sept. 27, 1978, 14.

God is our Father and the creator of the universe

God is an impersonal, physical energy.

Yahweh is God: the I-AM-THAT-WHICH-I-AM

God is the principle of creativity and action

The great diversity of conceptions of God led me to conclude that what people really meant when they professed "belief in God" was a personal allegiance to a particular *concept*. Invariably, the concept was flawed and limited because it was *abstracted* from a personal background of awareness and conditioning, as opposed to a total comprehension of *actual* being. In other words, the lack of understanding of the underlying entity (assuming there is one to understand) rendered all concepts relative. There is simply insufficient information to distinguish one person's deity as the *one true God* to the exclusion of all others. This then leads to the conclusion that asking a person: "Do you believe in God?" is a useless question, because there are no objective standards for defining the entity. The only rational question one can ask is: "What is your conception of God?" Or "What do you mean exactly when you claim to believe in God?"

This further supports the contention of philosopher Joseph Campbell[9] to the effect that:

'God' is an ambiguous word in our language because it appears to refer to something that is known.

All of which reinforces the point that when people use the word *G-o-d* they're not talking or writing about an actual entity but a limited construct or ideation configured as a noun, which we call a *God concept*. Further, because it's limited

---

9   Campbell.: *The Power of Myth*, 56

7

by content and comprehension, i.e. by finite minds with finite intelligence which can't grasp all aspects, then all such concepts must be relative and subjective. This means that the Jewish concept of Yahweh, the Muslim concept of Allah, the Hindu concept of Brahmin and the Christian concept of the Trinity all stand in the same epistemological relation. From an informational point of view, none can be selected as "true" to the exclusion of the others.

This is completely analogous to there being inadequate information to distinguish one religion's claims as true to the exclusion of all others. In the case of individual religions and religious traditions, the embodiment of the respective truth claim is found in a *sacred revelation*, or holy book. For example, the Holy Bible for Christianity, the Torah for Jews, the Koran for Muslims and the Upanishads for Hindus, each proclaims inherent truths. For many of the respective faiths' followers, these inherent truths are also absolute in the sense they dare not be contradicted.

The problem is that the early writers for each scripture suffered from the same limitation of comprehension as their modern counterparts. A finite neural capacity limited intellectual grasp, irrespective of the particular conceptual allegiance. Take the account in Genesis and how it describes God's behavior: one instant creating the world and calling it *good* and subsequently becoming disenchanted and wiping it out in a flood, while bemoaning that a *mistake* was made.

Now, a genuine God putatively doesn't make mistakes since perfection is surely a fundamental divine attribute. However, a human brain is quite likely to project its flaws onto its concepts and that includes beholding the contrived deity botching assorted events and actions. No one can blame (finite) brains for this propensity, but humans at least need to recognize that they do it!

What of the concepts or god-beliefs themselves? Well, they span the gamut from the pantheistic god of Spinoza, embodying natural laws as Einstein described it, to a personal

God that scrutinizes every deed a human does, to a Deist deity that created the universe then walked away. The point is that none of these can be defended absolutely, no matter how many biblical quotes or dogmas are invoked. They are all relative because our human capacities are relative and finite.

Is there any advantage to be gained by acknowledging that a God-concept is what people are really talking about when they use the noun "God"? I think there is. For one thing, the acknowledged use of the term *God-concept* reinforces the attitude of cautious forbearance mentioned earlier. The implicit relativism acts as a restraint, backing the believer away from a militant stance of absolutism. Ideally, this should dispose him or her to be more tolerant—tolerant toward unbelievers and tolerant toward those of different religions. Far from being wishy-washy, this affords humanity a hope that religious conflicts will one day come to an end. No more Jews versus Arabs, Catholics versus Protestants, or Hindus versus Muslims.

Reaffirming this stance is the take of Jacob Bronowski when he visited Auschwitz and pointed to the gas chambers, in the BBC documentary *The Ascent of Man* and the book by the same name. Bronowksi avers[10]:

This was not done by gas. It was done by arrogance. It was done by dogma. It was done by ignorance. When people believe they have absolute knowledge with no test in reality, this is how they behave.

Bronowski goes on to advise that humans embrace *the principle of tolerance* which he ties to the (Heisenberg) Principle of Uncertainty in physics. As he puts it[11]:

---

[10] Bronowski, *The Ascent of Man*, 235.
[11] *Op. cit.*, 232.

The Principle of Uncertainty or, in my phrase the Principle of Tolerance, fixed once and for all the realization that all knowledge is limited

Because knowledge is limited, and further, the human brain is limited in its processing of it, no absolutist propositions to do with morality or ethics can be entertained either. Nor can one claim an absolutist position in terms of punitive sanctions say if another doesn't accept his deity or beliefs. Hence, the evangelical assertion that an atheist or a pantheist will burn in Hell because he doesn't accept Jesus Christ as personal Savior, is insupportable given the context of a subjective God-concept.

The upshot is that, far from conceding to evil, the acceptance of relativity in God-concepts and their derivative ethics offers an escape from evil. It is an admission of intellectual humility. An admission that human brains are too limited in capacity and function to access the fundamental answers to life, or to have an exclusive grasp (somehow denied to all those of other faiths) of the "one, true God" is therefore liberating.

At the core of seekers' penchant for transcendent meaning, is the search for objective truth. Can such a thing exist, and is it accessible? That is the subject of the next chapter.

In the meantime, acknowledgment of the reality or at least practical primacy of God–concepts is what we're really talking about when using the word *God*. Such acknowledgement also takes us one step closer to a mature and realistic rational ontology devoid of childish wishes, superstitions and fantasies

Beyond that, the acceptance of subjective God-concepts, instead of believing one's use of a God-noun (Allah, God, Jehovah, Yahweh etc.) accesses the literal entity, allows a much needed tolerance to enter. This tolerance then tempers judgments and absolutist dogmas, positions. If we admit *a priori* that our particular God-concept is only relative and subjective then we must also have more respect for others' concepts and be less willing to lord it over them or insist they convert to our own. (The phenomenon of conversion and the missionaries who spend their lives working to achieve that is indeed the ultimate in God arrogance.)

Humility vis-à-vis God-concepts can help to assuage spiritual arrogance and the brash intolerance so prevalent in our culture. This is sorely needed, especially in the wake of the events of September 11, 2001. Not only did the Christian God-fearing denizens of the country demonize Muslims, but non-believers as well. We beheld a sort of jingoistic McCarthy-style religio-regression more strident than the original brand. While ninety percent or more of Americans sought refuge in their churches and prayer groups, atheists remained unfazed and determined not to be beaten into the fold by hysterical fear-mongering. Not surprisingly, atheists' patriotism was questioned, since many of us also stood front and center against the illegal, pre-emptive invasion and occupation of a sovereign state that had nothing to do with 9/11. This reinforced Sam Harris' accurate take on faith[12]:

> Faith is what credulity becomes when it finally achieves escape velocity from the constraints of terrestrial discourse—constraints like reasonableness, internal coherence, civility and candor . . .

Arguably, if God-concepts had been more in play the investment in irrational faith claims would have been much less. This might have prevented a misplaced, intolerant faith from achieving escape velocity post-9/11 to the detriment of all citizens. Non-believers might have felt a lot less like scapegoats, and been less likely to lash out with a more radical "New atheism".

---

[12]   Harris: *The End of Faith*, 65.

11

Sadly, all the monotheist religions reject the judicious temperance that ensures the cautious testing of reality. Each one instead proclaims that it and it alone has the handle on the One True God and all others are wrong, and its followers are unbelievers or heretics. This is a tragic prescription for never ending strife that our intertwined planet can no longer afford.

II. THE TRUTH HURDLE

If by this point it can be agreed that the God-concept is a valid basis for deity comparisons, then there is one more hurdle which must be confronted: that of finding or defining truth. It is recorded in the Bible that Pilate asked Jesus: "What is truth?" Alas, we have no indication a complete response was forthcoming. Perhaps Christ even recognized that the definition was either too open-ended or perhaps more convoluted than Pilate would accept.

The point is that a comprehensive examination of the underpinnings is essential in order to divest the word *God* of its immature overtones and examine it in the radical skeptical sense. This is preparatory to ascertaining if a non-contingent ultimate exists[1].

I begin, therefore, by invoking Gödel's Incompleteness Theorem as an initial barometer by which to show how truth must be limited, irrespective of context. The Theorem,

---

[1]   The attribute associated with this is *aseity*, and first propounded by Thomas Aquinas.

propounded by the mathematician Kurt Gödel in the 1930s, states when paraphrased in non-mathematical form[2]:

> In any consistent system which is strong enough to produce simple arithmetic there are formulae which cannot be proved-in-the-system, but which we can see to be true.

Some radical epistemological skeptics assert that the use of Gödel is obscurantist and intended to bamboozle. Let me be clear that this is emphatically not the case, and I would not be using Gödel's theorem if it wasn't relevant.

George Boole (b. 1815) was a professor of Mathematics at Queens College, Cork and pioneered the discipline of algebraic symbolic logic through two publications, the latest of which was *An Investigation Into The Laws Of Thought*. Basically, Boole showed that logical propositions can be put into symbolic form with no loss of generality. With this symbolic economy a vast array of logical propositions could be tested. For example, Boole in his *Laws of Thought* states[3]:

> We are permitted, therefore, to employ the symbols x, y, z etc. in the place of the substantives, adjectives and descriptive phrases subject to the rule of interpretation, that any expression in which several of these symbols are written together shall represent all the objects or individuals to which their several meanings are together applicable, and to the law that the order in which the symbols succeed each other is indifferent

---

[2]   Gödel: *On Formally Undecidable Propositions of Principia Mathematic and Related Systems*, 58.
[3]   Boole: *An Investigation of the Laws Of Thought*, 21.

14

Given x = white and y = sheep we can therefore say that: xy denotes white sheep, but also yx denotes white sheep, since the order of the symbol doesn't alter the meaning of the conception (combination). Thus: xy = yx

Boole was careful to emphasize that while this illustrates the *commutative law of algebra*, it is not in any sense an actual algebraic multiplication but rather a process of "logical combination" by which xy means a definite conception. More abstractly, Boole allows that since the logic is commutative for the conception, we need not use either xy or yx but simply 'x'. This assumes y has the same meaning as x so xx = x = x^2 [4]:

Again, I have to interject here that we are not seeing any violations of known mathematics, but rather the outcome for a logical process of combination. Boole has simply compacted and simplified notation for logical combinatorial operations, much like the inventors of tensor calculus did with their notation.

Boole's next law is stated[5]:

Signs of those mental operations where we collect parts into a whole, or separate a whole into parts

He illustrates this using the example of letting x = women and y = men. So all people living on Earth is:

x + y = y + x

In this case, the signification is by quality (sex) and numerically, since the total of men plus women (x + y) must equal the total of people living on Earth. Less generalized operations can also apply. For example, let z *denote European*, then:

---

[4]   *Ibid.*

[5]   Boole.: *op. cit.*

$$z(x + y) = zx + zy$$

Denotes European males and females, hence all Europeans! So we have the juxtaposition of two literal symbols to represent their algebraic product as one single population.

Clearly, all this is important given *Gödel's Incompleteness Theorem*[6], which sets definite limits on the extent to which one can extrapolate from an axiomatic system without producing contradictions. Consider then the form which (paraphrased) says: *This formula is unprovable-in-the-system.*

In a more generic sense, the applications of Gödel's theorem go well beyond mathematical formulae or arithmetic axioms to encompass any statements which can be framed in those abstract terms. This is so important to grasp that it behooves me to give examples, starting with a simple statement of logical transitivity:

$$X = Y$$

$$Y = Z$$

therefore $X = Z$

If instead we append an axiomatic statement that reads: *X=Y is unprovable-in-the-system* and this statement is provable-in-the-system, we get a contradiction, since if it is provable in-the-system it can't be unprovable-in-the-system. This means the original axiom:

---

[6]   Gödel, *op. cit.* This is actually the first of two theorems. That is, if an axiomatic system is arithmetically sound one can construct a true statement based on the arithmetic but which is not provable in the axiomatic system itself. Gödel's 2nd theorem assumes the axiomatic system is sufficiently strong and consistent, but that the consistency of the system can't be proven using only the axioms within it.

X = Y is unprovable-in-the-system is false. Similarly, if X = Y is provable-in-the-system, then it's true, since in any consistent system nothing false can be proven in-the-system.

Thus the statement, *X = Y is unprovable-in-the-system* is true.

With these preliminaries, let's examine the logical structure applied to the symbolic sequence of statements:

X = Y

But, $Y \cap Z = \varnothing$

Then, $X \wedge Z$ (contradiction)

Example: Epimenides' *All Cretans are liars* paradox, which itself perpetuates a causal loop with no closure.

Take the statement X = Y: *All Cretans are Liars*

Take the alternative statement X = Z: All Cretans are Truth tellers.

Clearly, Liars (Y) cannot also be Truth tellers (Z), hence the intersection of the set of all Liars with the set of all Truth tellers must be an empty set ($\varnothing$), i.e. there are no members in both.

More technically, if the speaker is a Cretan, then the statement is clearly *ipso facto* unresolvable. If a Cretan, he exists within the so-called abstract, formal system. Yet he's definitely making a statement (meta-) *about the system.* Is he lying? Or, is he telling the truth? This, alas, cannot be resolved, so an undecidable proposition exists as the Gödelian Incompleteness Theorem (II) indicates. Note that while simple and interesting, the Cretans= Liars example only serves to illustrate what a meta-statement is. It doesn't help us grasp the basis for a supernatural or religious concept.

Is there a way out of the meta-loop? Yes! Provided one uses realism-based science to assess statements. For example, in the Einstein equation, $E = mc^2$, scientific epistemology allows us to regard E, m and c as *constructs*, connected via operational definition to the P-(perceptual) facts of energy, mass and the speed of light, c. Thus, we expect a correlation like:

$$C \leftrightarrow P$$

This re-affirms logical closure, physical significance and *no* meta-linkage.

For instance, the operational definition of mass is accomplished by comparing inertias for two different bodies. We use the ratio of their detected accelerations to masses: $m2/\ m1 = a1/a2$ and Newton's 2nd law, say in a collision experiment.

In effect, even if a scientific or research hypothesis includes some open or meta-statements (evidently leaving enough room open for undecidable propositions) there are nevertheless empirical checks and tests that can close the system parameters. Nothing similar exists for supernatural claims embodied in religious concepts.

Consider the statement:

This consecrated bread wafer is the body of Christ

Here we have neither P-fact nor C-construct. There is no confirmatory device for example, to demonstrate that the consecrated bread is a human body. The statement is thus open-ended. It also permits the real cause of religious experiences to be attributed to *hallucinations* or maybe a micro-seizure in part of the brain's temporal lobes. Michael Persinger demonstrated the latter using an electrical helmet to stimulate subjects' temporal lobes[7].

---

[7]   Persinger, *The Neuropsychological Bases of God Beliefs.*

Note also that we can't even identify unique and distinguishing attributes that point to the validation of the preceding religious claim. Without venturing into the realm of P-facts, the set of C-constructs (bread, body of Christ) is ripe for self-reference as well as the intrusion of incompleteness.

What if one ignores this and assigns attributes willy-nilly? Say by insisting: Well you cannot detect the body because you are only able to ascertain the physical *accidents* using scientific analyses[8]. In this case the claimant commits *reification*. He imposes his preconceived percepts on what is in reality an open-ended field. For such an open field, discussion is fruitless, since it ends up being a mental Rorschach for the benefit of the proponent. In a mental Rorschach one can read anything he wishes into the field, and hence make any claim, e.g. *I've been saved by Jesus Christ so I know I'm not going to Hell!*

By contrast, the empirical advocate of $E = mc^2$ (e.g. from nuclear fission or fusion reactions) has no latitude or degrees of freedom to fill in anything, since all P-facts are already defined by specific constructs and operational definitions. Each of these has a very exact meaning in physics, e.g. c, the velocity of light. There is no wiggle room, and this absence demands a pre-defined context, as well as escape from lurking "Gödelianisms".

In the end, we're entitled to reject the religious concept posed in contradictory or meta-language terms Though something is claimed (if only a possibility statement) the logical framework remains open since:

i)   The claimant hasn't defined exactly what his terms mean.

---

[8]   According to the Catholic doctrine of Transubstantiation, the "accidents" refers to the outer, physical signs. For example, that the wafer when chemically tested yields starch presence, not protein.

ii) He lacks the critical, discriminatory P-facts to back up his claim; facts can be confirmed outside his reference frame.

iii) He uses circular arguments to return to his original claim.

On account of these difficulties, philosopher Herman Philipse has noted we may legitimately show respect for religions because they reflect deep human longings. However, we are not obliged to show any respect when they *put forward claims of knowledge*[9].

Given the above, one may inquire into the inherent problems in articulating any alleged true statement? Scott Soames clarifies the issue by appeal to more and less general schema to arrive at truth in a convergent way. Soames defines what is materially adequate by referencing "Level 1" or L1 statements, depicted as *partial definitions*.[10] The task of communicating truth in language then reduces to consistently generalizing partial definitions to cover every type of sentence and condition.

He goes on to note that Tarski's definition, i.e. that if an earlier iterate allows for additions without contradiction to the original proposition (truth statement), then we can arrive at materially adequate sentences. In this sense, most scientific explanations—while admittedly partial—are nevertheless materially adequate. But do they amount to true statements?

Consider the following sequence of L1 statements for solar flares and note the ascending hierarchy of information presented:

1) A class X-7 solar flare occurred last Tuesday.

2) A class X-7 solar flare occurred at 22h 33m GMT Tuesday.

---

9   Philipse.: *Free Inquiry* (Feb./Mar. 2007), 37
10 Soames: *Understanding Truth*, 69.

20

3) A class X-7, optical class 2B solar flare occurred at 22h 33m Tuesday.

4) A class X-7, optical class 2B solar flare occurred at 22h 33m GMT last Tuesday, and lasted 1440 seconds.

5) A class X-7, optical class 2B solar flare occurred at 22h 33m GMT last Tuesday, peaked 543 seconds after inception, and lasted a total of 1440 seconds.

Are all of the above statements, referencing the same event, true? Are they all *equally true*? If not, why not? Can one therefore have true statements which do not express the entire truth but rather only a partial truth? If a partial truth is expressed can it be said to be *the truth* without reservation?

Obviously, the statements given are successively more materially adequate by degrees, but none of the statements are wholly materially adequate unto themselves. For example, using any of the statements (1)-(3) one would not be able to obtain an estimate of the power or energy released which requires knowing the flare's duration. As one moves in ascending order each statement contains more material adequacy, hence arguably more truth than its predecessor, simply because one can obtain more from the information. Thus (5) is more true than (4), (4) more so than (3) and so forth. Is (5) the last word? Consider this description of the event:

A class X-7, optical class 2B solar flare, occupying an area 1800 millionths of a solar hemisphere and located at heliographic longitude 90 degrees, and latitude 22 degrees, occurred at 22h 33m GMT last Tuesday, peaked 543 seconds after inception, and lasted a total duration of 1440 seconds.

Thus, one is unlikely to deliver all the material and relevant truth on the solar flare at once since data generally aren't processed simultaneously, certainly about a complex physical event. Even in the course of normal human interactions, and particularly teaching, total conveyance of information is unlikely. Is this a lie by omission? Hardly! In the case of physics teaching, even attempting to convey the full basis of Newton's laws of motion would take one hundred times longer than the standard classical mechanics course if all details and exceptions were included. In the interest of time and convenience, therefore, one must often omit the whole truth, assumed to be a complete description of a phenomenon or the principle that governs it.

"The whole truth and nothing but the truth" may well be a fine courtroom bromide but it doesn't make the practicality cut. Can one have true statements which do not express the entire truth but rather only a partial truth? Yes, and these are none other than the L1 statements by Soames' definition. As Soames puts it[11]:

> If such insta nces (e.g. L1 statements) are thought of as partial definitions, then the task of defining truth for an entire language may be seen as finding a way of generalizing the partial definitions so as to cover every sentence of the language.

Carrying this further, there is no way any practical expression of language can encompass more than limited truth. Take this exchange between a boss and an office worker:

"Where is Mr. Jones, our accountant?"

"He had to go to the bank to cash a check".

But the more accurate statement might be:

---

[11]   *Ibid.*

"Mr. Jones had to go the bank on 18th street to cash a $100 check because the bank on 11th street was too crowded, so he had to take a detour around the 12th street Viaduct, and come in from the south side overpass. He then had to walk a mile, because the closest parking was a mile from the bank across the river."

Technically speaking, the response isn't materially adequate. This is in the sense of not providing adequate information to either account for Jones' lengthy absence or to locate him in case of emergency. But one can argue that the respondent's practical simplicity simply trumped delivering the whole truth, and omitted details not considered to be relevant or critical, say to cover every expectation. One reason is that such details that did not add to the substance of the original L1 statement.

Clearly, the way our language is conventionally conveyed and structured is designed to omit more information than is actually needed to communicate a materially adequate truth. In this way the language itself tends to limit the full exposure of any given truth statement unless it is almost a tautology.

The Gödel Incompleteness theorem (I) can be applied to all or most incomplete statements. A good way to test such statements is to try to write them in some symbolic language form then compare them. Consider the two statements below, pertaining to material evidence in the JFK assassination:

p: *All of the bullet fragments recovered were from a 6.54 mm Mannlicher-Carcano rifle*

q: *All of the bullet fragments recovered were from a 7.65 mm Swedish Mauser rifle*

We write the symbolic form taking both into account:

$\sim (p \wedge q)$ e.g.

Philip A. Stahl

Two statements p and q are contrary if they cannot both hold. Note, however, that two contrary statements *may both be false!* Note also that all contradictory statements are contrary, but many contrary statements are not contradictory, i.e.:

Lee Harvey Oswald was observed in a 6ᵗʰ floor window of the Texas Book Depository

and

A swarthy man was observed in a 6ᵗʰ floor window of the Texas Book Depository'

They are not contradictory because a man was observed in a sixth floor window. Thus, swarthiness is not fundamental to the falsity of the statement because a shadow may have fallen at the time of the observation engendering a darker hue.

Does this application allow for contradictions because of the latent incompleteness? Would such a partially true statement be unprovable, say in a court of law, for an eyewitness? In the case of the solar flare example, it's not very likely unless the flare was homologous, e.g. occurring almost simultaneously at two nearby locations. Then the L1 statements aren't refined enough to separate the heliographic locations. The residual statements would then remain unprovable only if no higher resolution observations were forthcoming.

What does all of this say about any truth claim?

It says that in general truth claims must be treated with great skepticism. At any rate, one must always assume the initial claim for truth is partial, or at the L1 level. The claimant must be then pushed as far as possible to disclose the maximum content of the truth as he understands it, especially if the truth claim is made dogmatically. For example, consider the claim:

The Bible is the actual verbatim word of God.

The critical aspects for ascertaining the degree of truth can be pressed in multiple ways. What Bible? If the King James version then we know it's subject to gross errors in translation from the Latin Vulgate[12]. What led to certain parts being omitted? Which God? What is the ontological basis for it? What are the necessary and sufficient conditions for its existence so that we may distinguish it from Allah, Brahmin, Yahweh, Jehovah?

Unless these questions are all addressed and answered fully, the person can't be regarded as having made an absolute truth claim, but rather a *casual subjective conjecture* about his personal reality, as *he* believes it. This places the claim more in the realm of God-concept than an abiding or absolute truth or identity.

A fundamentalist may believe, for example, that his bible holds one hundred percent of the absolute truth in every passage, but that's not what its partial truth statements disclose. Rather, not only are all the passages of the bible (any version) partial truth statements, they are also likely false partial truth statements as well. This is especially so when passages are paired off together yielding contradictions.

Consider the question: How did Simon Peter find out that Jesus was the Christ?

According to Matthew 16:17, it was by a "revelation from heaven". However, if reference is made to John 1:41, *Simon's brother* told him. This isn't the only example! Consider the Easter narrative of the resurrection, putatively the most important event in Christianity. According to one version of the story (Matthew 28:2) the stone was rolled away after the women arrived at the tomb, in their presence. However, Mark's Gospel says it happened *before the women arrived.*

---

[12] Ehrman: *Misquoting Jesus: The Story Behind Who Changed The Bible And Why*, 89.

Which version is the true one, or is there even a single version which meets the criterion of material adequacy?

Such contradictions don't prove that the resurrection didn't happen, but they do throw considerable doubt on the reliability of the supposed witnesses, assuming they even existed. After all, we do know that many passages were wholesale fabricated by subsequent biblical copyists or forgers. And let us not forget Thomas Paine's famous words[13]:

> I lay it down as a position which cannot be controverted. First, that the agreement of all the parts of a story does not prove that story to be true, because the parts may agree and the whole may be false; secondly, that the disagreement of the parts of a story proves the whole cannot be true

In a false partial truth statement one has a proportion of pure fable or myth mixed in with the actual facts. Such degraded L1 statements are plausibly impossible to plumb to get even a partial truth statement. These realities ought to alert us to take greater care when we bandy about the word *truth*. Such forbearance ought to prompt us to acknowledge it's much more difficult to isolate than many believe.

Another seldom mentioned fact is that certain religious orientations are strongly associated with a lack of education. The educational deficit is often such that the believers enthralled by Christian fundamentalism, for example, are unable to consider any kind of a nuanced format. Susan Jacoby has described this condition for American fundamentalists in terms of a "high correlation between poor education and biblical literalism[14]." This is particularly bad in

---

[13] Paine: *The Age of Reason.*
[14] Jacoby, *op. cit.,*189.

the Deep South where high school graduation rates "lag as many as ten points" behind the Northeast and West[15].

Richard Hofstadter carries this even further to the extent of associating fundamentalism with a whole mindset of prejudice. He writes[16]:

> There seems to be such a thing as the generically-prejudiced mind. Studies of political tolerance and ethnic prejudice have shown that zealous church-going and rigid religious faith are among the most important correlates of political and ethnic animosity.

The profound absence of critical thinking ability (tied to poor education) and the inability to see moral gray areas are part and parcel of the same phenomenon, As Hofstadter notes[17]:

> The fundamentalist mind will have nothing to do with all this: it is essentially Manichean, it looks upon the world as an arena for conflict between absolute good and absolute evil, and accordingly it scorns compromises (who would compromise with Satan) and can tolerate no ambiguities.

This is also why, like Ms. Jacoby, I disdain the use of the vanilla catchall term *evangelical* to describe fundamentalists. As she points out, this bland generic term can encompass *"both theological liberals and conservatives"*[18]. Hence, it is a disservice to forward-thinking evangelicals to conflate them with a regressive cultist group that would dispatch them

---

[15] *Ibid.*

[16] Hofstadter:, *Anti-Intellectualism in American Life*, 133.

[17] *Op. cit.*, 135.

[18] Jacoby: *op. cit.*,188.

to Hell as it does Jews, Roman Catholics, Mormons, and non-fundamentalist Protestants. It is also important not to be so cowardly in the use of terms, because in order to recognize the reach of the Religious Right one needs to know exactly what part of the ideological spectrum is subsumed and pandered to, by the likes of Ralph Reed, Albert Mohler, Jr., Pat Robertson and others.

Underlying the template of all vicious or vindictive deities is personalization. In his book, *The Spiritual Brain: Science and Religious Experience*[19], neuroscientist Andrew Newberg provides a putative basis for this by showing how the brain's orientation association area(OAA) determines the belief system for each of us. Since each human brain is different, and the OAA varies in cognitive function from brain to brain, then the beliefs we choose will reflect that biological brain disposition[20]. An atheist, for example, will manifest a very high reductive cognitive function, in addition to very low dopamine levels, according to Newberg. A fundamentalist will typically display a very high causality cognitive function, overlaid by primitive fears issuing from the amygdala.

If the God concept is then internally confected by the brain, the personality of the believer can project its own prejudices, fears and hatreds onto its deity. In *A History of God*, Karen Armstrong has observed[21]:

A personalized God can become a mere idol carved in our image. A projection of our limited needs, fears and

---

[19] Newberg: *The Spiritual Brain: Science and Religious Experience*, 18.

[20] Newberg distinguishes causality-based cognitive functions, from reductive and holistically-based cognitive functions, and abstract cognitive functions. Each brain will display a different bias toward manifesting each.

[21] Newberg and D'Aquili,: *Why God Won't Go Away: Brain Science and the Biology of Belief,* 163

desires. We just assume then that he loves what we love and hates what we hate, endorsing our prejudices instead of compelling us to transcend them.

Reinforcing this take, the authors of *Why God Won't Go Away* note[22]:

The God Armstrong describes is the God of witch hunts, Inquisitions, Holy Wars, fundamentalist intolerances, and countless other forms of religious persecution—all carried out with the confident presumption of divine endorsement. The authority to commit such atrocities is rooted in the assumption, made by believers—that their God is the only God and their religion is the single, exclusive path to truth.

The point of God-concepts is there is no single, exclusive path to truth. Everyone's God is real to the extent adherents believe it to be. This is what Newberg and D'Aquili's' findings show. For example, when one enters the *Absolute Unitary State* there is only one God experience. Hence, one undifferentiated ultimate Being transcends the Jewish, Catholic, Fundamentalist or Muslim brand. The authors rightly conclude that the notion of exclusive truth is only apparent *when incomplete brain states are attained*. These sort of incomplete brain transcendent states are more likely to occur in a person for whom absolutist attributes are accepted by his OAA brain region. The incompleteness of the brain state prefigures a weaker, more rudimentary god-concept.

If the God-concept is rudimentary, the probability is that it's furthest from any ontological truth. The truth hurdle for such believers is then perhaps insurmountable. Likely more so because their thinking is so circumscribed that they refuse to even explore the ramifications of their narrow concepts.

---

22   *Ibid.*

For this reason I also want to make clear that the god-concept I attribute to fundamentalists is at the lowest end of the nuanced-God concept scale, more in the realm of a cartoon than a credible deity. As my Barbadian religious friend John Phillips once put it, this is what happens when people latch onto a book (King James Bible), "using only eight thousand different words in all". The problem is that mass consumption is usually inversely proportional to mature understanding.

Metaphysical statements and testing:

We turn now to metaphysical statements, how to recognize them and how to test for them. Consider, for example:

Human existence doesn't end at death

This is a metaphysical statement. A key indicator is that adding more levels to the statement doesn't make it more true. In other words, either human existence ends at death, or it doesn't. There are no intermediary shades, though as I will later show (Part II) this doesn't mean the answer must be supernatural.

Assume an orthodox Christian writes:

Human existence doesn't end at death but leads to Heaven or Hell.

Contrary to appearance, this is no more substantive than the original statement. It has more words but not more meaningful content. The reason is that metaphysical claims, unlike physical ones, don't disclose more reality because they've never been proven. Also, like God-concepts, they are all relative and subjective. This is borne out by the fact that a majority of people can't even agree on the definition of

Heaven or Hell or what an afterlife is like in either one. Some say Hell is "eternal fire" but many Christian theologians assert it embodies the painful absence of the Beatific Vision. This creates a pain like insatiable hunger, never quenched. Which is correct? There is no empirical discriminator hence both depictions are uncertain, subjective and relative.

The Bible (*NewTestament*) is also of little use here, since the sole place one finds the words *eternal punishment* is in Matthew 25:46. The problem is that the original Greek translation (*Kolasin aionion*) means pruning, as to a tree, to bear fruit. *Aionian* itself is the adjective form of aionion meaning pertaining to an aion (*eon*). The latter, however, is for a defined and limited period of time, certainly not eternal or everlasting. The Bible actually references at least five aions in assorted places, e.g. Matt. 10:30, Galatians 1:4, Ephesians 2:7, Eph. 3:9. In each case only temporary periods are referenced, so the word cannot mean eternal in the literal sense.

Hence, fundamentalist believers have no basis on which to hang a Hell—based eternal punishment nor of claiming Jesus as Son of God (according to John 3:14). This again factors into why fundamentalism's God-concept can be regarded more as a god-cartoon. Because nuance is eschewed the product is deformed by an educational deficiency reflected in a total absence of critical thought.
Let us move on.

For a solar flare I can add more details of the event because each addition can be empirically validated. For example, if I say the flare occurred at heliographic longitude and latitude such and such, I can verify that position using a high resolution solar graticule placed over the Sun's disk as a transparent template (marked off in heliographic coordinates) so the location can be noted and confirmed. I can't do anything similar for the claim that: "Human existence doesn't end at death".

Thus, while physical claims are supported by data and objective evidence, the metaphysical ones can only be accepted on belief, or the belief that some textual authority said so. However, this commits the logical fallacy *of appeal to authority*. A peculiar element of all metaphysical existence claims is that they can always be partially proven with one concrete example. But they can never be disproven no matter how many counter examples are provided. This is because metaphysical claims require the would-be "disprover" to go or be anywhere and look everywhere. (I.e. "Prove to me there're no Brontosaurus ghosts anywhere in the universe!")

Consider the existence claim:

There are two-inch high green fairies that speak Greek and give out money for lost teeth

This statement is impossible to disprove, but that impossibility doesn't mean it's a truth. The reason is that additional L1 statements, with more details, don't transform a fantasy statement into a truth statement. The original statement exhausts whatever possibilities there can be and no added ones can enhance it. Even if a skeptic traversed the universe searching for such fairies, and looked in every nook and cranny, doubtless running out of time, there is no way he'd disprove it. The claimant will simply pick one more place, or a hundred, the skeptic hasn't been!

Ironically, the claim *could be partially proven* if one example of the entity were produced. Thus, the claimant only needs to display a single two—inch fairy, green in color, that speaks Greek and has the ability to give out money for lost teeth. This one step would remove the need to endlessly argue, which would be an exercise in futility.

We are therefore led to a generalization concerning all metaphysical statements:

Any given metaphysical claim can be partially proven if an example can be shown

This shows that the onus must always be on the metaphysical claimant to exhibit his entity precisely and fully. The reason is that the most exhaustive physical search or empirical inquiry can never disprove its existence, by virtue of the claim's nature and subjectivity. This also applies to the God-claimant. This is in regard to the extent he claims the entity is independent of word forms and exists unto itself. Then we need him to show his entity exists unambiguously, minus vague appeals to "creation" or "order". The error of most God claimants is demanding the atheist disprove he-she-it exists, which is logically impossible.

The atheist or rational skeptic can no more do that than the tooth fairy skeptic can for the two-inch tall fairy that speaks Greek and exchanges money for teeth. The absolute God claimant, however, could resolve the issue instantly by the simple expedient of trotting out his God for us to see clearly, no hocus pocus, excuses, or rationalizations. At the very least, even if the God claimant can't produce his deity, he needs to provide the atheist with the necessary and sufficient conditions for it to exist.

Most attempted definitions or descriptions of *"God"* rest on metaphysical statements that are contradictory, as well as incomplete. In this chapter I examined the difficulty posed when the human brain is confronted by the assumption of an ultimate reality, as denoted by a word, and then asked to define it.

The crux of the thematic and epistemological problem was probably first highlighted by Philosopher Joseph Campbell in his book, *The Power of Myth* when he noted[23]:

God is transcendent, finally, of anything like the name of "God". God is beyond names and forms.

---

[23] *Ibid.*

Campbell is suggesting that it's best not to project any sort of embellished descriptions onto the presumed entity especially "omni"—ultimate ones, like omnipresent, omniscient, omnipotent etc.

To fix ideas, look at a metaphysical statement about God:

God is omnipresent and condemns those who disbelieve in Him to Hell

This may superficially sound plausible to an orthodox religionist—maybe a conservative evangelical, but that's because he or she isn't thinking carefully enough about the implications of the attribute. "Omnipresent" means what it states—not half present, not a quarter present, and not in some places or conditions—but in ALL. If one uses the term, one accedes to the meaning.

My contention is that this is a statement of contradiction.

There are two parts to the statement, for which we may use symbolic form, a la George Boole:

$$G = O$$

$$G \rightarrow U \rightarrow H$$

The first equates "God" (**G**) directly with being *omnipresent*. If indeed omnipresence is a singular attribute and *only* God can have it, then we essentially have an identity between the attribute and the entity. If therefore something exists that's omnipresent then it must be God. (**G = O**). It cannot be anything else. (This creates another problem for certain believers when they attribute so much ability, e.g. in temptation of billions, to "Satan" that the entity rivals "God" in omnipresence!)

The transactional statement **G** $\rightarrow$ **U** $\rightarrow$ **H** meanwhile implies an action, such that God (G) acts on the Unbeliever (U) to dispatch him or her to Hell (H). The contradiction arises when one makes the appropriate substitution of G = O into the second statement so that:

$$O \rightarrow U \rightarrow H$$

But if Omnipresence now guides the transaction, all elements must be defined by it since there can be only one omnipresence.

Therefore **IF G = O.** It must be also true that:

$$O = U$$

$$O = H$$

So $O \rightarrow U \rightarrow H = O \rightarrow O \rightarrow O$

In other words, omnipresence (of G) extends to the Unbeliever, and also to H (Hell) Therefore, if the following statement is true:

"God condemns those who disbelieve in Him to Hell"

And if

"God is Omnipresent"

Is *also true*

Then:

"God condemns himself to Hell—which is also Himself"

Must also be true, since: $O \rightarrow O \rightarrow O$

Naïve believers may decry this as some kind of devilish trickery but it isn't. It is simply faithfully using the believer's own claim that his deity is omnipresent and following that through to its logical conclusion. If the believers don't like it, then they need to ditch the attribute. This is exactly why thoughtful Christian believers (such as my Barbadian friend John) are much more prone to adopt a limited deity which lacks any *omni* attributes.

Another pair of contradicting attributes is *omnipotent* and *omniscient.* To give a simple illustration: Richard Dedekind once noted that if God is omnipotent then by virtue of that He'd be able to confect or manufacture a rock of infinite mass. However, by being *omniscient*, he'd already know that if he attempted to lift it, he'd use up all his infinite energy in doing so. Hence, being omnipotent contradicts being omniscient. In this case, God's omniscience prevents him from even attempting to make a rock of infinite mass and lifting it!

On account of the mutually self—limiting properties of omni attributes, James Byrne acknowledges all statements made by humans to do with God must be either incomplete or more often contradictory. Byrne thus endorses French philosopher Jean-Luc Marion's ploy of only writing "God" with a strikethrough, e.g. ~~GOD~~. Thereby to indicate *no one* has the capacity to describe, grasp, conceptualize or manipulate the underlying entity. In effect, as Byrne observes[24]: *"to think ~~GOD~~ as unthinkable is to reject the idolatry of the God of onto-theology."*

If this entity is de-conceptualized, then it can't be debated, even by the most ardent or determined atheist. The latter ends up tilting at a windmill of the mind, like a modern Don Quixote. Hence, the reason for the other part of the book's title: 'Beyond Atheism". In other words, we need to look beyond facile word symbols and stop jousting

---

[24] Byrne.: *op. cit.*, 151.

at them if we're to get anywhere substantive. The alternative is that debate will invariably prove futile since incomplete definitions and contradictions inevitably emerge. This is one reason why demanding necessary and sufficient conditions from believers may be preferable, if the rational skeptic engages them at all. However, from my own experience, not even this particular demand works, since believers simply ignore it.

Note that what I am referencing above is a different thing from being *"beyond knowledge"* as the classic agnostic would define it. It is rather, *beyond any capacity for human thought at all!*

Thus, while the avowed agnostic may insist his position embraces *impossibility of knowledge* of God, this new category prohibits even naming the subject when expressing limitations of knowledge. It is more productive and practical, as Byrne avers, to regard *God* as a *"regulative ideal"*. Such an ideal for human use doesn't necessarily preclude a transcendent Being, but it doesn't require it either. Another point missed by teleological-vitalist deity apologists is that there has always been a profound confusion between the principles of sufficient reason and causation. According to the former, nothing happens without a sufficient reason. However, as Mario Bunge has observed[25]:

> Giving reasons is no longer regarded as assigning causes. In Science, it means to combine particular propositions about facts with hypotheses, laws, axioms and definitions. In general, there is no correspondence between sufficient reason and causation.

We'll carry forward this emphasis and approach as we explore the basis of causality and scientific Materialism.

---

[25] Bunge: *Causality and Modern Science*, 231.

III. UNDERSTANDING CAUSALITY

Perhaps the most formidable impediment to a rational transition from naïve God-concept to transcendent Being is a naïve, popular grasp of causality. One sees this manifested over and over in numerous blogs, websites and forums with the same childish arguments used again and again, i.e, *"God is the Uncaused Cause"*, or *"God is the First Cause"* or *"The universe had to have an outside cause"*—as if the mere proclamation (and repetition) confers credence.

So it is useful to consider causality in a mature rational light, in order to be able to move forward, say to comprehend the validity and value of embracing a scientific Materialism (actually *Physicalism*). Much general confusion inheres in conflating *efficient causality* and *regular conditionality* which is what *"necessary and sufficient conditions"* are really all about[1]. The other part of the problem resides in extrapolating conditions peculiar to general traits for scientific laws *into human domains*.

For now, I want to focus on the first of these. Originally, necessary and sufficient conditions were invoked by Galileo

---

[1]   Bunge: *op. cit*, 33-34.

to replace the concept of *efficient cause* [2]. In this regard, it was recognized from early on that "efficient causation" was often too limited or narrow a concept to be practical or workable. As for "necessary and sufficient conditions"—they are really a statement of regular conditionality that exposes no real criteria for causal efficacy.

Nonetheless, in many venues they are about the best we can hope for in approaching a feasible discussion of causes. For example, Robert Baum[3] correctly observes that n-s conditions are *practical replacements* (in logic) for causes. In other words, instead of saying or asserting "x caused y", one stipulates that a, b are *necessary conditions* for x to exist at all, and c, d are *sufficient conditions* for y to have been the sole effect of cause x.

Baum's reasoning is clear (ibid.): because cause (generic) can be interpreted as proximate or remote, or even as the "goal or aim of an action" and is therefore too open-ended, ambiguous and construed in too many different ways. Thus, "cause" is too embedded in most people's minds with only one of several meanings, leaving most causality discussions unproductive and confused. If my "cause" and your 'cause" in a given argument diverge, then we will not get very far.

Because of this one uses the more neutral term *condition* and specifies necessary and sufficient ones. The latter terms are specifically meaningful in the context of determining causal conditions, and hence, causes. If one eschews them, then one concedes he is incapable of logical argument incorporating the most basic affiliation with cause or causation.

Given this, let's further examine conditionalness or conditionality. The goal is to see if or how we can drive n-s conditions toward a firmer basis, say of causal efficacy. Generally four characteristics are assigned for *efficient*

---

[2]   *Ibid.*

[3]   Baum, *Logic*, 469-70.

causality: conditionalness, existential succession, uniqueness and constancy. The first, conditionalness is a generic trait of scientific law.

Applying conditionalness to the occurrence of large, optical class (4B) solar flares, one must include factors such as: steepness of the magnetic gradient in the active region, rate of proper motion of sunspots in the active region, magnetic class of said spots, magnetic flux, and helicity of the magnetic field. Each of the above allows a degree of determinacy in the prediction, once I make the measurements. For example, the *magnetic gradient*:

$$\nabla B = [+B_n - (-B_n)] / x$$

where the numerator denotes the difference in the normal (perpendicular) components of the magnetic field (between opposite polarities of the active region) as measured by vector magnetograph and the denominator the scale separation between them. If I calculate $\nabla B = 0.1$ Gauss/km, then I know a flare is 96 percent probable within twenty four hours. In the case of existential succession, in the physical case of the solar flare I know that when the magnetic gradient spikes or steepens to 0.1 Gauss/km a flare is imminent to greater than 96 percent probability in one day.

Unlike conditionalness, the attribute of uniqueness (or high level determinacy) is absent from certain kinds of laws, such as apply to statistical regularities. These laws are peculiar to statistical mechanics, for example, the Maxwell-Boltzmann distribution function or the empirical—statistical correlations that show how sunspot morphology is related to the frequency of certain classes of flares.

Uniqueness is also absent from those quantum phenomena, including the spontaneous inception of the cosmos, governed by quantum processes as well as quantum logic, as opposed to classical or binary (either-or) logic

The Problem of Employing False Conditionality—Hence False Causation:

While the preceding section may appear to be a rarefied discussion, it actually has significant practical application: namely in ferreting out false causation arguments. Most of these, in fact, mistake a false conditionality for an efficient causation. Some examples from the past are really extreme, but I will point out just one—the classic used by mathematician Leonhard Euler on the French atheist Denis Diderot (who also, alas was innumerate).

The story goes like this: On being informed of a "new proof for God's existence" Diderot expressed a desire to hear it from Euler. Euler then walked toward him and announced (without cracking even a slight grin)[4]: "*Sir, $(a + b)^n / n = x$, hence God exists! Reply!*"

The poor Diderot, lost in any abstract math, was so stunned—the story goes—that he nearly lost his mind and senses and had to leave Paris. In modern parlance one might say "his head was ready to explode".

However, had he basic training in logic and the nuances of causation, he could've easily peered calmly at Euler, and informed him:

Sir, the so-called proof is nothing but nonsense that has nothing to do with the entity you are trying to prove. You have merely given a mathematical equation, nothing more—and hence, a false conditionalness which you mistake for efficient causation!

Of course, any number of other examples can be substituted for Euler's false conditionality. For example, "God is two-dimensional in time" proves efficient causation.

---

4   Paulos: *Irreligion*, 43

Or "God is the uncaused cause", when in fact all that's being done is to insert a noun which hasn't even been vetted for the bare necessary and sufficient conditions for it to exist. Let's examine more closely the "uncaused Cause" claim, which is alleged to be an argument by naïve causality proponents. Mathematician John Allen Paulos has perhaps best summarized the challenge to such causal naïveté[5]:

> God's the one, according to a religious acquaintance of mine who 'got the ball rolling' . . . . So have we found God? Is he the Prime Bowler or the Big Banger? Does this clinch it?

> If course not! The argument doesn't even come close. One of the gaping holes is the assumption that either everything must have a cause or there's something that doesn't. The first cause argument collapses into this hole no matter which tack we take. If everything has a cause, then God must too, and there is no first cause.

What impediment exists to the naïve causality proponent, say in conceding that the universe is its own cause? Primarily, the mental block arises because the naïf doesn't grasp quantum acausality which governs something like the spontaneous emergence of the cosmos, say from nothing. Hence, instead of taking *nothing* as a false or quantum vacuum and being able to see from quantum mechanics how a universe would arise all of its own, the naïf rejects the reasoning outright.

Nothing in physics terms, of course, is not the same as the metaphysical nothing, which is taken to be literal. In physics we identify the quantum vacuum or Dirac Ether as nothing

---

[5]   *Op. cit.*, 4.

but it's really 'something' since it embodies and enfolds immense energy[6], though this energy is negative.

Another assertion put forward by the causality naïf is that *God is the First Cause*. This is intended to shut down all further comebacks by the act of mere proposition. God is First Cause, hence none can come before it. And all subsequent effects (and sub-causes) follow. Is it really that simple?

In this case the set of causal elements exists in an axiomatic system similar to those examined by of George Boole. So, call the set: $Z = \{C_1, C_2, C_3, \ldots C_n\}$) such that one element is uncaused, hence a "first cause". It matters not whether it is C1 or any other. The point is that the proof of its existence can't be rendered from within the axiomatic system that uses the set Z for a causal argument. Thus, one will inevitably find at least *one contradiction*, and this contradiction means the system is incomplete, so the set must be also.

In other words, asserting *God is a first cause* is technically *unprovable* within an axiomatic system based on cause!

Look at it this way: say $C_1 \rightarrow Z$ is equivalent to saying C1 is *"the first cause of all Z"*. But if $C_1 \rightarrow Z$ is really provable-in-the-system, we'd have a contradiction. If it were provable in-the-system, then it would *not be* unprovable-in-the-system, so that asserting: "$C_1 \rightarrow Z$ is unprovable-in-the-system" *would be false*. Again, it can't be provable in the system since C_1 is an element from a presumed *causal* set. So, the statement "$C_1 \rightarrow Z$ is unprovable-in-the-system" *is not provable-in-the-system (Z),* but unprovable-in-the-system (Z). Technically, one would require a *meta-set* such that $Z' = Z + k'$, e.g. including k' as the uncaused element, i.e. with Z purged of it. However, it can be shown that invoking such a meta-set *leads to an infinite regression.*

---

[6]   See, for example: Boi: The Role of Vacuum in Modern Physics in *The Quantum Fluctuation.*

This shows why, before one interjects false conditionality, he had first better be sure Kurt Gödel isn't looking over his shoulder!

A Foray Into Quantum Logic and Acausality:

Alas, Kurt Gödel and his Incompleteness Theorem(s) isn't the only daunting challenge to the naïve God-thinker. Quantum acausality will also have a role in tempering the naïve believer's simple causality propositions and claims. Though most of the quantum mechanics in this book is relegated to Part II, we must of necessity tackle a bit here since it is relevant to the content of this chapter.

It is generally widely accepted that quantum mechanics opened up an entirely new field of logic, which we now know as *quantum logic*. Hence, new rules and postulates arose for which the logical classical definitions (e.g. based on the binary conditions of Boolean 'laws of thought) hitherto invoked are inadequate.

Earlier, we saw that two statements p and q, are *contrary* if they cannot both hold, i.e. if:

~ (p / q) e.g. *"Sunspots precede solar flares"* (p) *"Solar flares precede sunspots'*(q)

Two statements: p, q are contradictory, if:

[p → (q)], [(~p) → ~q] e.g. *"CMEs are flares"* (p), vs. *"CMEs occur after flares"*(q)

And so on.

However, the fundamentals of quantum mechanics (validated by repeated experiments) diverge from this. Quantum mechanics can be regarded as *a non-classical probability calculus resting upon a non-classical propositional logic.*

More specifically, in quantum mechanics each probability-bearing proposition of the form *"the value of physical quantity A lies in the range B"* is represented by a projection operator on a Hilbert space $\hat{\mathbf{H}}$[7].

John von Neumann [1932], showed that each physical system can be associated with a (separable) Hilbert space $\hat{\mathbf{H}}$, the unit vectors of which correspond to possible physical states of the system. Each "observable" real-valued random quantity is represented by a self-adjoint operator $\hat{\mathbf{A}}$ on $\hat{\mathbf{H}}$, the spectrum of which is the set of possible values of $\hat{\mathbf{A}}$. If **e** is a unit vector in the domain of A, representing a *state*, then the expected value of the observable represented by $\hat{\mathbf{A}}$ in this state is given by the inner product. The observables represented by two operators A and B are commensurable if and only if A and B commute, i.e., AB = BA.

However, non commutation is also possible, and indeed even expected, hence the emergence of the Heisenberg Uncertainty Principle which is really a statement regarding non-commutativity. This can be expressed in quantum mechanics, using the momentum (p) and position (x) measurements via the Poisson brackets:

$$[x, p] = -i\,\hbar$$

where $\hbar$ is the Planck constant of action h, divided by 2π.

If two variables a, b commute, then one has:

$$[A, B] = (A \cdot B - B \cdot A) = 0$$

---

[7]   This is defined as a linear vector space V with an infinite number of dimensions, i.e. $V = \mathbf{v}1 + \mathbf{v}2 + \ldots \mathbf{v}n$ where $n = \infty$. In quantum mechanics it is assumed Hilbert spaces are used unless otherwise noted.

If not, then:

$$[A, B] = (A \cdot B - B \cdot A) = -1$$

and we say a and b are *non-commuting*.

(You may observe one aspect at any one time, but not the other).

In term's of Bohr's Complementarity Principle, the variables x (position) and p(momentum) are regarded as *"mutually interfering observables"*.

This is why only one can be obtained to precision, while you lose the other.

The binary $\{0,1\}$-valued observables may be regarded as encoding propositions about properties of the state of the system. Thus a self-adjoint operator **P** with spectrum contained in the two-point set $\{0,1\}$ must be a projection; i.e., $\mathbf{P}^2 = P$. Such operators are in one-to-one correspondence with the closed subspaces of $\hat{\mathbf{H}}$. Indeed, if P is a projection, its range is closed, and any closed subspace is the range of a unique projection. If e is any unit vector, then $[Pe]^2$ is the expected value of the corresponding observable in the state represented by e. Since this is $\{0,1\}$-valued, we can interpret this as the probability that a measurement of the observable will produce the "affirmative" answer 1. In particular, the affirmative answer will have probability 1 if and only if $Pe = e$; that is, e lies in the range of P.

What all this means is that the "universality" of a concept is a moot issue. It has no meaning or significance in the setting of quantum mechanics and quantum logic. Since a typical closed subspace, say representing a quantum ideation in the brain, for which we already know quantum mechanics applies[8], has infinitely many complementary closed subspaces, this lattice is not distributive.

What are we to make of this? Mainly that the empirical success of quantum mechanics calls for a revolution in logic itself. This view is associated with the demand for a realistic interpretation of quantum mechanics. Now, since philosophy hasn't yet progressed to a non-distributive, non-classical form, it can't have squat to say about ultimate reality. In effect it's a non-player, or perhaps more accurately, an ersatz player.

To be more specific, the formal apparatus of quantum mechanics reduces to a generalization of classical probability in which the role played by a Boolean algebra of events in the latter is taken over by the quantum logic of projection operators on a Hilbert space. The usual statistical interpretation of quantum mechanics demands we take this generalized quantum probability theory quite literally—that is, not as merely a formal analogue of its classical counterpart, but as a genuine doctrine of chances.

Let me give an illustration of how classical logic breaks down. Take the case of a single electron fired at a two-slit screen and ending up on the other side—impinging on a 2nd screen. (See Figure below):

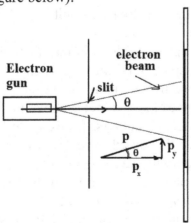

---

8   Stapp: *Mind, Matter and Quantum Mechanics,* 42

Prior to reaching the screen the electron exists in a superposition of states or "wave packets". Is this description statistical, or individual? This depends. The wave function has a clear statistical meaning when applied to a vast number of electrons. But it can also describe a single electron as well. In the example just cited, all the energy states refer to the same electron. However, if all electrons are identical, the statistical and individual descriptions coincide.

Without making this too long, it is found (in > 90% of cases) in numerous trials that the electron goes through both slits of screen (1) at the same time to reach screen (2). Thus, one is not able to say (designating the slits in the intervening screen as A, B respectively, and C as the final screen):

If A then C

OR

If B then C

But rather: *If BOTH A and B, then C*

This is a decidedly non-Boolean result.

The point emphasized here is that this deviation means that in specific spheres (mainly in science, specifically in modern physics) conventional logic and thinking are of little or no use. As you can see, it breaks down in this example. A number of researchers, authors, for example Hilary Putnam, have argued that the distributive law of classical logic is therefore not universally valid[9].

A more complex application might be to the premise or claim that *"no primary cause can be physical"*. The trouble is that this assumption is based on a classical system of logic

---

[9]   See, e.g. Putnam, *Boston Studies in the Philosophy of Science 5.*

that uses binary {1,0} or (yes, no) operators. Thus, since a careless person, perhaps attempting to execute a "proof" of a creator, will assert all physical entities *must be caused*, he'll make the classical error (*post hoc ergo propter hoc*) of applying this to the cosmos' origin.

But what if instead of classical mechanics and its deterministic provisions, quantum mechanics is incorporated, say at the level of quantum gravity? Can the proposition still hold? T. Padmanabhan in his quantum gravity model[10], showed that it's irrelevant, as much as regarding the electrons as hard tiny marbles.

Without going into all the complex mathematics entailed, Padmanabhan employed integrals related to the "action" (J) as a function of time. He proceeded by solving for the expansion factor S(t) using two separate energy equations, one of which (2.15 in his paper)bears a remarkable resemblance to the basic quantum wave potential equation. Moreover, his potential energy term is remarkably similar to that for the quantum harmonic oscillator with some critical differences (e.g. substituting a conformal quantum variable, α for the frequency f, and thence angular frequency $\omega = 2\pi f = 2\pi\alpha$)

The most masterful section in his paper is III. '*Geometry of the Quantum Universe*' wherein spacetime itself is taken to be in a particular quantum state U(q, t). He then assumes "stationary states" (given by the variable Q) for the early universe that are independent of time and for which all the dynamics *"are contained in S(t)"* (ibid., p. 28). The form of the expression for his "energy content" of the universe, **E** (t) also bears a remarkable structural similarity to the equation given earlier for total energy in an expanding cosmos. (Except other variables such as 'Q' appear)

The conformal factor Padmanabhan uses is α, which is a purely quantum mechanical parameter, defined from his equation (2.24): $\alpha = S^6(t)\,\omega^2(t)$

---

[10] Padmanabhan: *Physical Review D*, 28, 756

thereby fixing the state of the universe to be compatible with a harmonic oscillator of frequency ω. (Which we know has solutions in terms of Hermite polynomials $H_n(q)$) To make a long story short, and leave out lots of formalism, he then considers a series of different solutions for the respective energy equations, including for an open, flat and closed model cosmos. It's found all the spacetimes are non-singular (e.g don't have an associated singularity or infinity) and start with some minimum value of expansion factor. "Classical" (non-quantum) limits are achieved by setting $\alpha = 0$, thus $S(t) = 0$.

Physically, it's found that the conformal factor (α) contributes a *negative energy* **density**. Negative energy density may be cast in a relatively simple form of an equation of state, viz.:

$$w = (\text{Pressure}/ \text{energy density}) = -1$$

This is consistent with Einstein's general theory of relativity—which one could say approaches the status of a 'basic law of physics'. In this case, the existence of a negative pressure is consistent with general relativity's allowance for a "repulsive gravity"—since any negative pressure has associated with it gravity that repels rather than attracts[11].

The point is, the metric and treatment is feasible since non-trivial and matterless solutions exist. Thus, the cosmos can be incepted and proceed to expand because of the negative energy density of the conformal factor. It's also this basis that provides the dynamic scaffolding for the instantaneous formation of the universe by a possible quantum fluctuation that arises when a particular threshold is crossed near $\alpha = 0$ (from quantum to classical domains)

As Padmanbhan shows in his paper, such a cosmos from nothing is perfectly justified in the context of the

---

[11]   Perlmutter: *Physics Today,* April,(2003), 53.

model, and follows from the basis of the equations, the light cone, scale factor restrictions and so on. This means the limits at spontaneous inception must definitely be for acausal determinism and quantum cosmology, not classical determinism and causality.

Padmanabhan accomplished the use of quantum logic under very specific conditions (defined by his conformal variable, α) and subject to rigorous mathematical analysis, to establish that a physical entity (cosmos) can arise uncaused in the classical logical sense. By "uncaused", I mean in the same context (roughly) as pair production subject to the energy-time uncertainty relation, i.e.

$$\Delta E \, \Delta t \leq \hbar$$

Thus, given a primordial vacuum state, with conformal quantum variable α, one can have an "explosion" arising from the negative energy density and inception of the universe.

On Self-Reference and Circularity of Logic:

Yet another formidable problem for the naïve causality proponent (or causal naïf) is the danger of not recognizing self-reference and circularity of argument. This is a good place to end this chapter because it rounds out concerns to do with the use of both classical and quantum logic. In other words, in using either one must always be aware of the lurking twin demons.

As we saw earlier in Chapter II, the central problem for all axiomatic (classical logical) systems that are insufficiently rich is *self-reference*. These limits are imposed at the outset and lead to the classic example for the whole self-referential paradigm: the Epemenides' *All Cretans are liars* paradox.

Philosopher of Science Henry Margenau has observed that, in the absence of P-facts and defined C-constructs, any

51

syllogism or argument will have too many meta-statements, and break down to mere circularity.

What are these? Consider $E = mc^2$, which famous Einstein mass-energy equivalence constitutes a specific formalism for a very particular operational definition linking energy and mass. We say it is a *closed formalism*, embodying closed symbols and operational definitions.

Scientific epistemology allows us to regard E, m and c as *constructs*, connected via operational definition to what we call *P—(perceptual) facts*. That is, these facts are based on experimental measurement confirmed numerous times. Hence, these measurements provide an open avenue out of any would-be tautologies. Thus, we expect a correlation like:

$$C \leftrightarrow P$$

re-affirming closure, significance and *no* meta-linkage.

Now, consider the open-ended verbal statement:

"I see a desk"

There is here no connectivity between construct and perceptual fact. The words in quotation marks are a metaphor. The desk is *not* a P-fact, nor is seeing it a P-experience (experience wholly grounded in sensation). After all, a host of attributes (color, size, shape, density etc,.) are omitted, so we are left with an abstraction or mere shell of desk in terms of an actual, material correlate.

The open-ended process above creates a dynamic that yields an effective transition from a recurring complex of attributes, sensations to a simple, bare-bones construct, 'desk'. This process goes by the name 'reification'

In effect, the construct "desk" is part of no set or defined ensemble of sensations that can be precisely named, defined. (Since all attributes are omitted). To boil it down, "I see a desk" is devoid of any context since no attributes are assigned. It is left to the beholder to fill these in.

By analogy, saying "the small tree" lacks the necessary specificity or P-fact attributes to sufficiently distinguish it from the universal set of trees.

By contrast, anyone who invokes $E = mc^2$ has *no latitude or degrees of freedom to fill in anything*, and hence invite circularity. Since all P-facts are already defined by specific constructs—which have very exact meaning in physics. (e.g. c, the velocity of light, or about 300,000 km/sec)

There is no wiggle room, and this lack of wiggle room means a pre-defined context exists. In contrast to this, the proponent of a vitalist or supernatural cosmos offers a claim that is subjective because the observer must provide an assumed closure—unlike in the case of $E = mc^2$. where all symbols are fixed.

This subjectivity arises precisely because the claimant fills in the blanks—so to speak—and provides a subjective frame. For all intents, s/he may also give whatever definition desired for the supernatural or a "living universe", to try to have it every which way with no accountability. This is contrasted to a scientist, who—if he claims observation of a new quark or Higgs boson—must show empirical data that consistently confirms it.

In the absence of P-facts and a defined C-construct (e.g. which concretely answers : *'What is a living universe?*, *What specific attributes does it have that are recognized by all*) the claimant is in a parallel position to the Cretan. He claims something, even if only a possibility statement, but his system remains open since:

i)   He's not defined what exactly 'living universe' means

ii) He has no P-facts to back it up which can be confirmed (independently) outside his reference frame

iii) He uses circular arguments to return to his original claim

Hence, he is trapped within the realm of meta-statements.

At the same time, this 'vitalist' complains egregiously about a Materialist (or mechanist scientist) for not being "open to the cosmos" as a living system or whatnot.

But the claimant himself hasn't provided the contextual basis to do that, since he's only offered an open system with no closure. No C-constructs, no P-facts. To escape a Godelian loop, the vitalist or rigid causality naïf is obliged to:

i) Provide an operational definition for "living universe"

ii) Provide one single construct based on (i), showing how this construct makes use of the definition,

iii) Provide a single percept or perceptual FACT that would even allow for it to be compared to a scientific hypothesis—say to explain the same phenomenon. (Energy might be a starting concept here)

The above note can easily be adjusted in any argument to show that supernaturalism-vitalism doesn't hold up to logical scrutiny.

Logical Problems with the Intelligent Designer Claim:

Not discussed up to now are the sundry and serious logical-causal problems associated with the "intelligent design" claim. One often made generic claim is that *"intelligent causes exist"*, but in proposing this the ID advocate confuses the principles of sufficient reason and causation. According to the former: *Nothing happens without a sufficient reason*. Philosopher of science Mario Bunge has noted[12] :

---

[12]   Bunge, *op. cit.*, 231

Giving reasons is no longer regarded as assigning causes. In Science, it means to combine particular propositions about facts with hypotheses, laws, axioms and definitions. In general, there is no correspondence between sufficient reason and causation.

Thus, while intelligent causes may exist, they are not absolute prerequisites for a *scientific* hypothesis or explanation. Indeed, in fields such as quantum and statistical mechanics we have acausal determinism, such as in the behavior of the wave function for an atom, which confounds any conventional notion of cause leading to explicit effect. Thus, the problem entails using an unjustified generalization to describe *all* physical systems.

ID also punts by not identifying the nature of its "designer". A priori one must know what one is looking for. For example, consider the "intelligent cause" of a complex cosmic radio signal, which may contain what appear to be mathematical relations. As such a signal is being parsed (say for the signature of an extraterrestrial intelligence), certain assumptions are attendant—including whether the presumed originating "aliens" can actually exist at the source location.

Intelligent design by contrast *offers no insight* at all into their designer. Is it some kind of deity? If so, it is definitely in the realm of religious dogma, and probably beyond any measurement or scientific test. In which case, its pursuit is a waste of time.

Is it a space alien from Tau Ceti, or Zeta Reticuli? If so, we may demand the cosmic radio signals that unambiguously make the nature of the designer clear. If ID'ers can't specify their designer, why should we take it any more seriously than 'Bigfoot'?

In the end, irreducible complexity (which is the specious basis of ID) inevitably amounts to an argument from ignorance. Because a structure (e.g. eardrum) or a process (origin of life from inanimate matter) appears difficult from the inferior vantage point of the percipient, it's automatically assumed that no scientific appeal can be made. No model, however remotely probable, can be offered. Thus "intelligent design" is latched on to as a "god of the gaps". But history shows how absurd such an approach is.

For example, ball lightning used to be assumed to be a supernatural manifestation until its static electrical nature was exposed. Same thing with St. Elmo's fire appearing near the yard arms of ships. Diseases like plague were believed caused by "malefic influences" or even demons, until the microbial basis of pathogens was revealed by the use of microscopes.

A hundred years ago no one could explain how the Sun could give off so much heat and light for so long. Not until nuclear fusion was discovered, and evidence obtained – e.g. by specialized detectors—that they were occurring on the Sun.

Take the ear drum, ear canal, tympanic membrane and all. As Robert Ornstein showed[13], these all can be explained on the basis of development of repeated adaptations of form and function. No designer needed.

All these and more disclose that a long record of scientific history exists to demonstrate the wisdom of the materialist—physicalist view. And why special, ad hoc causes are to be dismissed as unfounded.

To consolidate these points and problems for Intelligent Design, I offer a number of other questions they have never been able to properly answer, or even address:

1) Why doesn't the designer insinuate itself into the domains of other worlds in the solar system to create life? Why isn't Mercury inhabited by designed creatures, or Venus? Or Jupiter?

   IF the designer is also omnipotent it ought to be able to design outside of purely natural (or terrestrial)

---

[13]   Ornstein: *The Evolution of Consciousness*,.

norms and limits. (Thus an organism on Venus, for example, that can live off sulphuric acid, CO2 in the atmosphere and an atmospheric pressure of 90 atm.)

If the designer is not omnipotent, and indeed doesn't exist in the first place—it makes more sense that life will only occur on certain planets within habitable temperature zones and containing the elements (oxygen, nitrogen, water etc.) needed for life. In such cases, it isn't "design" at work but a long, gradual process of chemical evolution that eventually leads to life forms. The only reason to invoke a designer in the first place is that it possesses ubiquitous power to design ANYWHERE! If it can't do that, or is limited by conditions already in place—we simply don't need it. It's redundant.

2) If the above limitations apply, then what are the necessary and sufficient conditions for a designer to exist? Do these conditions apply to a singular, unique entity or to multiple ones? If the entity is claimed to be supernatural, then what abiding properties must we look out for to substantiate it.

If the designer exists and is not a figment of the imagination, then it should be possible to predict what it can design in a totally novel situation. Say, operating under different planetary conditions: e.g. mass, gravity, atmospheric composition etc. This will demonstrate there is a real empirical basis to the entity compatible with the claim, and not merely a posteriori statistical hocus pocus.

The inability to deal with either of the preceding sets of problems, questions discloses proponents of ID still haven't produced the "goods" to warrant our taking it any more seriously than a bizarre creationist tract, such as the claim that humans cohabited the planet with dinosaurs in some early epoch. That means first establishing a base of facts and evidence unique to itself. Then, formulating testable predictions which can be made and that turn out to be more accurate than those of naturalistic evolution. Until ID's proponents accomplish that, preferably in the context of publishing in established scientific journals—it will remain rank speculation.

This brings us to a powerful alternative paradigm to the fantasy Intelligent Design narrative: the empirical one according to modern scientific Materialism.

IV. MODERN SCIENTIFIC MATERIALISM

In my original book on atheism and Materialism, I observed that[1]:

> The beauty of Materialism is that it is minimalist by definition. By its very nature, focusing on manifestations of matter, fields and energy, it excludes distracting an unverified entities such as spirits, souls and the rest of the supernaturalists' grab bag of ethereal inventions.

The emphasis here is on the minimizing effect on assumptions needed in explanations, say by adopting Materialism. I then had gone on (in the next chapter) to provide a rigorous definition of scientific Materialism. This represents an entire world view that encompasses naturalism and physicalism while rooting out vitalism, naturalism and teleologism. In the present context, it is also the ideal "astringent" or "disinfectant" to pave the way for a discussion

---

[1]   Stahl: *op. cit.*, 11-12.

about ultimate Reality untainted by human, anthropomorphic phantasmagorias.

Before continuing it is well to remind the reader that there are actually multiple forms of Materialism, that include:

- *Physicalist Materialism* (everything in the cosmos has a physical nature)

- *Epiphenomenalist Materialism* (non-physical processes occur that are contingent on physical origins, organs, etc.)

- *Panpsychic Materialism* (attributes a mental character to physical entities)

- *Emergent Materialism* (can attribute vitalist forces to physical nature)

- *Dialectical Materialism* (mental processes evolve from physical ones)

Only the first, physicalist Materialism (which is essentially identical to scientific Materialism), will be of use in ascertaining whether a path toward an ultimate transcendent entity is worthwhile. My role here is to show that the cosmos, minus the presence of humans or active conscious agents, is purposeless. That is, to show how scientific Materialism discloses a purposeless cosmos, neglecting the presence of humans.

The term *modern Materialism* (or *modern scientific Materialism*) I introduced in my first book, in connection with incorporating modern quantum mechanics into classical or Newtonian mechanics. Some Luddite-prone atheists have opposed this or found excuses to reject such inclusion, but their quantum exceptionalism is both irrational and counter-productive.

For example, it has been pointed out that the actual probability of a single fusion of 2 protons (e. hydrogen nuclei) to yield deuterium is almost nil. It is something like one fusion every 14 billion years, or a time exceeding the age of the universe! This is because one has two like charges trying to attach when we know from electrostatics that *like electrical charges repel.* Hence, by all rights and known physics principles the Sun shouldn't shine—but it does! How? Because of a process or phenomenon called quantum tunneling! Without the invocation of this quantum process we'd not be able to explain as simple a thing as sunshine!

Quantum tunneling may be illustrated as shown below:

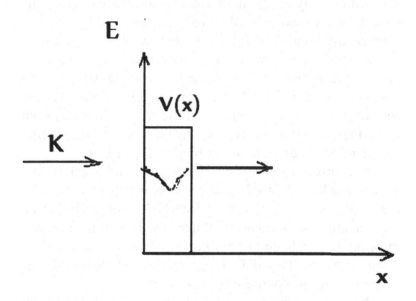

The idea being that a particle of relatively low incident energy (of kinetic energy K, say) can *actually penetrate a higher potential energy barrier*, say of energy V(x) > K. Note that the penetration of the barrier is a direct result of the wave nature of matter! (The matter wave form changes in the process of transmission through the barrier, say from an exp(-ikx) function to a sin (kx + φ) where φ denotes phase angle). In effect, this wave nature—which is uniquely quantum mechanical in origin—allows a higher energy barrier to be penetrated by a lower energy particle, something totally without parallel in classical, Newtonian physics! Note that if the barrier is not too much higher than the incident energy, and if the mass is small, then tunneling is significant. It was insights such as this that paved the way to apprehending how much subtler nature was than hitherto realized, and how many more technological advances could be achieved when the wave nature of matter was factored into designs.

This also opened the door to what one might call acausal determinism, which is radically distinct from causal determinism, say in Newtonian mechanics. It also opened the door to modern scientific Materialism as opposed to the naïve classical mechanical form originated by Galileo and Newton.

As we'll see in Part II, this also opened a new dimension for analyzing human consciousness, without which we'd have remained in the Newtonian paradigm. The key to bear in mind is that modern scientific Materialism has been liberating as well as restricting—in the sense of winnowing out neurological dross for describing reality or being.

Of course, from earliest times both philosophers and theologians have debated the question of whether the universe has a purpose. This historic debate hinged on requiring an external purpose independent of humans. Therefore, it existed irrespective of whether or not humans existed or evolved on Earth—but once they did—it became incumbent on humans to process and accept this divine purpose.

Those who beheld some divine purpose invariably believed the cosmos had to have been created. Most of these creationists appealed to a subjectively perceived evidence of "design" in the universe as an argument for the existence of a special divine creator. William Paley (1743-1805), for example, drew attention to the complexity of structures occurring in both astronomy and biology, arguing that they could not possibly be a product of blind chance.

In this respect, he may be said to be the father of *intelligent design* (ID) now making the rounds as the latest manifestation of the belief that some kind of "irreducible complexity" is embedded in physical—biological reality that dictates invoking an intelligent designer.

The viewpoint of Science in general, and modern physics in particular, is totally opposed to this. This opposition has arisen not merely from logical arguments, but from experiments and observations in quantum mechanics, statistical mechanics and cosmology. In the light of these advances, Paley's (not to mention ID's) deficiencies are now evident.

Both physicists and biologists, for example, now recognize many systems in which order and complex activity can emerge spontaneously. Thus, one of the objectives in this chapter is to show how such recognition leads the dispassionate observer to dispense with any notion of cosmic purpose that transcends mere existence in its own right. Both order and purpose, in other words, are the confections of an over-worked anthropomorphism projected onto the cosmos.

A biological example, based on in-vitro experimental studies of cancer tumors, is the individual tumor cell.[2] The cell appears as a fluctuation, able to develop by replication. A cosmological example is the instantaneous formation of the universe by a possible quantum fluctuation[3] that arises when one treats the conformal part of space-time as a quantum variable.

A more prosaic example is the aurora, such as I observed near Chena Hot Springs, Alaska in March of 2005. This particular aurora displayed two perfectly symmetrical parallel green "tubes", arcing from north to south horizon. Did an

---

[2]   Garay, and Levefer,: *J. Theoretical Biology*, 417, 73.

[3]   Padmanabhan:, *ibid*.

intelligent designer craft two natural fluorescent tubes in the sky? Not at all! The inimitable procession to order (observed over two hours) was dictated by the (pre-existing) presence of the auroral oval around the pole and the polar electro-jet, after impinging electrons from the solar wind began to decelerate into the oval and form currents in sheets. These were then shaped by the ambient magnetic field of Earth into the two parallel tubes visible near Chena Hot Springs.

Sunspot groups also display an inherent organization that has arisen spontaneously from the action of powerful local magnetic fields on ambient plasma. In the photo below, a large sunspot group I photographed in 1980, bears this out. Note the large central umbra in the leader spot, and the fainter penumbra. Some days earlier this region was merely a sea of small, dark magnetic specks of no discernible scale or configuration.

It was the subsequent action of powerful, twisting and localized magnetic fields (generated by a sub-surface dynamo action) acting on the ambient hot plasma, that shaped and organized the sunspot structure.

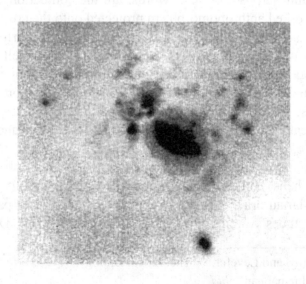

What do the above examples disclose? Basically, that William Paley's famously naïve argument: *"A watch must always have a Watchmaker, so also the universe must have a Maker or Creator."* is flawed and outdated.

The analogy is flawed, first, because the universe is not a mechanical contrivance like a watch. Apart from the fact that—for the most part (certain limited domains in celestial mechanics excepted) the clockwork universe was dispelled when quantum theory emerged. Unfortunately, while the practicing physicist has long since had to adopt an indeterminate, non-mechanistic world view (e.g. guided by the experimental results from quantum physics), the same cannot be said for non-physicists, including theologians, philosophers and multitudes of laypersons.

These groups continue to labor under erroneous assumptions of causality and "order" generated almost exclusively by an ignorance of modern physics. For example, an ignorance of the fact simultaneous measurements at the atomic level are fundamentally indeterminate. Technically, for one of the most common forms of the Heisenberg Uncertainty Principle, this may be expressed (in terms of position x, the Planck constant h and momentum p = mv):

$$[x, p] = -i\, h/\, 2\, \pi$$

In term's of Bohr's quantum (Complementarity) Principle, the variables x (position) and p(momentum) are regarded as *mutually interfering observables.* This is why only one can be obtained to precision, while you lose the other.

In another sense, one can think of approaching a particle in such way (or with such apparatus) that it suddenly gets 'wavy'. At a particular stage of resolution, as the late David Bohm noted, the particle aspect vanishes and you apprehend a wave. But during some interim threshold one can regard it as a *wavicle.*

Philip A. Stahl

Of course, if Heisenberg's principle didn't apply—meaning we could know both the position and momentum to the same degree of accuracy, then: [x, p] = 0

Such that x• p – p•x = 0 spells out non-interference.

In cosmological terms, the whole concept of order has been relegated to a minor and tiny niche of the extant cosmos. For example, the recent balloon-borne Boomerang and MAXIMA UV measurements to do with Type Ia supernovae, have disclosed a cosmic content:[4]

7%—ordinary visible matter

93%—*dark component*, of which:

—70% is DARK (vacuum) energy and
—23% is dark matter

In effect, *93% of the universe can't even be assessed for "order" since it isn't visible*. In the case of dark matter, one can only discern its presence indirectly by the visible effects on neighboring matter. In the case of dark energy, the underlying physical basis isn't even known—though we know the result is an increase in the acceleration of the universe (arising from a cosmic repulsion attributed to dark energy)[5].

This is all critical, since in the past apologists of teleologism (the belief that purpose and design are part of nature) have cited a perceived "orderliness" as a revelation

---

[4] See, e.g.: *Physics Today*, July, 2000, 17.

[5] Specifically let ρ be energy density and p the pressure, then (ρ + 3p) acts as a source of gravity in general relativity. If we set: $0 = (\rho + 3p)$ we have $p = -\rho/3$ (or $\rho = -3p$) and if: $p < (\rho/3)$ we have gravity that repels.

for the "handiwork" of an intelligent Mind, or Creator. Alas, this falls through the cracks if most of the universe is disorderly, or dark-energy-matter. Indeed, by current assessment—and discounting plasma abundance, one may reckon that even rudimentary order is evident in barely 0.00001% of the cosmos. And this can all be explained or accounted for by appeal to scientific reasoning or hypotheses. For example, the nebular hypothesis, whereby the original solar nebula progressively collapsed under the force of gravitational attraction, can account for the formation of the solar system.

Another point missed by these apologists is that there has always been a profound confusion between the principles of sufficient reason and causation. According to the former: Nothing happens without a sufficient reason. But as Mario Bunge has observed[6]:

Giving reasons is no longer regarded as assigning causes. In Science, it means to combine particular propositions about facts with hypotheses, laws, axioms and definitions. In general, there is no correspondence between sufficient reason and causation.

As an example, let's say I fire electrons from a special electron gun at a screen bearing two holes some distance away. At first glance, one might reasonably conclude that the electron motion is singular and follows one unique path. That is, that each fired electron traverses a single, predictable path, following stages 1, 2, 3 and so on, toward the screen. This is a reasonable, common-sense sort of expectation but alas, all wrong!

According to the most widely accepted interpretation of quantum theory[7], the instant the electron leaves the gun it

---

[6]   Bunge,: *op. cit.*, 231.

[7]   Feynman. *The Feynman Lectures in Physics*, (III), 1-4.

takes a large number of differing paths to reach the screen. Each path differs only in phase, and has the same amplitude as each of its counterparts, so there is no preference. How does the electron differ from the apple? It takes *all* paths to the screen, the apple takes only one (at a time) to the wall. And the electron exhibits phases (as a wave) while the apple doesn't. The electron's wave function can be expressed:

$$\Psi = \Psi\,(1) + \Psi\,(2) + \Psi\,(3) + \ldots . \, \Psi\,(N)$$

Here the total wave function for the electron is on the left hand side of the equation, while its resolved wave amplitude states (superposition of states) is on the right-hand side. If they are energy states, they would correspond to all possible electron energies from the lowest (1) to the highest or Nth state (N).

There is absolutely no way of knowing which *single state* the electron occupies until it reaches the screen and an observation is made, say with one or other special detector (D). This is illustrated in the diagram below, based on the electron double slit experiment which Richard Feynman once referred to as the cornerstone of understanding quantum mechanics. Below, I use different numbers for each of three wave forms though we understand that these are merely three of an infinite set.

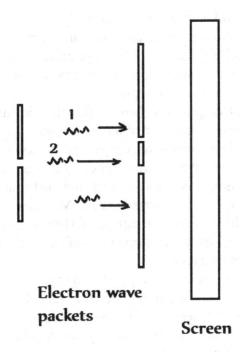

Electron wave packets

Screen

Prior to reaching the screen the electron exists in a superposition of states or "wave packets". Is this description statistical, or individual? This depends. The wave function has a clear statistical meaning when applied to a vast number of electrons. But it can also describe a *single* electron as well.[8] In the example just cited, all the energy states refer to the **same** electron. However, if all electrons are *identical*, the statistical and individual descriptions coincide.

Germane to the point made earlier, i.e. that there is no correspondence between sufficient reason and causation, one finds that in a large number of cases, the approaching electron goes through both holes in the screen—not just one. This is totally counterintuitive to one steeped in the traditions of Newtonian or classical mechanics. For example, if a baseball were hurled at a wall with two six inch diameter apertures

---

[8]   Herbert: *Quantum Reality—Beyond the New Physics*, 115-117.

near to each other it would go through one or the other but not both! Of course, the electron deviates from such classical behavior precisely because of its wave nature as demonstrated in the famous Davisson-Germer experiment that verified that particles exhibit wave properties.

The point emphasized here is that this deviation means that in specific spheres (mainly in science, specifically in modern physics) conventional logic and thinking are of little or no use. A number of researchers, authors, for example Hillary Putnam, have argued that the distributive law of classical logic is not universally valid[9] Much of his reasoning has to do with the peculiar nature of Hilbert spaces that are part and parcel of the underpinning of quantum mechanics. (See previous chapter).

Interestingly, it is this very indeterminacy that also resides at the core of many quantum bootstrap models, allowing for the spontaneous inception of the cosmos. People have serious problems with such models and ways of thinking because: a) they fail to appreciate the lack of correspondence between sufficient reason and causation, and b) they fail to understand that causality predicated on classical logic is no longer applicable to many areas of modern physics.

While further conceptual/conceptual development remains (the work of science is never final) it is clear that any postulated purpose in the cosmos can already be regarded as a redundant anachronism. If the cosmos can bootstrap itself into existence via a quantum fluctuation, and acquire order via the implicit laws of statistical and thermal-quantum physics, then it has no need of a creator or designer and no purpose other than to exist. No extraneous being is necessary to ensure its continued stability or existence. More bluntly, the addition of such a being doesn't advance the quality of our research, or improve our predictions by the most remote decimal place.

---

[9]   Putnam, *op,.cit.*

Hence, to all accounts such a being (or purpose) is totally superfluous.

Thus do humans, as generic offshoots of the cosmos, have any purpose other than to be. If they seek an additional purpose, they must craft and forge this subjectively of their own accord—rather than looking for it on high. Does this imply that the concept of "God" is outright null and void? No. It merely requires that we re-think the concept so that it is consistent with the absence of higher or extraneous purpose.

As Bernard d'Espagnat notes [10]:

> The archaic notion that is conveyed by the words 'Lord' and 'Almighty' will presumably never recover its full efficiency for lulling the ontological qualms of mankind. For a religious mind, turning towards being should therefore become a subtler endeavor than the mere acceptance of the heavenly will stated in the Bible, formulated by the priests, and exhibited by miracles.

Finally, the abolition of extraneous higher purpose should not incur any psychic loss for humanity. As French has aptly observed[11]:

> It is a loss of dignity to define humanity as a race defined to please a higher Being, rather than as a race whose only end is to please itself. The 'gift' of purpose to the human race is thus very expensive: one can fulfill one's God-given purpose only by sacrificing felicity while one is alive.

---

[10]   d'Espagnat,: *In Search of Reality*, 158.
[11]   French: *Beyond Power: On Women, Men and Morals*, 254.

Philip A. Stahl

Thus does scientific Materialism pave the way for a purposeless cosmos, in the sense of removing the need for all deity concepts that act to impose external purpose, as from above. What I will show in Part II of this book, is that the arrival of humans—the human species—paves the way for intrinsic conscious agents of purpose within the universe itself, and these agents can command a creative potential.

V. ETHICS, MORALITY & SCIENTIFIC MATERIALISM

On several occasions, I've been telephoned or emailed by orthodox religious types who've asked me: *If you don't believe in God what's stopping you from going out and raping, robbing, murdering or doing anything else? If you don't believe in God, then you don't believe in God's laws!*

Invariably, I respond that decent, civilized and even moral behavior doesn't depend on god—belief or adhering to laws of a god. Rather, it depends on rational and objective analysis of a situation, and sound decisions maximally promoting the welfare of all concerned. In other words, moral choice and moral integrity rests on an internally consistent moral or ethical order.

In forging a coherent and pragmatic ethics, Materialism is rigorously economical in the choice of memes applied to the task. It relentlessly excises all extraneous considerations in arriving at a practical good to benefit the maximum number of people. No distractions exist to clutter the issues, such as: invisible entities to deflect responsibility for an action (e.g. the devil's temptations), or erroneously mistaking a personal preference for an ethical value applicable to all.

In deliberating over possible alternate courses of action, the Materialist asks the following questions in determining acceptability:

- *Does the intended action harm anyone?*
- *If so, how, specifically?*
- *Is a communal (civil) law being violated?*
- *Is the communal (civil) law a just law?*

These are the four chief criteria, embodied in four questions, which the scientific Materialist considers before deciding on an action.

In formulating an ethics or morality consistent with Physicalism or scientific Materialism, one must first inquire into the origins of evil, with the intent to dispatch all supernatural or unphysical agents and replace them by physical explanations. The basic premise of scientific Materialism is that *no moral order can exist apart from and outside of humans* and that in every case of personal evil, humans are the active agents. Hence, evil emerges as an ubiquitous possibility from innate human actions, not from some external, invisible, non-physical entity, e.g. Satan. As previously noted by other authors, e.g. John Kekes, this external moral order is therefore a groundless assumption. As Kekes observes[1]:

> If there is such an order it would have to be supernatural, since in the natural world with which we are familiar, no morally good order is discernible. The most casual reading of history makes us see, as Hegel says, 'the evil, the ruin that has befallen the most flourishing kingdoms which the mind of man created.

[1]   Kekes: *The Roots of Evil,*. 141.

This implies that the moral basis of orthodox Christianity (as well as the god extrapolated from it), must be rejected. Moreover, it can easily be shown that unless this is done a kind of moral inconsistency or ethical chaos results. So from whence comes human morality? The easiest and most direct response (of the Physicalist) is that it arose as an offshoot of human evolution. As humans evolved, especially from individual hunter-gatherers to settled agrarians—farmers, the cohesion and survival of human communities began to depend on adherence to a moral order that preserved the welfare of all. If then one or more in the community stole or committed violent actions against others, it undermined the security and survival of the whole. Repeated recognition of this then led to the enunciation of a fixed moral coda, such as embodied in the Ten Commandments but more succinctly expressed in the fundamental tenet of Hammurabi's law as well as dozens of others embodied in different religions: *Do unto others as you would have them do unto you.*[2]

This sort of communitarian moral order later became endemic in more organized and sophisticated human communities and indeed, formed the basis of settled societal laws, legal systems. No supernatural law or commandment ordained specific moral or legal behavior. Instead it was the conscious and deliberate recognition that the promotion of the welfare of others was directly linked to the one's own welfare. Compromise others' security, and you compromise your own. No god is necessary, for crafting morality, or creating civil laws.

By contrast, external religious morality is predicated on some formal codification of expected human behavior in terms of absolutist propositions, not subject to debate. The typical moral code of an orthodox religionist, whether Muslim, Pentecostal, Catholic or Jewish, isn't subject to evolution or variation based on contingencies, or externalities.

---

[2]   Epstein, *ibid.*

75

Philip A. Stahl

This blindness probably results from a 'control' meme that proclaims the morality as 'god-ordained' or revealed in some scripture or other. If ordained by a god—whether Allah, Jehovah, Yahweh or whoever, it cannot be compromised or altered no matter what.

Kai Neilsson has rightly asked[3]:

Is an act good because God did it, or is it good independent of such action?

For a genuine ethical basis, any human action must be totally independent of whether a god did it (in scriptures) or ordains it. It must be good on its own merits. A first test, as Neilsson observes, is ethical choice predicated on a generally accepted humane standard. Consider: if a human parent knows his child is trapped in a burning house, s/he will try to save it however s/he can. There is no way the human parent will simply walk out and allow 'fate' or "free will" of the child to make the decision. If the human parent has an ounce of common decency s/he must intervene.

By contrast, does the orthodox God (actually God-concept) of Christianity always intervene? Evidently not, if one peruses history, even as recently as the genocide of 6 million Jews by the Nazis. Could not all the gas chambers have been made to malfunction, after all?

Thus it follows, even from the most generic examples (presupposing a supernatural, omnipotent force) that human ethics or a human moral order must exist independent of an external pervasive moral order which always sees humans as good or godly if they just believe the right things.

What the religionists have done is to take the natural code of (humane) ethics most people follow and embellish it with a blizzard of superstitious precepts and injunctions. These are

---

[3]   Neillson, Kai: *Ethics Without God,* 72.

superstitious since, inevitably, they are linked to the supposed dictates of a supernatural being who will not hesitate to punish those who disobey "him".

Many Christians, especially of the fundamentalist mold, actually believe or point to their Bibles for moral answers. But if they knew the actual content, I can't see why they'd do that! For instance, *2 Kings 2, 23:24* allows children to be slain by wild animals if they insult their elders or any authority (in this case a prophet). Thus, the Bible is not offering any kind of absolutist moral teaching, but rather more plausibly regurgitating the bloodthirsty thoughts of the vengeful, limited-minded human who wrote it.

By *Deut. 22:22* both John Edwards and his former girlfriend (Riele Hunter) would have been stoned to death. The bible fails here by flouting the absolutist code for *'No killing'* (in the 10 commandments) and even worse, allowing it *for adultery.*

Meanwhile, by *Deut. 21: 18-21* we read[4]:

If a man have a stubborn and rebellious son, which will not obey the voice of his father, or the voice of his mother, and when they chastise him, he will not even listen to them, then his father and mother shall seize him, and *that*, when they chasten him will not hearken unto them; Then shall his father and his mother lay hold on him, and bring him out unto the elders of his city, and unto the gate of his place. And they shall say to the elders of his city, 'This our son is stubborn and rebellious, he will not obey us, he is a glutton and a drunkard.' And all the men of his city shall stone him with stones, that he die; so shalt thou

---

4   Deuteronomy, *The Old Testament*, 321 (The Authorized King James version)

put evil away from among you, and all Israel shall hear and fear,

So, any insolent or intemperate son would have to be taken to the outskirts of a city by his parents who'd let the elders stone him to death. While the modernist may think this insane, there are Christian apologists who seek to parse it in a way that makes it palatable! The Website for *The Christian Apologetics and Research Ministry* (CARM) claims, for example[5],

In the Old Testament God appears harsh for three reasons. First, it was to demonstrate the exacting requirements of the Law, a perfect and demanding standard. Second, it ultimately demonstrates the need for grace that would eventually be manifested on the cross. Third, should rebellion take root the very heart of the gospel would be at risk since the prophecies of the Messiah coming to and through Israel could be undermined should rebellion become rampant and society fall apart causing the prophecies to fail. Therefore, we can conclude that this harsh requirement was a necessary legality to instill and designate the necessity of family order and respect and to ultimately provide another safeguard that would ensure the sacrifice of Christ.

But these rationalizations amount to nonsense. "Exacting requirements of the law" is in reality no different from the harsh Muslim Sharia law where thieves see their limbs hacked off or women are whipped to death for adultery. Just because "God" allegedly proclaimed it doesn't make it morally right and indeed, this is a justifiable basis to question whether this

---

[5]   See, e.g. *http://carm.org/bible-difficulties/ genesis-deuteronomy/stone-rebellious-son*

is any real God at all, as opposed to a phantasm percolating in the temporal lobes of an ancient brain. Somewhat similar to the modern schizophrenic or psychotic who claims: "God told me to kill that child!"

The appeal to "grace" is also fulsome and not required, nor is any invocation of the cross, since even if a historical Jesus actually existed and suffered crucifixion there's no evidence of a God-man or Savior[6]. The obsession with rebellion and family order isn't compelling either, given multifold alternatives existed that didn't require slaying the son. In addition, one can rightfully argue that the apologists are resorting to a slippery slope logical fallacy with the claim that a simple family issue would metastasize into a national rebellion and putatively "failure of prophecies" if the extreme sanction hadn't been enforced. In any case, the matter of the reality of biblical prophecies also must be questioned, especially whether their fulfillment isn't more in terms of ex post facto confabulation by zealous scribes using already existing Old Testament pointers.

My point is that the bible cannot be *an arbiter of moral authority*, far less absolute authority.

The Physicalist Model for the Origin of Evil:

Evil exists, but not as an infinite negative absolute, or personified in a spirit entity, but rather as a dynamic of our own brains. What most ordinary people refer to as "evil" is easily explainable by the scientific Materialist in terms of brain evolution. Thus, Homo Sapiens is fundamentally

---

[6]   This is the take of Biblical scholar and member of the Jesus Seminar, John Dominic Crossan, with whom I concur when he refers to the historical Jesus as a Mediterranean "peasant Jewish Cynic". Such Cynics were "hippies in a world of Augustan yuppies". See: Crossan: *The Historical Jesus: The Life of a Mediterranean Jewish Peasant*, 421.

an animal species with a host of animal/primitive instincts residing in its ancient brain or paleocortex. The paleocortex sits evolutionarily beneath the more evolved mesocortex and neocortex, the latter of which crafts concepts and language[7]. One clever person has compared this tri-partite brain structure to a car design welding a Lamborghini to a Model T Ford chassis, with a 1957 Chevy engine to power the Lamborghini. If an automotive engineer can conceive of such a hybrid beast, I'd be interested to know exactly how he thinks it would run.

Given the preceding brain structural defect, there is much evidence that human behavior will get progressively worse as the complexity inherent in technological and globalized societies increases, but brain evolution is unable to keep pace with it. Basically, we are a species with the capability of making nuclear weapons and intercontinental missiles but with an R-complex imbued with reptilian tendencies[8].

Indeed, in terms of adaptability to technological society, the hybrid brain design is already theorized as one major cause of depression and mental illness in such societies[9].

The behavior resulting from this hybrid brain is bound to be morally mixed, reflecting the fact that we literally

---

[7]   Author Arthur Koestler, to the best of my knowledge, first coined these terms in the 1967 edition of his book, *The Ghost in the Machine*. Since then they've been revived in other books but with differing nomenclature. For example, Carl Sagan in *The Dragons of Eden*, incorporates the paleocortex –limbic system into what he calls "the R-complex". Robert Ornstein in his 1991 work, *The Evolution of Consciousness*, incorporates the haphazard neurologic expression of one or more of these regions as "simpletons".

[8]   R-complex is the term used by Carl Sagan to denote the brain region with the most primitive tendencies, i.e. "performing dinosaur functions". See, Sagan: *The Dragons of Eden*, 60.

[9]   Solomon, *The Noonday Demon: An Atlas of Depression*, 401.

have three brains contending for emergence in one cranium. Behavior will therefore range from the most selfless acts (not to mention creative masterpieces) to savagery, carnal lust run amuck and addictions that paralyze purpose.

The mistake of the orthodox religionist is to associate the first mode of behavior with being human and not the latter. In effect, disowning most of the possible behaviors of which humans are capable.—and hence nine tenths of what makes us what we are. Worse, not only disowning these behaviors—but ascribing them to some antagonistic dark or negative force ("Satan") thereby making them into a religious abstraction.

The neocortex then goes into over-drive, propelled by its ability to craft words for which no correspondents may exist in reality. Suddenly, our "souls" are at risk of being "lost to Satan" who will then fry us in "Hell". In effect, the religionist's higher brain centers divide reality into forces of darkness and light, just like the ancient Manicheans.

As the divide grows and persists, certain behaviorally idealistic expectations come to the fore, and a mass of negative or primitive actions is relegated to "evil". Humans tuned in to this Zeitgeist, which is soon circulated everywhere, being to suppress all behaviors that they regard as defective or sinful. They don't realize or appreciate that humans are risen apes, and not fallen angels.

Are we all sinners as assorted fundamentalists and zealots claim? No, we're an animal species saddled with a tri-partite brain whose higher centers often become self aware of the chasm between the base, atavistic and primitive behaviors (emanating from the reptilian brain) and the ideal behavior conceived by the neocortex. The neocortical language centers then craft the term *sin* to depict the gulf between one and the other.

In this context, the concept of sin makes eminent sense. Sin emerges as the label placed on specific brands and forms of evil. In reality, sin is predicated on an exaggerated importance of humans in the universe. Thus, it elevates (in a perverse way) the importance of humans in an otherwise meaningless cosmos. With sin the overly self-important and morally smug, self-righteous human has at least the potential of offending his putative deity—thereby getting its attention—as opposed to being relegated to the status of a cosmic cipher. Sin is thus an attention getter to a mentally conceived Big Cosmic Daddy.

Despite this, sin is an invariably localized and reactive behavior at the personal, individual level. Sin impinges on and affects the deity (God-concept) that so many believe in. Take away the deity, and sin loses its allure and quickly becomes redundant. How can there be sin if there is no deity to offend or to notice sin and to tote up all the little black marks in its book of future judgment?

The Devil or Satan is simply the mental projection of the most primitive brain imperatives onto the external world. And yes, this imperative (which I will soon get to in more detail) is capable of mass murder as well as genocides. A supernatural Satan need not be invoked here, only the ancient brain residue of reptiles—acting collectively—aided and abetted by the language—obsessed neocortex, which finds it as easy to create neologisms to represent non-existent phantasms as to think. It thereby does the reptile brain's bidding, manufacturing sins, as opposed to attempting to halt it.

In fundamentalists' parlance, this projected entity is like a lion seeking someone to devour. Think of the T-Rex and its insatiable appetite for flesh. Think of components and aspects of the T-Rex brain in each of us lying in wait for the right trigger to set it off, like in the Virginia Tech massacre. Now, project that horror and its instincts to tear, rip and kill anything different or vulnerable outside your being. Voila! We have *the Devil* incarnate. Only really a psychological embolism adorned in reptilian tendencies (traced to our own brain's reticular formation) *we have within us*. So alien and terrifying we have to project it outside to a nameless supernatural Devil.

At the same time, Christian Apologists like C.S. Lewis have employed facetious representations to depict the moral quandaries facing demonic "tempters". In a kind of reverse theological psychology, Lewis, in *The Screwtape Letters*, fabricates an exchange of letters between Uncle Screwtape and nephew Wormwood, wherein the mentor demon attempts to educate nephew on the fine points of tempting humans[10]. Lewis at the time of the original writing (1942), probably expected the serious rationalist to believe that such a clever parable could entice people to accept evil manifest in personal demons.

At face value Lewis' unconventional morality lesson emerges as a creative masterpiece at getting the unwary to accept demonic reality. But even a minimal application of reason and numerical logic would disclose it is nonsense. By way of example, in May of 1990 during a debate at Harrison College, Barbados with a Christian who invoked Lewis' Screwtape narrative I had occasion to do the math for him. I noted that given Lewis' original likely demonic population of two-thousand, then it followed that when the human population hit six billion each demon would have 3 million humans (each) to try to tempt into a Hell—bound act each day. Given a uniform load, and dividing the labor equally, each demon would only have about 0.028 seconds per day for each temptation. Obviously, if the world began with only a couple of thousand agents of temptation, they'd never be able to keep up with the temptation burden as the human population increased to hundreds of millions then billions! In this way I used an argument analogous to *reduction ad absurdum* to show Lewis' Screwtape fable to be just that, an elaborate fable[11].

---

[10]   Lewis: *The Screwtape Letters*.

[11]   Of course, some Christians have attempted to escape this by proposing even more fantastical claims, i.e. "demon

Worse, Lewis' justification for Inquisitional tortures is mind-boggling and effectively renders whatever morality he espouses as useless, and indeed dangerous! In this case, in his book *Mere Christianity,* he pardons the witch burners for making a "mistake of fact", i.e. in believing women described as witches were evil incarnate[12]. To quote one critic[13]:

> If Lewis is willing to accept that witches do not exist, and that, while believing in them, it was right to put them to death, what other "ungodly" transgressions can we forgive as mere "mistakes of fact"?

Interestingly, Lewis' pseudo-morality would easily have been incorporated into the Third Reich's justifications for genocide. I mean, they really believed the Jews were "vermin"—as so much of their propaganda portrayed—so by Lewis' standards they'd be excused for making a "mistake of fact". Lewis might well reply here that the Nazis really knew better than that so their actions were inexcusable. But how do we know there were also not more percipient Inquisitors who *also knew better* than to believe more than a quarter million women burned as witches did not really embody evil or have pacts with "Satan"? It amounts to mere question begging.

Some authors turn these concepts back on their heads and arrive at mind-boggling conclusions. The authors of the book *Mean Genes,* for example, make the case that genetic imperatives drive the most fundamental (epigenetic)

---

reproduction" to inflate the demonic population to more effective levels of temptation. Perhaps the first authors to do this were Kramer and Sprenger in *The Malleus Maleficarum,* 26-27. They advanced the entities known as *succubi* as the likely agents to explain demonic babies.

[12] Lewis: *Mere Christianity,* 14.
[13] Inniss: *The Secular Humanist Newsletter,* (Spring, 1998), 1

morality[14]. The hybrid brain in this sense is merely the facilitator of the genes' imperatives. Perhaps there is a method behind the madness of the brain's disjunctive function: To aid and abet a primal, epigenetic morality.

In the larger societal sense and deformed to an extreme, the epigenetic imperative leads to horrors such as the Holocaust, where Jews were depicted as inimical genetic aliens or pests to the German Fatherland. Hence, once de-humanized, Jews could be dispensed with by the Reich as serious threats[15]. Likewise, the genetic imperative running amuck explains the Rwandan genocide, where Tutsis could be dispensed with as the genetic aliens to the real Rwandans, the Hutus. In this case, Hutu talk radio played a key role in spreading the memes for the epigenetic morality, by dismissing the Tutsis as *cockroaches*.[16]

Examining these genocides at the detached, objective level one cannot but help notice the analogies with ant (or bee) species that invade the habitats (e.g. hives) of others, kill them, make off with their queens and seize their resources. In this sense, the epigenetic morality and imperative emerges as the real "god" articulated in the Bible, while the perfecto, "goody two shoes" posturer (invented later by the clever, angelic leaning neocortex) is the fake. This was the contention of author Lloyd Graham in the last chapter of his contrarian book, *Deceptions and Myths of the Bible*.

For example, as Graham observes[17]:

Satan is matter and its energies and the (Temptation of Jesus in the desert) story is but a mythologist's way of

[14] Burnham and Phelan: *Mean Genes*.
[15] Livingstone-Smith, *Less Than Human—Why We Demean, Enslave and Exterminate Others*, 145.
[16] *Op. cit.*, 151.
[17] Graham: *Deceptions and Myths of the Bible*, 315.

telling us . . . that in the inanimate world matter and energy dominate . . . . The only consciousness here is the epigenetic and this is—as yet—wholly incapable of controlling violent forces. This explains why our imaginary God of love and mercy allows these forces to destroy us.

Graham's depiction of the material and epigenetic god is one embedded in carnal lusts, revenge and avarice—so how can humanity be any different?

Graham earlier notes[18]:

Man owes God nothing, not even thanks. Whatever is, exists because of necessity and not divine sufferance. And whatever exists suffers because of nondivine Causation. Our world is full of suffering, tragedy, disease, disaster, pain; we demand a better reason than religion has to offer.

Perhaps for this reason, Graham insists that it is the de facto creations—*humankind*—who are the genuine authors of workable morality (*dynamic justness* not moral justice) not the claimed Maker.

Religious scholar Elaine Pagels makes much the same point in her book, *The Gnostic Gospels,* pointing out that the Gnostics regarded the biblical deity as a degenerate sub-being which they called *demiurgos.*

Again, both Graham's epigenetic god and the demiurgos are crude God-concepts, hence must be viewed in the light of limited human brains, deficient in their own aspirations to truth or even testability. The danger is that when moral or ethical testability is absent, then uncontained absolutism can result with devastating consequences. Jacob Bronowski

---

[18]   *Op. cit,*. 272.

has maintained that because human knowledge is limited, and further—the human brain is limited in its processing capacity—one must temper expectations and especially refrain from absolutist moral judgments. The reason is that only partial aspects will be glimpsed and then be invoked to fabricate a false or pseudo morality. As he put it[19]:

> The Principle of Uncertainty or, in my phrase the Principle of Tolerance, fixed once and for all the realization that all knowledge is limited.

One of the practical outcomes of such insight is surely to ignore trivial infractions or random moral deviations, including[20]: *masturbation, playing cards, dancing, working on Sundays, etc.* Condemnation of any of these can therefore be described as arbitrary moralizing.[21]

A classic example that highlights the moralizing instinct in humans was described by Dacher Keltner and presented to students to gauge their level of moral revulsion. Keltner presented them with the case of a man who goes to the supermarket each week, purchases a packaged chicken and then takes it home for sexual relations, before cooking and eating it[22].

Keltner reported that after his posed example he observed the students to "react with *the full blown Darwinian-Jamesian emotion of moral disgust written across their faces*"[23]. The nature of the reaction, presumably, discerned an innate moral right, said to be inextricably bound to the "moral gut." Keltner's examples include moral philosophers (e.g. Jonathan

---

[19] Bronowski: *op. cit.*, 232.
[20] Kekes,: *op. cit.*, 130.
[21] *Ibid.*
[22] Keltner:, *Born to be Good—The Science of a Meaningful Life*, 46.
[23] *Ibid.*

Haidt) that "prioritize the moral gut"[24]. In other words, millions of years of human evolution have embedded such disgust—revulsion reactions into us and we ought to heed them as a criterion for moral judgment when aroused.

But why? To the scientific Materialist one is then allowing emotions to rule and if these are codified into law many nasty consequences can ensue. In the case of the man abusing his purchased chicken, Keltner expressed relief to report that—after their initial disgust—the students agreed the behavior could be placed in the category of a personal perturbation or even idiosyncrasy. And so long as practiced in the man's own home—presumably with blinds drawn—there were no laws broken. Oh, it would also be best if he had no dinner parties featuring abused chickens!

The scientific Materialist concurs with this, labeling such initial reactions to peculiar acts as emotive moralistic trivialization. If such moral trivialization is permitted to metastasize into law then we describe it as *Moralism*, For the most part, moralism isn't founded on species survival but on an unsubstantiated and subjective belief in a uniform human sensibility to external stimuli. In this way it becomes the conscious vehicle of behavior modification, used by any group with political or economic power.

For example, the latest rage in many U.S. communities is to shut down medical marijuana or pot shops because they will lure kids. Of course, this is hogwash and unsupported by any data. The truer fact is that kids' lives are more in peril from over consumption of alcohol, especially in fraternity and sorority hazing in colleges. At least medical marijuana laws in most states, such as Colorado, provide stiff regulation to avoid use by minors.

---

[24]   *Ibid.*

Another driver of moralism is the Catholics' *natural law,* which is neither natural nor any kind of recognizable law[25]. The putative basis for it more appears to be the presumption of some kind of natural moral order which is theoretically known to humans and so their knowledge will lead them to avoid infractions. For the scientific Materialist this is nonsense, as the only natural laws we recognize are those which form the underpinning of our natural sciences. For example, the tendency of systems to increase in disorder (entropy) is a natural law, as is the inability of any mass to travel faster than light speed (300,000 km/s).

Masturbation is a controversial but important example of a theological natural law proscription, with near universal applicability. It's also very useful in an era of spreading HIV-infection, AIDS and the recent campaigns for teenagers to embrace virginity (abstinence) and 'just say no'. This is where masturbation enters as a sensible option to teen sexual intercourse. Note that for a Materialist, abstinence is only applicable to intercourse. *Absolute abstinence* (i.e. from *all sex*) is regarded as not only impossibly utopian, but quite probably harmful.[26] In this regard a Materialist ethic offers pragmatic alternatives rather than no alternatives.

In terms of the four criteria given earlier, there is no demonstrable harm arising from masturbation, nor does it harm anyone else by definition. Moreover, once done in private (as is normally the case) it does not violate any civil laws. Hence, the Materialist regards it not only an innocuous act, but also a highly desirable alternative to casual intercourse with its inherent risk of HIV-infection, and

---

[25] The use of the term can itself be confusing to non-Catholics who may confuse it with scientific natural laws.
[26] See, e.g. author Dorothy Baldwin's remarks in her monograph *Understanding Male Sexual Health,*. 46.

unwanted pregnancies (which can lead to abortion).[27] Clearly, all practical solutions to the problems of adolescent sexuality, including self-stimulation, merit attention.

Typically, however, natural law proponents attach guilt, or impute sin, and thereby imbue a normal human sexual activity with ethical import where none exists. For example, according to ethicist Leslie Dewart:[28]

It is unnatural precisely as a moral object, for it contains a moral defect against the generative powers and the use of the sexual organs. The moral perfection of the use of these organs requires the congress of man and woman . . .

Subsequently quoting St. Thomas Aquinas, from the same article:

It is contrary to the natural order of the sexual act as befits human beings.

It is wrong because of the sexual isolation in which its practitioner places himself.

Viewed from a scientific Materialist's perspective, these statements reflect an exaggerated, over solicitous concern

---

[27] One of the most horrendous statistics in 1995 was that a full 30 percent of children born in the U.S. were to teenagers, out of wedlock. The burden to society is an enormous one, whether in terms of abortions—or paying to support so many babies. While the numbers have gone down a bit, they are still much too high compared to say, The Netherlands, where condoms are regularly distributed as part of sex education classes. This embodies a Materialist mode of thinking.

[28] Dewart: *Contraception and Holiness: The Catholic Predicament*, 187.

for the biology of one primate relative of the chimpanzee, on one ordinary planet. Worse, they signify a brazen attempt to intrude in personal affairs that don't concern moralists or theologians. They also raise a host of questions for the skeptic and rationalist. For example, what exactly is a *moral defect against the generative powers*? By what specific criteria is a moral defect measurable, or even knowable? I can determine an optical defect, say in a lens or a telescope mirror, but how do I determine moral defects? How does one verify moral perfection in sexual organs? What is the empirical basis for this? What *observables* characterize this perfection', so one may distinguish it unequivocally from 'imperfection'? What are the precise criteria?

Devoid of any answers, the natural law underpinning Catholic sexual morality amounts to so more balderdash than ballast. But unless these pointed questions are answered, one cannot know whether the language used has any correspondent to objective reality. Nor can one know whether any valid experiential basis exists under the academic disguises. If we don't know these things the moral precepts are probably masquerading as an excuse for interference in human lives. In this case, they all add up to a *sophisticated moralism*.

Aquinas' views, in his reference to *the natural order of the sexual act as befits human beings,* betrays an allegiance to Aristotelian modes of thought. These tend to fix behaviors within very limited and fixed definitions and categories, as has already been pointed out by Julian Pleasants.[29] While Aquinas can be excused on the grounds of living in more backward times, modern (Catholic) theologians and their ilk can't escape blame so easily. They should know better than to pander to ancient ideologies simply to be able to exert control over their flock's collective gonads.

An even more potent indictment emerges from the fact that not so long ago, Catholic theologians justified slavery

---

[29]   Pleasants, *op. cit.*, 88.

as wholly consistent with natural law [30]. Considering both slavery and the subsequent artificial birth control proscription, we clearly see where the Church is coming from. Natural law was invented purely as a theological sophistry; a device to control and manipulate people's lives. Again, as with disinfecting God-concepts of their supernaturalism, the warp and woof of scientific Materialism is to disinfect morality of its dross, redundancies, irrelevance and trivia to enable a more objective manifestation which serves the welfare of all humans, not just a special subset. And not only merely to serve in the meeting of basic needs, but to encourage a broader felicity in life and within community.

A more recent example of ecclesiastical moralism occurred with the Christmas, 2012 holiday message of (then) Pope Benedict XVI. In a time of the year that ought to promote unity, the pontiff—directing his remarks at the Vatican—denounced gay and lesbian progress (as seen in the results of the Nov. 6, 2012 U.S. general election) as a *manipulation of nature* and *an attack on the family.* But note the same generic moralistic framework used to attack masturbation: that nature is somehow being subverted, manipulated or overturned. Of course, the pontiff's message amounts to so much codswallop, and for basically the same reasons as Aquinas' attacks on the solitary "sin". Like Aquinas before him, the pontiff has no clue as to the richness and diversity of nature, including the sheer number of non-human species that exhibit homosexual behavior!

What about abortion? Where does scientific Materialism come down on that? Here natural law doctrine declares some *natural right to life of the unborn.* However, if such right really exists, is there not also a natural right to life for the *already born*? The *just war* concept says no, since it sanctions certain killings for already formed personalities, who may be innocents in just wars. Clearly, the Church's moral authorities can't have

---

[30]   *Ibid.*

it both ways. If they declare a reverence for life and accord it to the unborn, they must do at least as much for the already born.

One suspects that the main defect in this thinking, pivoting on special rights for the unborn, arises from a logical fallacy. As Antony Flew observes[31]:

> The Genetic Fallacy consists in arguing that the antecedents of something must be the same as their fulfillment. It would be committed by anyone who argued, presumably in the context of the abortion debate, that a fetus—even from the moment of conception, must really be because it is going to become, a person

Given such a glaring logical misstep, it seems clear why Catholic doctrines concerning abortion and just war are inchoate and incomprehensible. Added to that is the fact the Church didn't always hold abortion to be sinful. Anne Druyan and the late Carl Sagan pointed out that John Connery, S.J, a leading Catholic historian, showed that up to 1869 the Church's Canon Law had historically held abortion to be murder only *subsequent* to the end of the first trimester.[32] The interesting thing is that for the bulk of Church history the practice of abortion was allowed, at least up to the first three months of pregnancy. More interesting is that the doctrine of papal infallibility was pronounced in 1870. Could it be that the latter doctrine was introduced to back up the Church's change in its moral position on abortion? If so, one wonders who really controls the Church, the Holy Spirit as is so often claimed or zealous prelates in positions of high power who fear relinquishing vise-like grips on their congregations[33].

---

[31]   Flew: *Thinking About Thinking*, 101.

[32]   Sagan and Druyan: *PARADE*, (April 22, 1990), 6.

[33]   And (most recently), nuns, mainly belonging to The Leadership Conference of Women Religious, which was issued

The question for us now is: If scientific Materialism disavows any received morality (as in scriptures), or accepts any assumed to arise from an external supernatural order or deity, or any "natural law", then what remains as a guide? Well, I already provided four question-based criteria for action, but it's appropriate now to flesh that out using a basic architecture.

Michael Shermer gives what is perhaps the best solution under *moral provisionalism* or what I would call *ethical incrementalism*. As Shermer notes[34]:

Provisional ethics provides a reasonable middle ground between absolute and moral relative systems.

He adds that *they are applicable to most people most of the time* and so require no invocation of external invisible spirits or agents.

Materialist-based ethical incrementalism also allows increasing moral oversight when current scientific evidence warrants it. Consider these examples:

1) *Abortion*:

According to ethical incrementalism, abortion cannot be ethical *in all circumstances for all conditions*. Thus, since Sagan and Druyan have noted that fetal brain waves appear past six months, it follows that no abortions should normally

a reprimand by the Vatican for straying outside the purview of Church teachings—especially after they defended the inclusion of contraceptive services in Obama's Affordable Care Act. The Vatican has also censured Sr. Margaret Farley (of Yale Divinity School) after publication of her book, '*Just Love*'. Farley evidently stepped on Vatican toes when she justified artificial contraception as well as masturbation within marriage as an aid to preserving fidelity.

[34]   Shermer: *The Science of Good and Evil*, 168.

be allowed in the third trimester. The only (provisional) exceptions would be: a) the health of the mother (e.g. if she were to have the child she'd die), or b) case of incest or rape—wherein having the child would create extreme mental trauma for the victim. (By that I mean possible psychosis or severe depression, including attempted suicide).

2) *War*:

In the judicious application of ethical incrementalism no war would be casually conducted by a random presidential edict, or pseudo-doctrine (i.e. *Bush doctrine*). Instead, we'd have an actual *declaration of war* by congress. This gives congress the opportunity to exercise its constitutional rights, while imparting moral and ethical authority in rendering a war truly just. In this light, we'd have no more Vietnams, Iraqs, Afghanistans or other adventures of choice, finagled outside the parameters of congressional authority. For too long wars have been waged through the back door at great financial and moral cost to the U.S. The Iraq invasion, for example, never would have been allowed had an actual declaration of war been demanded by congress, as opposed to it meekly rolling over for the executive branch.

3) *Teen sexual behavior*:

In the domain of ethical incrementalism, teens are warned that *actual intercourse* outside of a stable permanent relationship is morally toxic. As a midway position, however, teens are allowed (as former Surgeon General Jocelyn Elders suggested) to obtain sexual relief via self-stimulation. This balance would immediately stop the increasing rates of teen pregnancy, though likely not without the benefit of a good sex ed. course, which must also include removing the stigma attached (by the teen peer culture and larger society) to masturbation.

These are just a few examples, and many more might be cited or found. The point is that there is a middle way, and ethically conscientious humans ought to seek to pursue it as opposed to pretensions to either a facile absolutism or equally facile relativism.

This chapter has been an extensive one, mainly because the foremost objections to any deviations from orthodox Christian God-concepts and moral norms, hinge on morality. The chapter is therefore intended to show that a coherent and credible provisional ethics can be consistently practiced by the scientific Materialist. This is irrespective of whether one is an atheist, secular humanist or a subscriber to a generic and impersonal deity.

PART TWO

PURSUING AN IMPERSONAL-
PHYSICAL TRANSCENDENT VIA THE
QUANTUM THEORY

(HYPER-REDUCTIONISTS NEED NOT
APPLY)

VI. FROM GOD-CONCEPTS TO QUANTUM MECHANICS

The tendency to posit a superior, supernatural being to account for physical existence is nearly universal in every human culture. Indeed, every major sacred book, whether Bible, Torah, or Koran, attributes a (supernatural) divine origin to the universe. The problem inheres in taking this literally, and then extrapolating to an entity 'God'—that allegedly *is involved at a micro-manager level in the cosmos*. Even the staunch atheist physicist, Victor Stenger, acknowledged in a recent article concerning lack of evidence that[1]:

> That is the situation with the Judeo-Christian-Islamic God. Until recent times, absence of evidence for his existence has not been sufficient to rule him out. However, we now have enough knowledge that we can identify many places where there should be evidence, but there is not. The absence of that

---

[1]   Stenger.: *Huff Post* (Religion Blog), Aug,. 23, 2012

evidence allows us to rule out the existence of this God beyond a reasonable doubt.

Now, I am not talking about all conceivable gods. Certainly the deist god who does not interfere in the world is difficult to rule out. However, the Judeo-Christian-Islamic God, whom I identify with an uppercase G, is believed to play such an active role in the universe that his actions should have been detected, thus confirming his existence.

Stenger clearly concedes that *some God-concepts can't be ruled out* as possible transcendent realties. He names the Deist concept, but surely one can include any pantheistic, or impersonal variant, say like Bohm's *holomovement* (elevated to God—concept status).

In this latter case, the universe emerges as more than the sum of its parts by virtue of being holographic. This is based on an explicate or divisible order being enfolded into a higher-dimensional *implicate order* through which consciousness is enfolded as well. Hence, Bohm's deity at least has some scientific legs, since quantum mechanics has been used to fashion the end product. (Bohm uses a mathematical device he calls the *quantum potential* which I will get into in subsequent chapters.)

The relation of explicated individual forms to Universal Mind (Dirac Ether or holomovement) might be depicted as I show below:

INDIVIDUAL FORMS (EXPLICATE ORDER)
__∩__∩__∩__∩__∩__
DIRAC ENERGY SEA (IMPLICATE ORDER)

The relation is holographic in the sense that each of the individual forms contains the information of the whole holographic field. The Dirac Ether is equivalent to Bohm's

Implicate Order, or what he calls the holomovement, and is a pure frequency domain[2] The ripples on this sea are the distinct material forms perceived as separate entities in the universe because we are generally unaware of the implicate order. Nonetheless, the remarkable insight is that within this order separate forms (individualities) emerge as purely illusory. By analogy, the separate waves one sees on the ocean surface are illusions—at least in the sense they cannot be removed and placed on the beach for inspection! So also, material forms cannot be abstracted from the energy background of the Dirac Ether.

If then a god exists, it will not be a personal being, but more realistically a subtle manifestation of energy and fields that may be resonant with a developed consciousness, but to different degrees. In many ways, use of the term *God* is totally redundant and useless, because as a Catholic priest friend once put it (during a seminar in which we exchanged views) it's really *the ALL*. All of being, all of energy, all of every conceivable field, including the Higgs and hence of mass itself[3]. In effect, in Part One I invoked atheism in conjunction with scientific Materialism to purge any lurking subjectivity for the path to follow. The additional objective is to purge our minds of all naïve constructs of God and to think instead in terms *of impersonal energy*, and the evolution of that energy in ways our consciousness can apprehend.

---

[2]   Frequency (F) is related to time (T) by: $F = 1/T$. Thus, $T \to 0$, for a "frequency domain".

[3]   Of course, a logical problem with this was first explicated by philosopher Alan Watts (*Behold The Spirit*, 146). Thus, if God or God-entity is deemed *coterminous* with the universe—as a definite pantheistic concept—then this implies (according to Watts): "God minus the universe equals nothing". This confuses the contingent nature of the universe with the non-contingent nature of a genuine transcendent entity. I will come back to this issue in Chapter VIII.

Philip A. Stahl

The present chapter recruits modern quantum mechanics to this task, for the simple reason that we need a nonlocal paradigm and context, and this is afforded by quantum theory but not by classical mechanics.

After some astronomy lectures I've been asked: *Well, be that as it may, where's the harm in at least acknowledging the possibility of a supernatural origin for the Big Bang—admitting that while the detailed evidence may not be available, the possibility cannot be dismissed?*

This is a fair question, but misses the point. As a limited human enterprise, in terms of funds and resources, science is compelled to make a narrow and judicious selection of problems to investigate. Indeed, the problems posed by the natural world often tax the resources of science beyond its capability to extract practical solutions. Now, add to this the (pseudo-) problems of a realm that no one can be certain exists, and it becomes clear why scientists are averse to venture beyond their domains. At least this is the attitude of most natural scientists, competing for scarce funding.

At another level, science excludes all hypotheses which are judged impractical in terms of confirmation, or empirical test. God is such a hypothesis. What determines whether a hypothesis belongs in the excluded category? For one thing, we must know whether the proposed entity is defined in terms recognizable by science. For scientists, definitions are *operational*, which means they are framed in terms of other (familiar) scientific concepts: energy, fields, mass, volume or whatever.

However, if a concept falls within the purview of *Godel's Incompleteness theorems*, then it isn't addressable by science. God is such a concept, since there aren't enough testable axioms or tenets to prove it or even to identify the necessary criteria for adequacy of operation. Thus, the sort of transcendent personal deity of Christians is unprovable by any system of axioms that can be conjured up by the finite human brain or collection of brains.

Put another way, the typical human brain can make 'x' statements about God but these will always be at least (N—x) short of encapsulating the concept in fullness and adequacy. The gap between all the statements that *can be given* and the essential core that must be given is usually referred to as the space of undecidable propositions.

Now, some say that just as they may have a faith in deity or supernatural, personal God, I have faith the Sun will rise each morning. This is not quite the same thing. In my case it isn't so much any faith but rather confident *pre-supposition predicated on a host of predictable past behaviors—as in thousands of years of first hand, observable evidence!* This is always the case when experience repeatedly validates that the probability of controversion of the underlying physical laws is null.

Stenger's complaint (and mine as well) is that the Judeo-Christian-Islamic God is not supported by evidence that matches the outsized nature of the claims made for it. In other words, it fails the most basic criteria for meeting necessary and sufficient conditions. This deficiency could be redeemed if the concept was modified, for example to *the Socinian deity*, which is limited by never knowing more than the most advanced consciousness existing in the universe at one time. If limited in consciousness, this deity will also make errors. Physicist Freeman Dyson describes an entity almost like a child[4]:

> The main tenet of the Socinian heresy is that God is neither omniscient or omnipotent. He learns and grows as the universe unfolds.

Dyson adds that the beauty of adopting this construct is that it *leaves room at the top for diversity.*[5] As this entity

---

[4]   Dyson: *Infinite in All Directions*, 119.
[5]   *Op. cit.*,120.

grows to fill the universe it becomes as much a diversifier as a unifying force[6]. In a manner of speaking, it would be something like an evolving holomovement. The evolution, by the nature of the role of consciousness with in it (as a kind of integrated creative agent) would then advance as consciousness advances.

Nevertheless, to grasp more of this relationship, and how the nonlocality implicit in quantum mechanics is the key to it, one must understand at least some of the basic quantum mechanics on which it hinges!

Looking at Some Basic Quantum Mechanics: The De Broglie Wave:

A good beginning is with the matter waves of Louis de Broglie. Around 1926, a young French physicist named Louis de Broglie actually postulated the basis for material particles, such as electrons, acting *as waves*. This was experimentally verified in the (1927) Davisson and Germer electron diffraction experiment sketched below:

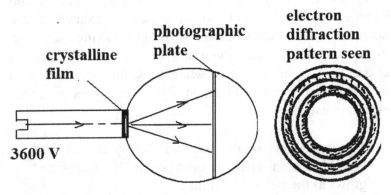

The Basic Davisson andGermer experiment

---

[6]   *Ibid.*

In the experiment, electrons moved through a potential difference V = 4,000 volts, so the kinetic energy gained would be equal to the work done, or:

$$\tfrac{1}{2}\,m\,v^2 = eV$$

Where m the mass of the electron is: *9.1 x 10⁻³¹ kg*

And the electron charge e = 1.6 x 10⁻¹⁹ C

The velocity then is:

$$v = \sqrt{(2eV/m)}$$

The momentum $p = mv = m\sqrt{(2eV/m)}$

The *de Broglie wavelength* λ_D is:

$$\lambda_D = h/p = h/\sqrt{2eV/m}$$

For a voltage V = 3,000 V one would find:

$$\lambda_D = (6.626 \times 10^{-34}\ \text{J-s})/[2\,(1.6 \times 10^{-19}\ \text{C})(9.1 \times 10^{-31}\ \text{kg})]^{1/2}$$

$$\lambda_D = 2 \times 10^{-11}\ \text{m}$$

Which is *the de Broglie wavelength* of the electron in this experiment.

A first step to uncovering the original quantum mechanical wave model (of Neils Bohr) is to examine his quantized relationship, where the left hand side is the angular momentum of the electron orbit around the nucleus of the hydrogen atom:

$$m\,vr = nh/2\pi = L$$

where L is the angular momentum. Re-arranging:

$h/\ mv = 2\pi\ r/\ n = \lambda_D$ or $2\pi\ r = n\ \lambda_D$

Showing the radius is scaled into n (standing) waves of wavelength λ_D

In the preceding, $\hbar = h/\ 2\pi$ is the *Planck constant* divided by 2π[7].

A visual reference for this orbiting wave electron atom can be represented as shown below, in Fig. 2, with the de Broglie wavelength noted, and emphasizing that an integral number of such wavelengths form the circumference of the atomic orbit, as required by $2\pi\ r = n\ \lambda_D$.

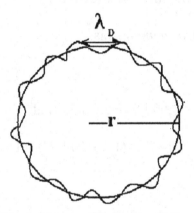

Standing wave model for the Bohr atom.

By extension of the concept of these standing waves, but for different n and r, one can arrive at the *probabilistic wave model* of the atom. This also factors into the basis for the Heisenberg Uncertainty Principle (See Appendix A), as well as *the wave-particle duality.*

---

[7]   The Planck constant, first proposed by Max Planck, is:
       $h = 6.626069 \times 10^{-34}$ J-s Then the value of $\hbar = 1.0546 \times 10^{-34}$ J-s

The point of all this is that particles of mass m have wave properties and actually can be deemed waves. Hence, every material particle has associated with it a de Broglie wave with a wavelength

$$\lambda_D = h/\,mv$$

where h is Planck's constant, and m the mass, v the velocity.

Louis de Broglie, and later Physicists David Bohm and Basil J. Hiley[8], not only concurred with the physical reality of de Broglie waves (or B-waves) but also put forward that they were guided by a clock synchronism mechanism. This was set at a certain rest frequency, f_o, and also for frequencies in non-rest frames. This mechanism would provide a "phase locking" as if guided via "synchronous motors". I invite those mathematically inclined to check out Appendix B for a more complete development.

Problems for Diehard Reductionist-Atheists:

While it may appear that I've been overly hard on theists, especially Christians, reductionist atheists are not out of my crosshairs by any means. One of the most outspoken, against any role for quantum mechanics in modern theories of consciousness, for example, has been Victor Stenger. Indeed, Stenger goes so far as to argue vigorously against any remote form of emergence that might arise from considering quantum theory in physical processes.

One of his arguments is[9]:

---

8   Bohm, and Hiley:*Foundations of Physics*, (10) 1001-1016.
9   Stenger: *God and the Folly of Faith*, 155.

It does not matter whether you are trying to measure a particle property or a wave property. You always measure particles. Here is the point that most people fail to understand: Quantum mechanics is just a statistical theory like statistical mechanics, fundamentally reducible to particle behavior.

Stenger goes on to write that in statistical mechanics one uses the *averaged behavior* of a mass of particles to "determine collective quantities like pressure and density". He compares this to quantum mechanics, asserting we use the average behavior of particles (e.g. electrons) "to calculate collective quantities such as the wave function field".

To fix ideas, I show below (Figure 3) the probability distribution for an electron in the 1s hydrogen orbital. Contrary to some definite sequence of positions, as might have applied in the naïve Bohr model of the atom, we have instead a smeared presence which is a function of the distance from the Bohr radius, a_0. Thus, the probability for finding the electron is maximized near this radius but minimized as one moves way from it in either direction. This probability P_{1s} is the result of squaring the wave function for the orbital. If the wave function is defined: $\psi (1s) = 1/\sqrt{\pi} (Z/a_0) \exp (-Zr/a_0)$,

And the probability function (wave function squared) is expressed:

$$P = |\psi (1s) \psi (1s) *|$$

Where $\psi (1s) *$ *is the complex conjugate*, then the graph shown in Fig. 3 is obtained:

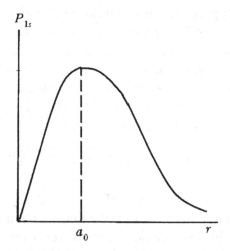

Fig. 3: Probability Distribution for the electron in the 1s Orbital of Hydrogen

Next, we look at an example from statistical mechanics, and specifically the case of electrons in a plasma—an electrically conducting gas. The diagram in Fig. 4 shows the Maxwellian distribution for a set of n electrons in a solar medium.

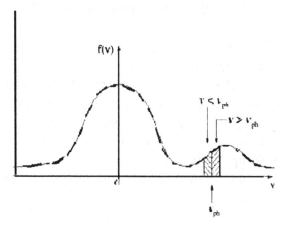

Fig. 4: A velocity distribution for a plasma with a beam instability

Note that f(v) is the distribution probability for plasma particles with specific velocity, say v_{ph} (phase velocity). In this distribution this velocity is defined at the sort line within the shaded region to the right. Resonant electrons (at $v_{ph} \approx \omega_e / k$) are the first to be affected by the local wave-particle interactions and have distributions altered by the wave electric field, E1, such that the total energy:

$$\Sigma E_{tot} = \tfrac{1}{2} E1_w + E1_k = \tfrac{1}{2}[\tfrac{1}{2} \varepsilon_0 \mid E1\mid^2] + \tfrac{1}{2} \rho \mid \tilde{v}\mid^2$$

Note that *the wave energy* (E1 $_w$) is balanced against the kinetic (particle) energy (E1 $_k$). We know such a small hump far from equilibrium (center point of the main distribution) can be created when an energetic beam of particles is injected into the plasma. We don't know how many particles overall are injected or precisely where, but we can find the number occurring at the phase velocity, v_{ph} since:

$$v_{ph} \approx \omega_e / k, \text{ where } \omega_e = (4\pi n_o e / m_e)^{1/2}$$

is the electron plasma frequency. The base frequency, f_e can usually be obtained from observations of associated radio waves, via $f_e \approx [9000]^{1/2}$ MHz, and thence: $\omega_e \approx 2 \pi f_e$.

Thus, the electron charge, e, is known, as is the electron mass (m_e) and the wave number vector, k (= $2\pi / \lambda$) can be estimated from observations. In this case the number density of the plasma at the phase velocity v_{ph} can be estimated. Note that *this is different* from the quantum example, because in that case the probability is computed using a complex number, or complex conjugate.

For quantum mechanical position in one-dimension (x) and momentum p_x:

$$x \cdot p_x - p_x \cdot x = -i \hbar$$

With the operator p_x (op) $= -i\,\hbar\,(\partial/\partial x)$

Similarly, for the energy-time form of the uncertainty relations:

$[E, t] = i\,\hbar$ or **E t – t H = i $\hbar$**

So for the energy operator,

$E(op) = i\,\hbar\,(\partial/\partial t)$

Physicist Max Born's achievement was to see that the presence of the imaginary number (i) in both the time-dependent and time-independent solutions to the equation meant that the wave function could not be real! However, normalization (say by multiplying ψ by its complex conjugate ψ^* and integrating, would yield a real result (say if $\psi(x) = C$ exp i px $/\hbar$) So,

$\int \psi(x)\,\psi^*(x)\,dx = 1$

In Born's statistical interpretation, it was useful for describing the changing probability of finding a micro-system in a particular quantum state but not to be taken literally, as a physically real entity. This is what led Born and the Copenhagen theorists to dismiss the notion that de Broglie waves are actual physical waves. (See also Appendix C for more on the quantitative development using the operator equation)

However, this (Copenhagen) view isn't supported in the foundations of quantum mechanics. One of the foremost quantum theoreticians, J.S. Bell, in one remarkable paper[10], pointed out that in the conventional quantum distribution for position "the probability *enters only in connection with initial*

---

[10]   Bell,: *Foundations of Physics*, 989.

conditions, as in classical statistical mechanics. Thereafter, the joint evolution of Ψ (the wave function) and X (position) is perfectly deterministic" Bell, goes on to note (importantly!) that Ψ: *"has the role of a physically real field, as real as Maxwell's fields were for Maxwell"*[11].

In other words, the field is not merely a statistical artifact as the Copenhagenites claim. Importantly, Bell observes that Maxwell *"had fields extending over all of space, and particles located at particular points."* Most critically, the field at the particular point is that most relevant for the motion of the particle.

The biggest contradiction to Stenger's particle interpretation is also from Bell[12]:

Although Ψ is a real field it does not show up immediately in the results of a 'single measurement', but only in the statistics of many such results. It is the de Broglie-Bohm variable X that shows up immediately each time.

Hence, the particle position as a function of time, X(t) always exists even when no measurement is made. Bell adds that the fact X is *called a hidden variable* and not Ψ is *"a piece of historical foolishness."* This is because there is a joint evolution of Ψ and X, which is *"perfectly deterministic"*. In Stenger's view, by contrast, the evolution is perfectly probabilistic and indeterminate—based on the perspective of specific particle position[13].

---

11 Ibid.

12 *Ibid.*

13 According to Stenger (op. cit.):Quantum mechanics doesn't specify the motion of any given particle. "only the statistical behavior of the ensemble". In other words, no X(t) is feasible.

The truth is that Stenger is appealing to the most popular (among quantum physicists) of *several quantum interpretations: the Copenhagen Interpretation of Quantum Theory*. In this interpretation, the wave function Ψ is purely statistical in nature, following the original proposal of Max Born. We cannot use it to effect specific computation concerning individual particles of a quantum system but are constrained to work only with collective properties.

The principle of *probable position computation* is based upon the wave function ψ itself not being a quantity one can measure. One instead measures: $[\psi]^2$ [14]

In general, the probability $P = [\psi]^2 \, dV$, where dV is a differential of volume, say $dV = dx \, dy \, dz$ in x-y-z space.

For a one-dimensional system: $P = [\psi]^2 \, dx$

The probability P_{ab} of finding a particle between locations a and b is:

$$P_{ab} = \int_a^b [\psi]^2 \, dx$$

By contrast, the basis of the de Broglie-Bohm interpretation—also called the Stochastic Interpretation of Quantum Mechanics - is a description such that: *$\Psi + X(t)$ and $X(t)$ always defines the particle's position for the associated B-wave.*

Problems with the Copenhagen Interpretation:

It's instructional to examine in more depth this interpretation of quantum mechanics with which so many reductionists, atheists are infatuated. Probably the

---

[14]   Once more, the brackets [ ] denote *the absolute value* of the quantity.

one physicist who most refined the limiting aspects of this interpretation was Paul Dirac, in his book *Quantum Mechanics*. Accordingly, he defined first *the principle of superposition* which lies at the core of the Copenhagen Interpretation[15]:

A state of a system may be defined as a state of undisturbed motion that is restricted by as many conditions or data as are theoretically possible without mutual interference or contradiction

By undisturbed motion Dirac meant the state is pure and hence no extraneous observations are being made such that the state experiences external interference effects to displace or disturb it. In the Copenhagen Interpretation, disturbance of mutually defined variables, say x, p or position and momentum, occurs when the following condition is met;

$$[x, p] = -i \, \hbar = -i \, h/ \, 2\pi \text{ (or more generally, } [x, p] \neq 0)$$

where [x, p] denotes a particular operation for a Poisson bracket[16], e.g. such that:

$$[x, p] = (x \bullet p - p \bullet x)$$

And h is the Planck constant of action.

If instead one found that [x, p] = 0, one would say the variables "commute" and hence there's no interference. If the condition doesn't hold, then interference exists. Hence, Dirac's setting of an upper limit in the last portion of his definition, specifying as many conditions as theoretically possible "without mutually interfering interference." This state is undisturbed.

---

[15]   Dirac, P.A.M.: *Principles Of Quantum Mechanics*, 11.
[16]   These *Poisson brackets*, of course, are not to be confused with the absolute value ones for the wave function!

We need to clarify ideas and concepts further to see what the Copenhagen Interpretation is all about and why many regard it as even more metaphysical than the competing interpretations, including Bohm's. Let's say electrons are fired from a special electron gun at a screen bearing two holes some distance away, as depicted earlier:

At first glance, one might reasonably conclude that the individual electron motions follow separate, unique paths. That is, each electron *traverses a single, predictable path*, following stages 1, 2, 3 and so on, toward the screen. This is a reasonable, common-sense sort of expectation but alas, all wrong!

According to the Copenhagen Interpretation of quantum theory, the instant the electron leaves the gun it takes a large number of differing paths to reach the screen. Each path differs only in phase, and has the same amplitude as each of its counterparts, so there is no preference. How does the electron differ from an apple, say tossed at a wall? The electron takes all paths to the screen the apple takes only one (at a time) to the wall. And the electron exhibits phases (as a wave) while the apple doesn't. The electron's wave function can be expressed:

$$\psi = \psi(1) + \psi(2) + \psi(3) + \ldots \psi(N)$$

Here the total wave function for the electron is on the left hand side of the equation, while its resolved wave amplitude states (*superposition of states*) is on the right-hand side. If they are energy states, they would correspond to all possible electron energies from the lowest (1) to the highest or Nth state (N). There is absolutely **no** way of knowing which single state the electron has until it reaches the screen and an observation is made, say with one or other special detector (D).

Prior to reaching the screen the electron exists in a superposition of states or wave packets. Is this description statistical, or individual? This depends. The wave function has a clear statistical meaning when applied to a vast number of electrons. But it can also describe a single electron as well. In the example just cited, all the energy states refer to the same electron. However, if all electrons are identical, the statistical and individual descriptions coincide.

Germane to the point made at the end of Chapter III, i.e. that there is no correspondence between sufficient reason and causation, one finds that in a large number of cases, the approaching electron *goes through both holes in the screen*, not just one. This is totally counterintuitive to one steeped in the traditions of Newtonian or classical mechanics. Of course, the electron deviates from such classical behavior precisely because of its wave nature—as demonstrated in the famous Davisson-Germer experiment that verified that particles exhibit wave properties.

While the Copenhagen Interpretation looked airtight on paper, Hugh Everett III and others were bothered by the claim that all such differing states for an electron, say associated with $\Psi(1)$, $\Psi(2)$, $\Psi(3)$ etc. *exist simultaneously in the same observational domain for a given, specified observer*. Then all but one of the (superposed) states magically disappears when the actual observation is recorded, say by a detector on the screen.

This seemed too contrived and artificial to Everett. What if, he asked himself, one used instead the basis of *many worlds*? Not literal worlds, but rather worlds in the sense of different quantum states separated from each other. Instead of thinking of all quantum wave states co-existing in one phase space (meaning differing x-y-z coordinates assigned to each electron in one system) one could think of each phase attached to another world: a quantum world. Then all these "worlds" co-existed for the total duration of time T before an observation. At the actual observation the choice of one world became a reality. (However, in other quantum worlds those choices could still materialize in slightly different formats).

While seemingly fantastical, the Many Worlds Interpretation thereby eliminated the troublesome issue of observer disturbance of observations so peculiar to the Copenhagen Interpretation. The core problem was best summarized in Dirac's own words[17]:

> If a system is small, we cannot observe it without producing a serious disturbance and hence we cannot expect to find any causal connections between the results of our observations.

In other words, the observation itself *disrupts causation*. For if the observed state is interfered with such that the observables don't commute, i.e. $[x, p] = 0$, then one cannot logically connect states in a causal sequence. To quote Dirac again[18]:

> *Causality applies only to a system which is left undisturbed*

In other words, one for which $[x, p] = 0$ which we now know can only be a macroscopic or classical system.

The Copenhagen solution for many of us is obviously no solution at all. It's more a mathematical recipe book to churn out results without any grasp of the real underlying mechanics. There is no effort to peel back the layers of what quantum physics exposes, but merely to use the results as a kind of "cook book". For those like David Bohm, Basil J. Hiley and others, this would not do. But in order to change the dynamic from the current orientation, we need to examine the complaints of the fiercest critics.

---

[17]   Dirac: *op. cit.*, 4.

[18]   *Ibid.*

VII. QUANTUM QUACKERY OR ANTI-QUANTUM MYOPIA?

A novel phrase that appears to have entered the lexicon of some secularists and diehard atheists is *quantum quackery*. This probably got its legs after an article by the same name written by Michael Shermer[1]. I like Shermer's take on many issues, such as his concept *of moral provisionalism* for a balanced ethics, but I fear he is far off base here.

Of course, he can't be blamed too much for going after the lowest hanging fruit, in this case the 2005 movie, *What the Bleep Do We Know?* Having watched it twice, I found it quite entertaining but nothing on which I'd base a perspective of the world. This includes Physicist Amit Goswani's take that *the material world is nothing but possible movements of consciousness*. However, I believe Shermer was a tad too rough on Amit when he challenged him to *"leap out of a 20 story building and consciously choose the experience of passing through the ground's tendencies."*

---

[1] Shermer, *Scientific American*, January, 2005, 4.

Huh? I don't believe that's what Amit actually meant, but we will get to that in the upcoming chapters, as I deal with consciousness from a quantum perspective.

Where Shermer gets himself in deeper trouble is in criticizing the collaborative work of Physicist Roger Penrose and anesthesiologist Stuart Hameroff. Their theory (some would say "conjecture") is that within neurons are tiny structures called microtubules "which initiate a wave function collapse that results in the quantum coherence of atoms in the brain."

Before exploring the Penrose-Hameroff conjecture in more detail, let me first deal with Shermer's claim that: "there is too large a gap between subatomic quantum systems and large scale macro systems" for any quantum processes to bridge. However, in my first book, *The Atheist's Handbook To Modern Materialism*, I described this interpretation as inaccurate. In particular, the synaptic cleft dimension (of about 200-300 nm[2]) is exactly the scale at which the *Heisenberg Uncertainty Principle*[3] would be expected to operate. That necessarily implies quantum mechanics!

The action then is centered around the brain's synapses, and their dimensions, but not exclusively. Physicist Henry Stapp, for his part, has also pointedly noted that uncertainty principle limitations applied to calcium ion capture near synapses. Stapp cites a reference model for which a calcium ion travels about 50 nm (i.e. 50 billionths of a meter) in about 200 μs (i.e. 200 millionths of a second) en route from channel exit to release site. He then elaborates by noting that:[4]

---

[2]   1 nm = 10^{-9} meter, or one billionth of a meter.
[3]   This states that one cannot know both the position (x) and momentum (p) of an electron, for example, to arbitrary precision. If you know position exactly you know nothing of the other. In one dimension: $\delta p \, \delta x \geq \hbar$
[4]   Stapp: *Mind, Matter and Quantum Mechanics*, 152.

Uncertainty principle limitations on body-temperature ions diffusing this way shows the wave packet of the calcium ion must grow to a size many orders of magnitude larger than the calcium ion itself

Hence, *the idea of a single classical trajectory becomes in appropriate.*[5]

It's critical to point out that the locations can't be computed from classical Newtonian mechanics but rather are based on the probability density we saw earlier, viz.

$$P_{ab} = \int_a^b [\psi(Ca^{+2})]^2 dx$$

Where the brackets denote what's called *an absolute value*. So the location is given by what we call the "expectation value" of where it most probably is, or:

$$<x> = \int_{-\infty}^{\infty} x [\psi(Ca^{+2})]^2 dx$$

Where $\psi(Ca^{+2})$ is to be defined for the particular synapse site. This nullifies the use of classical trajectories or classical mechanics to trace the path of the ions.

Thus we can represent the ion *uptake superposition* (assuming a Copenhagen basis) as a separate contributor to the aggregate assembly[6]:

$$\psi (n \in A, B \ldots E) = \Sigma_{Ijklm} \{\psi(Ca^{+2}) [n_i(A), n_j(B) \ldots n_m(E)]\}$$

wherein all possible states are taken into account. The total of these taken in concert enables a quantum computer modality to be adopted for a von Neumann-style consciousness. In quantum neural networks it is accepted that the real world

---

[5]   Stapp: *ibid.*

[6]   Stahl, *op. cit.*, 157.

brain generation of consciousness is more along the lines of a quantum computer-transducer than a simple collective of switches. As S. Auyang has observed, consciousness is: *more than a binary relation between a Cartesian subject and object.*[7]

Stapp carries this deficiency of the Cartesian dichotomy further, in exposing it as a prime defect of classical mechanics, say in coming to terms with consciousness[8]:

That classical mechanics is not capable of integrating consciousness into science is manifest. Classical physics is an expression of Descartes' idea that nature is divided into two logically unrelated and non-interacting parts: mind and matter. However, the integration of consciousness into science requires instead, a logical framework in which these two aspects of nature are linked in ways that account for both the observed influence of brain processes on mental processes and the apparent influence of mental processes on brain processes.

Further, the incorporation of quantum mechanics into brain function enables the much more effective basis of a quantum computing basis for processing[9]. That means that rather than limit storage to bits, one can work with *qubits* (truncated for <u>qu</u>antum <u>bits</u>) where the *superposition* of a combined data element $(1 + 0)$ applies:

$$\psi = \psi(1) + \psi(0)$$

---

[7]   Auyang,: *How is Quantum Field Theory Possible?*, 112.
[8]   Stapp: *op. cit.*, 146.
[9]   Stapp, *op. cit.*, 132.

The storage capacity dramatically expands as a result. For example, an ordinary computer register only holds one of eight possible 3-bit combinations at a time, say: 001, or 010, or 011. By contrast, a qubit register could accommodate *all* eight possible 3-bit combinations:

$$000, 001, 010, 100, 110, 101, 011, \text{ and } 111.$$

In general, for any given n-bit combination—with n a whole number, a qubit register can accommodate 2 to the nth power total combinations at one time. Thus, 16 combinations could be held in memory for 4-bits, 32 for 5-bits, and so on. This change marks an *exponential* (two to the n or 2^n) increase over any classical counterpart. Since human brains typically hold the equivalent of whole libraries in memory, it seems that qubit processing is at least worth consideration to get beyond the deliberately delimited potential of brains to which reductionists subscribe.

Shermer next claimed that Victor Stenger, in his book, *The Unconscious Quantum*, showed that in order to describe a system quantum mechanically, the product of its mass m, speed v, and displacement d, *must be on the order of Planck's constant, h.* (Where h is 6.6×10^{-34} J-s)

But this is exactly the error Alan Chalmers exposed as being too strong a falsification criterion. Chalmers observed:[10]

. . . if we make our falsificationist criteria too strong then many of our most admired theories within physics fail to quality as good science while if we make them too weak few areas fail to qualify.

One example of too strong a criterion would be requiring any falsified theory to be rejected outright. But

---

[10] Chalmers: *Science and its Fabrication*. 16.

if that is accepted, all of Newtonian physics is sacrificed merely because it cannot compete with Einsteinian General Relativity at a given prescribed scale.[11] Lost forever would be the powerful utility for all earth-based applications, or even the basic (celestial) mechanics needed to get to the Moon or Mars!

Conversely, too weak a criterion may require that any non-falsifiable theory be accepted. For example, the theory of cold fusion,[12] which lacked falsifiability for over a year, would have been accepted.

The problem evidently lies in how particular criteria for testing are identified and articulated. Who actually set or defined the thresholds of acceptance or rejection? To the extent that this is a subjective operation, those whose theories inevitably fall out of favor will complain about 'subjectivity' and 'bias'.

In the case of Stenger's (m) x (v) x (d) criterion, it's clearly too strict in terms of falsification. A much more realistic criterion is that used by Henry Stapp in ascertaining that calcium Ca^{++} ions in the brain display a scale that is amenable to quantum description. Stapp further notes that the synaptic cleft's dimension of 200-300 nm is of a scale to admit application of the Heisenberg Uncertainty Principle.

Shermer quoted Stenger[13]:

---

[11]   Newtonian theory cannot account for the advance in Mercury's perihelion (about 43 seconds of arc per year) while General Relativity can.

[12]   Cold fusion is the theory/hypothesis that nuclear fusion can be obtained from special ('heavy') water in a test tube. That is, under certain conditions, more energy is given out than is absorbed.

[13]   Shermer, *ibid.*

If mvd is much greater than h then the system can probably be treated classically

That is, from a Newtonian perspective. Shermer then goes on to state that[14]:

Stenger computes that the mass of neuro-transmitter molecules and their speed across the distance of the synapse are about two orders of magnitude too large for quantum effects to be influential.

The problem is that if the dimension of the synapse itself is 200nm—300nm or within Heisenberg Uncertainty Principle dimensions, the computation is meaningless for the reason that Stenger would not be able to calculate accurate v and x, or d (position in relation to v) at the same time.

The form for the Heisenberg Uncertainty Principle, say in one dimension, is:

$$\Delta x \, \Delta p_x \approx h$$

Where Δx is the uncertainty in position in the x-direction and Δp_x is the uncertainty in momentum. But what do we see with Stenger's" mvd formula? Well, we see immediately that $mv = p_x$ or the momentum in the x-direction, and Stenger's d variable is just x, the synaptic gap distance with Δx the associated uncertainty.

The stark reality is that as intent as Stenger is on proving no quantum threshold, his calculation is amiss, because (under Heisenberg's Uncertainty Principle) he can't obtain simultaneously accurate values of both p and x (or in this case, mv and d) since if he estimates or knows one

---

[14]   *Ibid.*

to perfection, he loses all information on the other[15]! Thus, rewriting the Heisenberg relation (in 1-dimension) to find the indeterminacy in momentum:

$$\Delta p_x \geq h/\Delta x$$

If Stenger's d were really known to perfect accuracy ($\Delta x = 0$) then:

$$\Delta p_x \geq h/0 = \infty$$

i.e. no localization is possible because the indeterminacy in the position is now infinite.

Shermer himself misrepresents the Penrose-Hameroff efforts (to show a physics basis for neurology) by accusing them of *"physics envy"*, which is balderdash. Shermer describes this as the *"lure of reducing complex problems to basic physical principles"*. But, in fact, this is precisely the violation of which reductionists like Stenger and Shermer are guilty. After all, *they are the ones* insisting we need not go beyond Newtonian or classical mechanics to describe processes in the brain! By way of physics principles, these are about the most basic there are, more so than those of quantum mechanics. The only thing more basic is to hearken back to the notion of atoms as composed of hard little particles, as per the ancient Greek philosopher Demokritos.

---

[15]   Bohm, *Causality and Chance In Modern Physics*, 85. Here, David Bohm makes the strong case that the "indeterminacy principle" is more apropos than uncertainty principle. Thus, for any physical observables it isn't merely that they're uncertain to us—because we can't measure them with complete precision—but rather that "their very mode of being requires them to be indeterminate". Henceforth then, I shall refer to the *Indeterminacy Principle*, or indeterminacy only.

Stenger, in an article entitled *Is the Brain A Quantum Device?*, takes some heart in Hameroff agreeing with him in an earlier criticism that "*synaptic chemical transmission between neurons is completely classical*". But this is shaky refuge indeed, given that Hameroff has always admitted that he himself is not a physicist, and doesn't know much about quantum mechanics. However, Henry Stapp—a long time professional quantum physicist—has shown clearly how the transfer of calcium (Ca^{++}) ions across the synaptic cleft is indeed quantum in nature[16].

The issue, again, gets back to the nature of the extreme reductionist beliefs upheld by Stenger and consistently displayed in all his recent books, including: *The New Atheism, God—The Failed Hypothesis, Not By Design*, and *God and the Folly of Faith*. This isn't to say that in these books Stenger hasn't marshaled compelling arguments for some of the claims (e.g. such as the ID crowd invoking the *anthropic principle*) but rather that the overuse of extreme reductionism often makes his strategy appear more like a dialectic one trick pony. As if any remote possibility of non-reductionism—say in emergence of one property or other beyond what particle assemblies provide—is enough to over react to any and all claims that don't fit neatly into the hyper-reductionist, proto-positivist mold.

By contrast, bold thinkers like David Bohm (whose work I'll examine in more detail in the next chapter), Roger Penrose and Henry Stapp aren't convinced that all complex problems can simply be reduced to the base level of collisions of particles, or simple Newtonian scale interactions. Indeed, Stenger is on record as criticizing one of the foremost physicists (and a 1977 Physics Nobel Prize winner), Philip Anderson, for his challenge to ardent reductionism[17]:

---

16   Stapp: *op. cit.*, 42.
17   Stenger: *God and the Folly of Faith*, 208.

In 1972, Philip W. Anderson, the eminent condensed matter physicist who won the Nobel Prize in Physics in 1977, wrote an article in Science' with the title 'More is Different'. In the article, he complained about the reductionist notion that all animate and inanimate matter of which we have detailed knowledge, is controlled by the same set of fundamental laws. In that case, Anderson noted, 'The only scientists who are studying anything really fundamental are those working on those laws.

Stenger then takes umbrage at Anderson's next remark that many properties of complex systems cannot be derived from particle physics.

According to Stenger[18] : *Wow! No one ever realized that before*

Stenger's final take is[19]:

the fact we cannot derive these emergent principles from particle physics does not prove that everything cannot be just a collection of particles.

So we humans, despite possessing incredible creative aspects to consciousness, are mere "collections of particles". Well, *who* is really reducing complex systems to the most basic physical principles here?

Stenger also claims[20]:

---

[18]   *Ibid.*
[19]   *Ibid.*
[20]   Stenger, *op. cit.*, 205.

While notions of a holistic science are bandied about, nothing much has come of them (recall S-matrix theory). The dominant methodology of science remains reductionist.

This is true, but only to the extent reductionism has been consciously chosen as the best way to not only analyze problems, but also *interpret* them. It is in the interpretations that the real problems inhere. For example, David Bohm's holistic physics as wonderfully outlined in his *Wholeness and the Implicate Order*, is a majestic work that discloses all that fundamental quantum mechanics can do in exposing our eyes and other senses to higher dimensions—not taken into account. Physicist Henry Stapp's *Mind, Matter and Quantum Mechanics* plays an equally crucial role. Indeed, Stapp goes so far as to provide a mathematical model (in the Appendix to his book) integrating consciousness with quantum physics. Any hard core skeptic, especially a hardcore atheist, needs to read it.

Apart from all this, Alain Aspect's twin photon (correlation) experiments clearly show a fundamental nonlocality which in the next chapter will be examined in more detail, including further Stenger objections. Why doesn't Victor Stenger accept these results as evidence of nonlocality? Well, primarily because he fears such acceptance will open the door to holism, and then all manner of religions and supernaturalism, God-seeking and general religious irrationalism. He avers[21]:

In the holistic view of life, every event is part of a grand scheme that applies, under divine guidance, to the whole system, from bacteria to humans and from millions of years ago to the present and indefinite future.

---

[21]   *Ibid.*

But this errs by inflating worries beyond their actual bounds. It also does a gross disservice to those physicists working at the frontiers, depicting them as little more than quantum spiritualists or high priests of an obscure cult. Moreover, none of those quantum physicists who've pursued an integrative physics have claimed any divine guidance. This is Stenger's own particular bugbear, worry and insertion.

It isn't difficult to parse Stenger's reductionism because I once shared it too, in three atheist books I wrote. The pinnacle of reductionism, not surprisingly, was achieved in classical physics, based on Newton's laws of motion. Its quintessential form, Mechanics, ultimately became the model for all of science by virtue of its sophisticated and elegant mathematics. Its power, particularly to make predictions, was so beguiling that it led to an entire mechanical paradigm for the universe.

An illustration can help to clarify why mechanical reductionism became so beguiling to later scientific minds. One of the more interesting systems is the Attwood machine in which we have two masses suspended at opposite ends of a string on a single pulley, but with one mass exceeding the other, e.g. $m2 > m1$. Then, when set up, the masses will accelerate *in the direction of the greater mass*, since an unbalanced force is now acting. See diagram:

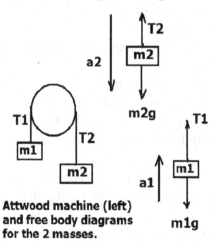

**Attwood machine (left)
and free body diagrams
for the 2 masses.**

The problem for this simple pulley system is to find the acceleration resulting. Since m2 > m1 the acceleration is in the direction of a2, and using two free body force diagrams (right side of graphic) we may write (since T1 = T2 = T) 2 separate equations of motion:

$$m2a = m2g - T$$

$$m1a = -m1\ g + T$$

Adding the two equations:

$$a(m1 + m2) = (m2 - m1)g$$

And the acceleration is just:

$$a = (m2 - m1)\ g/\ (m1 + m2)$$

In other words, the difference in the two masses times g, the acceleration of gravity, divided by the sum of the two masses. This Newtonian paradigm reached its most extreme form in the theories of Pierre Simon de Laplace, who asserted that the past, present and future positions *of all particles in the universe* were within the purview of Mechanics. The universe as automaton!

And what of Man? According to physicist Henry Stapp[22]:

Classical physics portrayed man as a puppet controlled by the iron hand of destiny ordained at the beginning of time. Man was thereby removed of all responsibility for his acts.

In fact, if one carried reductionism even further he'd end up with the meaninglessness highlighted by authors

---

22   Stapp: *Foundations of Physics*, (15), 35

like Alex Rosenberg.[23] This isn't meaninglessness of the cosmos, but something more fundamental: the essential meaninglessness of any brain product including: thoughts, words, book content, whatever. To believe Rosenberg's hyper—reductionism would be to make the writing of this book an exercise in futility and symbolic nonsense. Since I happen to think words have meanings and hence convey significance that can be apprehended by brain neurons, this is unacceptable. Thus began my departure from hard Atheism or the ridiculous notion of an atheist universe.

Other Confusions Displayed by the Reductionists:

While I've focused on Victor Stenger, because he's perhaps the most outspoken reductionist—who's waged endless combat against theists and emergence adherents—there are other examples that can also be cited. Consider a 2011 conference convened at The Philotetes Center, where physicist Mark Alford attempted to rebut Deepak Chopra's claim of a quantum mind (i.e. one unified mind field on the basis of quantum nonlocality) by arguing no quantum mechanics (QM) is needed to parse brain function. Of course, he is quite wrong (not on the "quantum mind" aspect) since one can find numerous ways QM enters as I showed earlier.

Alford remarked that[24]:

It seems improbable that these very delicate processes are the crucial feature in the functioning of the human brain which is not a suitable environment for quantum subtlet".

---

[23] Rosenberg: *The Atheist's Guide to Reality:—Enjoying Life Without Illusions.*

[24] Alford: *Skeptical Inquirer*, (May-June, 2011) 8

But in fact, he's quite mistaken. For example, as I noted earlier, if the synaptic cleft scale is on the order of 200-300 nm it's subject to the Heisenberg Indeterminacy Principle. This is precisely a *quantum scale* so it makes sense that the Heisenberg Principle would apply at this level, and one can therefore surmise all the mutual interference effects that are attendant. This point is emphasized by quantum physicist Henry Stapp[25]:

Brain processes involve chemical processes which must, in principle, be treated quantum mechanically. In particular, the transmission process occurring at a synaptic junction is apparently triggered by the capture of a small number of calcium ions at an appropriate release site. In a quantum mechanical treatment, the locations of these calcium ions must be treated quantum mechanically: a quantum mechanical component must be added to the other uncertainties such as those generated by thermal noise, that enter into the decision as to whether the synapse will fire

In term's of Bohr's Complementarity Principle, the variables x (position) and p(momentum) are regarded as *mutually interfering observables*. In terms of brain function it would mean that those electrons configured into brain dynamics can exhibit wave-particle complementarity in the course of neural transmissions that always entail electrical signals. Of course, if Heisenberg's principle didn't apply—meaning we'd know both the position and momentum to the same degree of accuracy then:

$$[x, p] = 0$$

---

[25]   Stapp. *op. cit.*, 152

Is this really the case? Absolutely not, because the parameters and scales applicable don't support it! Not at the specific synaptic sites! Henry Stapp observes[26] that while some classical descriptions and models are fine for certain neural contexts, i.e. *locations of neurons and their macroscopic electrical activity* (such as relayed to an EEG), they break down when one tries to apply them to the firing of synapses.

Beyond this example, the vast information capacity of the typical human brain is more readily explained by appeal to quantum bits (qubits) rather than ordinary bits.
Alford is quoted as also asserting:[27]

It's more likely that consciousness arises from other, more conventional bits of science, and you don't need to reach all the way to this, the most exotic, the most delicate, the most bizarre bit of modern physics.

And yet, despite being bizarre, this "exotic bit of physics" has reshaped our entire modern scientific and technological landscape! It's given us high-powered lasers and also enables us to put solid state electronics to practical use employing something called quantum tunneling—whereby a lower energy wave can penetrate a higher energy barrier, as well as explaining why solar fusion occurs more than once every fourteen billion years in the Sun's core. It has also enabled us to probe the inside of the atom and atomic transition processes, including being able to associates discrete energy levels with atomic states! Hence, it is nowhere near the abstract, incomprehensible theory that Alford claims.

His argument that *we don't need to go that far* is also somewhat puzzling. Why not, if it can be shown to work?[28]

---

[26]   *Ibid.*

[27]   Alford: *op. cit.*

[28]   See, for example, David Bohm's excellent presentation in his book, *Quantum Theory.*

His argument is analogous to asserting we don't need to go all the way to use differential calculus to compute rocket trajectories! That the latter is "way too exotic". Well, true! One could rely on just algebra to attend to rocket flight (with finite differences substituted for where differentials appear) and come away with at least some basic info. But it'd be much cruder than what the dy/dt's would yield, and you'd not be able to land on Mars, even after ten years of computations!

His other remark is also rather disappointing for a physicist[29]:

If you rely too much on the current scientific paradigm, wait a hundred years—it's been replaced. So I don't think you want to be using quantum mechanics as a foundation.

Here he conflates a scientific paradigm with scientific theory (e.g. Quantum theory). The two are not one and the same. The current paradigm, if one needs to articulate it, is more accurately a form of *reductionist mechanism*. That is, no emergent properties are presumed to issue from basic material interactions or processes. In this sense, Alford and his cohort who subscribe to it are the ones on less than firm scientific ground, since we know paradigms do shift as documented in Thomas Kuhn's *Structure of Scientific Revolutions*. Thus, in a hundred years, the reductionist mechanical model may be totally replaced by an emergent or holistic model, say of the type proposed by the late physicist David Bohm in his *Wholeness and the Implicate Order*.[30]

Further, Alford is mistaken in how he portrays the fate of theories. Genuine theories, which start out with solid evidence and predictions, are seldom permanently complete.

---

29   Alford, *ibid.*
30   Bohm:, *Wholeness and the Implicate Order.*

For a quick example, look at Newtonian Mechanics. Did we replace it with the advent of Quantum Mechanics? Not at all! It remains a valid theory to apply, say to launch an artificial satellite into Earth orbit, or to put a Rover on Mars. It has not been wholesale "replaced" and indeed, in the standard Schrödinger equation, quantum mechanics is found to revert to Newtonian mechanics in the limit of very large principal quantum number (n → oo).

Another reason why quantum mechanics can't be conflated with the current paradigm is because it is only one of two props for modern physics, the other being relativity (special and general theories). I note that Alford has said nothing on those, though granted Chopra didn't incorporate them into his "quantum mind" either. However, if one is going to make reference to "the current scientific paradigm", one is at least obligated to include relativity as part of it!

It was David Bohm who first pointed out the very close analogy of quantum processes to thought[31]. In particular, the quantum wave packet collapse which is exactly analogous to the phenomenon of trying to identify what one is thinking about at the instant he seeks to pin it down. More often than not, when one does this, as Bohm notes: uncontrollable and unpredictable changes are introduced into the thought process, disrupting the pinpoint attempt.

Bohm also provided a putative basis for a holistic quantum consciousness which he referred to as *the holomovement*. This was done by positing a hyper-dimensional reality (e.g. 5-dimensional) in which mind was enfolded as part of an *implicate order*. To enable a unified mental field within this higher dimensionality, Bohm appealed to hidden variables obeying Heisenberg relations such that:

$$(\delta p)(\delta q) > h/ 2\pi$$

---

[31]   Bohm, *op. cit.*, 169

where p, q denote two hidden variables underlying a sub-quantal scale indeterminacy relation. From this (leaving out lots of details) he developed an agent to assist in the nonlocal action of distal variables, and called it the *"quantum potential"*, defined:

$$V_Q = \{-\hbar^2/2m\} \, [\nabla R]^2 / R$$

for a wave function, $U = R \exp(iS/\hbar)$

where R, S are real.

While all this looks fascinating, even Bohm admitted the plausible acceptance of his conjecture rested on the outcome of a particular experiment. The experiment he proposed was actually designed by Rapisarda and Gozzini and became known as the Gozzini experiment. It was originally to be conducted near Pisa, Italy ca. 1995. Alas, up to now—so far as I know—it hasn't been carried out. But if it had, and real de Broglie waves had been detected then this would be at least an indirect basis for Bohm's claim, as well as a feather in the hat for the claim of quantum mind. Without it, we have no valid basis to assert such a claim, and can only adopt Bohm's vision as inspiration or maybe a useful insight.

The bottom line on Alford's take: He was correct is rejecting Chopra's quantum mind but used the wrong reasons, which amounted to tossing out the baby (quantum mechanics) with the bathwater (quantum mind + QM). If he had refined his arguments a bit more and had more knowledge of the background issues, in particular on Bohm's work, he could have quashed Chopra's claims without having to resort to nullification of QM in brain processes as well!

Conclusion:

The gist of this chapter and the best way I can summarize it, is that hard core reductionist thinkers need to tread carefully in the degree to which they renounce nonlocality or emergence. In particular, they need to be more temperate and control their knee-jerk responses any time quantum mechanics is proposed for application to the human brain and consciousness. In this sense, derogative phrases like *quantum quackery* serve no constructive purpose and render the users more in line with modern Luddites.

Some physicists, aware of the adverse effects of hyper-reductionism, use another term: *Scientism.* This incorporates all aspects of the doctrinaire, reductionist-classical Newtonian approach with which many skeptics are fascinated, and which justifies their rejection of anything resembling holism or emergence.

Physicist Bernard d'Espagnat poses the problem thus[32]:

Is it not true that, 'reductionist' thinking strongly inspired by scientism has subtly taken hold of the diffuse mentality in each of us, compelling even, for example, non-materialists to think somehow of their own mind using concepts borrowed from the technique of electronic computers?

Of course, I admit to being guilty of this very overt simplification in my first book. Totally enchanted by the hyper-materialist and reductionist meme, I actually consumed up to half of a chapter invoking operational amplifiers and logic gates, to apply to human consciousness. In one segment, I actually suggested self-awareness in humans could

---

[32]   d'Espagnat, *In Search Of Reality*, 56.

be represented by a compound logic gate (called an XOR or exclusive—or gate) of the form[33]:

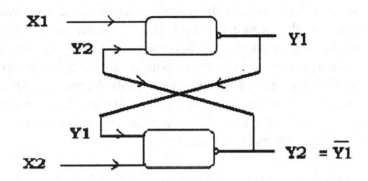

Classic Logic Gate for Self-Awareness

I claimed that irrespective of output, be it Y1 or Y2, the signal was fed back as a novel input, i.e. to X1 or X2. I then assumed that one, say X1, arose from internal data already stored while X2 arose from some mix of outside data and other internal data kept in hidden registers somewhere which could be likened to a human's subconscious. In each case, outputs would be produced that were then fed back into the system providing it with the capability *of self-recursiveness* and a degree of self-regulation.

Where I went off the rails, and exposed my hard core scientism (probably because the book was originally written to be published by The American Atheist Press) was in using this ridiculously simple logic element to suggest human self-consciousness could result from an indefinitely large macro-assembly of such. Obviously, I no longer buy that or I'd not be writing this book. But the point is it reveals the degree of ontological derangement to which one can be

---

[33]   Stahl,: *op. cit*, 149

vulnerable if he allows reductionism to cloud his thinking and fuel his opposition to emergence, or deity constructs. The associated logic can perhaps best be described as a form of *reductio ad absurdum*.

But I'm not done with this cautionary tale for reductionists who've resisted the call to be changelings. This applies to those who claim to be atheists and tend to hang on to reductionism like a permanent crutch. D'Espagnat again[34]:

> If scientism were correct, or more precisely, if the view of the world it proposes so forcefully, that of a world ultimately consisting of myriads of small localized objects merely endowed with quasi-local properties were correct, then such an evolution of our mentality would admittedly be excellent. It is always good for man to know the truth! But on the other hand, if the ultimate vision of the world which scientism proposes is false, if its conceptual bases are mistaken, then this development is—on the contrary—quite unfortunate.

d'Espagnat then states, matter of factly, that the presumptions of "common scientism" are false in his estimation, and he bases this not on subjective opinion but on specific scientific facts. This is a conclusion with which I must concur. But then as the book title implies, just as Beyond God must imply moving beyond all significations or symbols for deity, so also *Beyond Atheism* must move beyond reductionism and the lure of scientism in describing a more nuanced physical reality which again, doesn't mean veering into supernaturalism or accepting any kind of religion.

---

[34] D'Espagnat, *ibid.*

VIII. THE PHYSICAL BASIS FOR A NONLOCAL UNIVERSE

The Quantum Insight of interconnected wholeness and non-separability is primarily predicated on the experiment of Alain Aspect and associates. What we perceive to be a fragmentary, divided world is, in fact, a seamless and unitary whole. This is perhaps the singularly most important contribution of quantum mechanics, over and above modeling the hydrogen atom, or the application of 'tunneling' to electronic diodes.

This insight, not surprisingly, is the basis for what many of us now regard as a more honest appraisal of our universe, and going beyond the tendency to reduce everything to simple assemblies of atoms and their interactions. We saw in the previous chapter how critics have sought to impede this, perhaps out of a real fear it will provide grist to the ardent religious to use as they will.

But this is a mistake! The reason is that a holographic or nonlocal cosmos is not the same as a supernatural one, nor can it be invoked to support supernaturalism. What it does, instead, is to provide for the possibility of emergence of more organized physical forms that can then make way for a superior explanation of consciousness.

The Contribution of David Bohm:

At the time of his re-interpretation of quantum theory, David Bohm may never have been aware of the radical conception of reality he'd proposed. Or that he was (arguably) formulating the foundation of Holo-Physics, a foundation that showed how all manifest forms are interconnected in one unifying reality. Central to this, were: 1) his development of the 'implicate order', and 2) his inclusion of the quantum potential, as well as 3) his interpretation of the quantum wave function as real.[1] More than that, he integrated all of these as the basis of a *holomovement*.

None of this would be possible without David Bohm's re-invention of the philosophical basis of the quantum theory. Since the 1926 Solvay Conference in Denmark, a majority of quantum theorists including the influential Neils Bohr and Max Born, had come to believe that the best interpretation of quantum theory was no interpretation at all. That is, they offered the sterile prescription: 'Just make the measurements, and don't worry about what they mean'.

Central to this 'Copenhagen Interpretation' was the postulate that the quantum wave (which was described by the Schrodinger equation, for example) was simply a

---

[1]   The quantum wave function in one dimension is given as: $\psi(x) = \exp(ikx)$, and is interpreted as being 'fictitious' or purely statistical because of the presence of the imaginary number i. $(= \sqrt{(-1)})$

mathematical artifact—not a real wave. Their reasoning was that since it seemed to show unfolding probabilities, it could not possibly be physically real.

Bohm and Louis de Broglie[2] argued, however, that the Schrodinger equation gave way to a physically real wave that unfolded deterministically in time, while also doing so in a probability sense. They called this *'The Stochastic Interpretation'* of quantum theory. The quantum waves are physically real, but undergo random motions in a high-energy background (called 'Dirac Ether'). The distributions of these random particle-wave motions are what the quantum probability functions refer to.

Perhaps the most fundamental attribute of Bohm's holomovement is the *implicate order* which enables the integration of mind and matter. This is totally distinct from the Cartesian—classical physics point of view that splits mind from matter as two unbridgeable realms, whose apologists we saw in the previous chapter. The problem of confining brain operation to classical physics is that it inevitably invites Cartesian dualism, where matter is that which occupies space (*res extensa*) and mind is that which thinks (*res cogitans*). In the implicate order of Bohm both are unified in a higher dimensionality. If this is the case then for the purpose of organizing a coherent theory of consciousness, we can do no better.

In a beautiful demonstration of implicate and explicate order, Bohm used a cylinder filled with glycerine. The cylinder is designed so that the glycerine can be rotated in either clockwise or anti-clockwise directions. An ink drop is put into the glycerine, and represents an explicated (or

---

[2]   Louis de Broglie proposed the de Broglie wave as the basis for all matter. In effect, each material particle possessed a wavelength $\lambda = h/mv$, where h was the Planck constant, m was its mass, and v its velocity. The de Broglie hypothesis, validated in a 1927 experiment by Davisson and Germer, showed that matter had a wave character just like light.

unfolded) form. If the cylinder is now rotated, say clockwise, the ink drop apparently disappears. In fact, it is merely *enfolded* in an implicate order. This can be deduced when the cylinder is now rotated in the anti-clockwise direction, causing the ink drop to re-appear once more. Thus:

Disappears = enfolded (implicate order reality)
Re-appears = unfolded (explicate-order reality)

In the more general sense, Bohm postulated that all material forms are the unfolded or explicated order of a fundamental implicate order reality. This explication arises at the limit that the waviness (defined by de Broglie waves) of the cosmos gives way to particles. Particles bespeak the separation of the cosmos—waves (quantum waves) its unity. The problem with traditional thinking, of which most modern theology is the embodiment, is that it has treated reality in a particulate rather than wave context. In a sense, the false theology of the orthodox theologians (along with their false God concepts) fits hand in glove with the false physics reflected in the Cartesian-Newtonian viewpoint of too many modern physicists. (Though the latter would vigorously deny this)

Not surprisingly, the universe is perceived to be fragmented: galaxy from galaxy, star from star, each man from every other and even man from himself (body vs. Soul, mind vs. Body, etc.). It is out of this background of a false theology that conceptual theological horrors like 'heaven and hell', 'damnation' and 'salvation' arise. The reaction of the false physicists to this is also natural and understandable: they wholesale reject all of the false theology as puerile rubbish so like the ancient Greek Epicureans they cut the false theologians off at the pass by proclaiming everything ends at death. No afterlife, no souls, hence nothing to punish.

In the implicate order proposed by Bohm, the separateness of the universe is ultimately submerged within its wave nature. All seemingly separate entities are ultimately unified into one, much like the apparently separate 'waves' seen on the ocean ultimately dissolve and submerge into the vastly greater background sea that spawned them. The waves are the implicate sea explicated or unfolded. This is where the often used term *oceanic reality* originates.

In human terms, this implies that at a higher dimensional level all matter, especially as embodied in human forms, along with human minds, becomes interfused into one reality, one whole without division. As Bohm describes it[3]:

> In the implicate order we have to say the mind enfolds matter in general and therefore the body in particular. Similarly, the body enfolds not only the mind but also in some sense, the entire material universe.

Within this putative *Universal Mind*, humans exist not as separate beings at the particulate level of reality, but as conscious monads or centers of action that incorporate attributes of the undivided whole. This is what Bohm referred to as a "*more inward actuality that is neither mind nor body but rather a higher-dimensional actuality . . . . with a nature beyond both.*" (mind and body)[4].

Another nice illustration of this (originally conceived by Bohm) is as follows: You walk into a room and see two television monitors. Each shows the image of a fish, one in lateral view, the other face-on. The casual observer may simply deduce that he's seeing two different fish, one on each screen, each in a separate fish tank. The observer then walks

---

[3]   Bohm, *op. cit.*, 209
[4]   *Ibid.*

into an adjoining room where he confirms that each monitor is receiving input from two distinct camcorders trained on one aquarium, with only one fish inside it. One camcorder is aimed at the front of the aquarium, the other at the side. The fish is resting with its face to the front.

At that point, the observer has recognized that at the higher (three)-dimensional) reality there is one fish, seen in two different (two dimensional) perspectives. By analogy, Bohm has suggested a similar error of perception applies to how we perceive the particulate (unfolded) world around us. We see only fragmentation and separation because our senses can't access the higher dimensional reality that discloses all entities are unified.

How can we surmount the obvious wall of separation? One would need a means that transcends time, or the perception of time (which is itself fragmentary). Such a means already exists and is called meditation. Bohm himself observes:[5]

> I think that meditation would even bring us out of all the difficulties we've been talking about . . . . the actuality of this 3n-dimensional consciousness could not be attained by studying physics with our 3 dimensional consciousness. It might form a bridge or pier of some sort that moves us a certain way but, somewhere we've got to leave thought behind, and come to this emptiness of this manifest thought altogether and of the conditioning of the nonmanifest mind by the seeds of manifest thought. In other words, meditation actually transforms the mind. It transforms consciousness.

Bohm's reference to *bringing us out of the difficulties* etc is in response to questions posed concerning the role of meditation in respect to: space-time, the holomovement, and '3n-dimensional reality'. In effect, meditation permits a

---

[5] Bohm, in *The Holographic Paradigm* (Ed. K. Wilber), 103-104.

bridge by which to escape the plurality of objects and enter a realm of unity.

The full emptiness of non-manifest thought implicit in meditation requires rational thought be left behind. In normal practice meditation accomplishes this by providing a thoughtless void. In this effective conditioning of non-manifest thought, the substratum of the wave universe or oceanic reality is made possible. In effect, meditation acts as an amplifier to empower our minds toward higher dimensionality and the Universal Mind.

The beauty of meditation is that it is accessible to all of us, without regard to class, race, income level or IQ. It is the one indispensible access point to Universal Mind and submergence within that Mind. It is, in other words, an intuitive and personal tool to accomplish the foremost practical goal of Theo-Physics: unity with Universal Mind and *Christhood*.

Ken Wilber (who interviewed Bohm) observes:[6]

. . . the core insight of this holistic experience is that man's innermost consciousness is identical to the absolute and ultimate reality of the universe,

Bohm, in this same interview, alludes to meditation as a possible means to *go from the explicate to the implicate, thence to some vast ocean outside of space as we ordinarily experience it.*[7]

Bohm's Persecution:

Like many earlier bearers of light and conscious evolution, e.g. Meister Eckhardt and Giordano Bruno, David

6   Wilber: *Journal of Transpersonal Psychology* 2.
7   Wilber, K. (Ed.) *The Holographic Paradigm*, 213.

Bohm was made to suffer grievously for his pursuit of truth, holistic insight and seeing physics in a more unified light. The result was a very real professional martyrdom in which Bohm saw his career nearly destroyed.[8]

This persecution began amidst the anti-communist hysteria that swept the U.S. during the McCarthy era. Bohm, then a fellow at the Institute of Advanced Study in Princeton, became caught up in the furor when he was asked to testify against colleagues in front of the House Un-American Activities Committee in 1949.[9] He refused and immediately became a pariah, including being ruled 'persona non grata' at the Institute for Advanced Study in Princeton. Thus, despite being acquitted of all charges, his employment potential on American soil was forever shattered thereafter.

However, this was not to be the end of it. Now working overseas (in England) and mainly alone, Bohm in 1952 saw the publication of his new model of quantum mechanics employing physically real waves and hidden variables. The reception was less than enthusiastic and no less than his earlier mentor J. Robert Oppenheimer remarked: *if we cannot disprove Bohm, then we must agree to ignore him*

Indeed Oppenheimer, a leading light in quantum and nuclear physics, left a bitter legacy behind for Bohm. In my own case, I recall asking a professor in a graduate-level quantum mechanics class about Bohm's hidden variables theory. He sneered then pointedly replied: *"We don't discuss such nonsense in a serious class on quantum mechanics. If you wish to pursue science fiction then by all means do so, but not on my time."*

That prof's emotive, small-minded response showed me more than he intended. It enabled me to see an outwardly serious rationalist who was inwardly terrified of the very possibility that Bohm's theory might be true. All of

---

8   Goldstein, *Science*, (275), 1893.
9   *Ibid.*

which indicates that professional scientists are nowhere near being the dispassionate and objective persons they fancy themselves. If a novel idea or concept violates their temperaments, they are as likely to become dogmatic and doctrinaire as anyone else. This is most unfortunate, because it retards progress for everyone else in the human family.

For my part, I took the Professor's words with a grain of salt and continued my own individual research into Bohmian quantum mechanics without his help. Assorted papers I received directly from Bohm (then at Birkbeck College, University of London) also helped. These major papers, generally published in the journal Foundations of Physics, dealt with his updated theory. Accompanying the papers is a personal note signed by him. For now, it is important to examine more closely the demonstrable basis of holo-physics.

Quantum 'Spookiness' and the EPR Paradox:

The genesis of the experiments leading to the Quantum Insight began as long ago as 1935. At the time, Albert Einstein began to feel a growing unease at the new turns quantum theory had taken. In particular, he was bothered by the seeming nonlocalizability implicit in Neils Bohr's vision of the universe as an 'unanalyzable whole'. Einstein—determinist that he was, fully recognized that an absence of 'locality' as it was called, translated into an absence of analysis. One had to be able to isolate a system or process in order to distinguish it from competing ones, else no analysis could be done.

In 1935, Einstein along with two colleagues, Boris Podolsky and Nathan Rosen, devised a thought experiment.[10] This has since been called the EPR experiment based on the first initials of their names. Einstein, Podolsky and Rosen

---

[10]   Einstein, Podolsky, and Rosen.: *Physical Review*, 777.

(E-P-R) imagined a quantum system (atom) which could be ruptured such that two electrons were dispatched to two differing measurement devices. Each electron would carry a property called 'spin'. Since the atom had zero spin, this meant one would have spin (+ 1/2), the other (–1/2). The diagram below illustrates this, the atom being disrupted inside the box, with its opposing spin electrons sent to the left and right.

$$(+1/2) \uparrow <\text{-----------}|\text{-----------}> \downarrow (-1/2)$$
$$[BOX]$$

Orthodox quantum mechanics forbade the simultaneous measurement of a property (say different spin states) for the same system. If you got one, you could not obtain the other. This was a direct outcome of the Heisenberg Indeterminacy Principle which stated that simultaneous quantum measurements could not be made to the same precision.

E-P-R argued that this showed the incompleteness of quantum mechanics. It was not the 'paragon' of physical theories its apologists claimed, if such indeterminacy was fundamentally embedded within it. At the same time they conceived an 'experiment' in which both spins could be identified—with the sole assumption that both were in definite states from the instant of their parent atom's disruption.

Then, we need only know one spin to obtain the other. Say we know or can measure one spin to be (+1/2).[11] Since the total atomic spin is zero, the other electron must have spin (–1/2) since: (–1/2) + (+1/2) = 0

Thus, we manage to skirt the Indeterminacy Principle, and obtain both spins simultaneously without one measurement disturbing the other. We gain completeness, but

---

[11]   More technically, this is what is referred to as 'the z-component of electron spin', since the electron is visualized as a spinning top, with z-axis (i.e. component) in the axial or z-direction.

at a staggering cost. Because this simultaneous knowledge of the spins implies that information would have had to propagate from one spin measuring device (on the left side) to the other (on the right side) instantaneously! This means faster-than-light communication, which violates special relativity. In effect, a 'paradox' ensues: quantum theory attains completeness only at the expense of another fundamental physical theory—relativity.

Bell's Theorem and Bohm's Solution:

Years later, mathematician John S. Bell asked the question: 'What if the E-P-R experiment could actually be carried out? What sort of mathematical results would be achieved?' In a work referred to as "*the most profound discovery in the history of science*", Bell then proceeded to place the E-P-R experiment in a rigorous and quantifiable context, which could be checked by actual measurements.

The crucial significance of the Aspect experiment and earlier the Clauser experiment in 1969 had not been lost on physicist David Bohm. Both experiments reinforced for him that a novel concept had to be introduced to account for these nonlocal results. The old answer of the Copenhagen theorists: '*Leave it alone!*', wouldn't do any more. In essence, Bohm had become convinced that the entrenched vagueness and philosophical abdication of the standard Copenhagen Interpretation could no longer be supported.

Regarding the various violations of the Bell Inequality, Bohm considered an alternative quantum world, based on different orders of manifestation which he called explicate and implicate.

To Bohm, the readily observable order of the macrocosm had *unfolded or explicated*. That is, its host of apparently diverse objects and processes constituted a divergence from unified order. This is the order at which Einsteinian locality and determinism would have some relevance. (After all, Newtonian mechanics can also be used to make predictions about the motions of bodies—such as pool balls and artificial satellites).

However, this plurality of objects (subatomic particles, planets, stars, galaxies) is ultimately enfolded in a higher dimensional implicate order. This order is hidden or unseen (hence 'implicate') and not perceived by lower dimensional beings.

To render this more concrete Bohm devised a number of excellent analogies such as the fish in the aquarium filmed from two different directions, noted earlier, as well as the glycerine rotated in two different directions with an ink drop.

Bohm offered this in the hope of showing how we can be deceived into thinking the explicate order is the valid one. Such an error is costly—in terms of confining our attention to a limited realm of fragmentary illusion, instead of seeing beyond it. For example, like the casual observer of the two TV monitor images, a casual observer of the Aspect experiment might conclude that the two photons (registered at separate detectors) are themselves separate. Bohm's implicate order prevails upon the observer to think instead of the photons to have always been connected as one whole—but perhaps in a higher dimension.

What is observed as a 'particle' is actually much more. The use of *particle* bespeaks a false image conveyed by excess attention on one order (the explicate). Bohm's interpretation makes redundant all of Einstein's objections to faster than light signals as the basis for "spooky" actions at a distance. Certainly, if a higher dimensional (implicate) connection already exists, then 'signal' is superfluous. Signal is a relevant concept only if systems are genuinely separated.

Bohm, of course, did not leave his radically different quantum interpretation as mere conjecture or speculation. His achievement was to interweave a number of concepts into a single coherent theory which has been referred to as "Bohm's Model of Quantum Mechanics" and *Bohmian Quantum Mechanics*.

Testing Bell's Theorem – More on the Aspect Experiment:

Because it is so very crucial to the concept of a nonlocal cosmos, it is worthwhile to examine the Aspect experiment in much greater detail than we did in the previous section. To test quantum conformity to Bell's Theorem, Alain Aspect and his colleagues at the University of Paris, set up an arrangement as sketched below.[12] In these experiments, the detection of *the polarizations*[13] of photons was the key. These were observed with the photons emanating from a Krypton-Dye laser and arriving at two different analyzers, e.g.

```
P1 ↓| <-----------|-----------> |↑ P2
A1           D              A2
```

Here, the laser device is D, the analyzers (polarization detectors) are A1 and A2 and two representative polarizations are given at each, for two photons P1 and P2. The results of these remarkable experiments disclosed apparent and instantaneous connections between the photons at A1 and A2. In the case shown, a photon (P1) in the minimum (0) intensity polarization mode, is anti-correlated with one in the maximum intensity (1) mode.

Say, twenty successive detections are made and we obtain, at the respective analyzers (where a '1' denotes spin +1/2 detection and '0' spin (−1/ 2):

A1: 1 0 1 0 1 0 1 0 1 0 1 0 1 0 1 0 1 0 1 0
A2: 0 1 0 1 0 1 0 1 0 1 0 1 0 1 0 1 0 1 0 1

---

[12] Aspect, Grangier, and Roger: *Physical Review Letters*, 91.
[13] Polarization is the orientation in space of the electric field E, associated with light. This can be altered, subject to the imposition of different filters and devices.

On inspection, there is a 100% anti-correlation (i.e. 100% negative correlation) between the two and an apparent nonlocal connection. In practice, the experiment was set out so that four (not two—as shown) different orientation 'sets' were obtained for the analyzers. These might be denoted: (A1, A2)I, (A1, A2)II, (A1, A2,)III, and (A1, A2)IV.

Each result is expressed as a mathematical (statistical) quantity known as a 'correlation coefficient'.[14] The results from each orientation were then added to yield a sum S:

$$S = (A1, A2)I + (A1, A2)II + (A1, A2,)III + (A1, A2)IV$$

In his (1982) experiments, Aspect determined the sum with its attendant indeterminacy to be:[15] $S = 2.70 \pm 0.05$.

What is its significance? In a landmark theoretical achievement in 1964, mathematician John S. Bell formulated a thought experiment based on a design similar to that shown. He made the basic assumption of locality (i.e. that no communication could occur between A1 and A2 at any rate faster than light speed). In what is now widely recognized as a seminal work of mathematical physics, he set out to show that a theory which upheld locality could reproduce the predictions of quantum mechanics. His result predicted that the above sum, S, had to be less than or equal to 2 ($S \leq 2$). This is known as *the Bell Inequality*.

Little did Bell realize that when his thought experiments finally became practical (via Aspect and colleagues at the University of Paris) they would show violations of his Inequality. Evidently, we cannot continue to think of the universe as an ensemble of separate parts and pieces.

---

[14] For example, if a set of data: 1, 1, 1, 1 is correlated with another set: 0.5, 0.5, 0.5, 0.5, the correlation coefficient is 1.0. The range is between 0 (no correlation) and 1.0 (perfect correlation).

[15] Aspect, A. et al, *op. cit.*

Attempts to Reject the Experimental Basis of Quantum Nonlocality:

It wasn't long before a number of attacks and objections were made by physicists determined to retain locality. The late physicist Heinz Pagels, in a 1982 book[16], attacked the basis for *real nonlocality* by arguing that the separate polarization records at each analyzer are themselves totally random sequences.[17] Hence, one cannot obtain any useful information except by correlating two sets of records in the manner shown.

However, at genuinely vast distances—say 10 light years between A1 and A2—such correlation can never be practicable. In that sad event we are left with either one totally random record (say for A1) or another, but with absolutely no prospect of comparing the two and getting positive information. In this way, Pagels insists, real nonlocality is avoided.

But is it? One can object first to Pagels' exclusion of a real nonlocal influence on the basis of rejecting definite polarizations before the measurement.[18] This excludes all null measurement techniques. For instance, say we know a polarizer will yield two processes, one of reflection, r> and one of transmission, t>.

Then: $P(U >) = r > + t >$

If then only r > is observed at some detector after interaction with P, it is concluded t > = 0. But this is by inference, not actual measurement.

While this is consistent with the Copenhagen Interpretation of Quantum Mechanics (see part (iii) below)

---

[16] Pagels, *The Cosmic Code*.

[17] Pagels,: *op. cit.*, 144-152.

[18] Pagels,: *op. cit.*, 150.

it is not consistent with any other interpretation. For example, from the standpoint of the *Stochastic Interpretation of Quantum Mechanics* (SIQM), Pagels' exclusion is inapplicable. A mathematical treatment of the Aspect results from an SIQM perspective shows that the photon polarizations can be considered as *"always* to have been defined and nonlocally connected".[19]

One can also attack Pagels' objection based on his definition of randomness. He uses the same definition as Richard von Mises, a German mathematician.[20] In von Mises' conception, randomness emerges as an *irreducible lawlessness*.[21] That is, it is defined without regard for regularity of place or pattern. Let me give an example, in which a coin is tossed ten times in a row and heads (H) and tails (T) registered:

T H T H T H T H T H

Is the sequence random? Based on only ten tosses it is difficult to say. However, a pattern of sorts appears to have emerged: each H and T alternate over one cycle. In von Mises' definition this isn't random, since a given event (in this case T or H) is required to be independent of place. This means I'm unable to predict the next place for an H or T (which is to say, the next event.) Gaming tables in Las Vegas are based on this principle.

The key point, missed by Pagels is that even the assertion of what constitutes randomness is based on an idea of what does not. In other words, a non-random pattern or regularity is required to define randomness! There must be an awareness of what is *non-random* before there can be awareness of what is random!

---

[19]   Cufaro-Petroni and Vigier *Physics Letters*, (93A), 383.

[20]   Pagels,: *op. cit.*, 91.

[21]   von Mises: *Probability, Statistics and Truth*, 23-25.

Since a unique definition of randomness is nonsense, or at least meaningless, one cannot maintain a priori (as Pagels does) that a sequence of polarizations will necessarily be a random sequence. The reason is that this assertion demands vastly more information than can be accessed in the experiment. Even a seemingly endless random sequence could merely be the subset of a vastly larger orderly sequence. So—something like:

$$0110111111001$$

That appears apparently random, could be a subset of the orderly sequence:

0110111111001 **0110111111001** 0110111111001 . . . .
(One hundred times)

It is impossible to know the pattern *unless the totality of information is available.* Unfortunately, the observer is never in a god-like position to state categorically one way or the other, by examining one record. However, a priori there is no reason why the nonseparability disclosed in the Aspect experiment should not apply over a distance of ten light years or more. The quantum potential, in fact, permits this.

Victor Stenger's words, criticizing such nonlocality, are a more pointed example of reductionist naysaying:[22]

This is a point that hardly anyone, including most scientists recognize: holism violates Einstein's theory of relativity. If simultaneous holistic connections between separated events exist, then either the whole foundation of twentieth century physics must be destroyed, or these connections must be supernatural.

---

[22]   Stenger: *Physics and Psychics*, 221.

Stenger makes the erroneous assumption that holism equates to faster-than-light propagation as in a signal concept. It does not. Nor do Aspect's experiments (or any others) show a faster-than-light (FTL) connection! What holism shows is not superluminal *transfer* of information, but rather *pre-existing connections in a higher dimensionality*! This is totally different, since it doesn't require *separate localizations* from which FTL signals emanate.

The point is that the two photons detected by A1, A2 in the Aspect experiment are *already connected in a higher dimensionality*, not readily accessible to us. The experimental results unequivocally show this, but we insist on using fragmentary language to refer to two photons—one at each analyzer, as if they are distinct entities separated by distance.

What Stenger perceives as some kind of relativistic cheating is really the normal behavior of a *higher dimensionally—unified entity.*[23] This is why the notion of superluminal signals, or indeed any signals, serves no useful purpose in discussions of holism vs. locality. In fact, it only serves to confuse the issues.

Nonetheless, the preceding examples enable us to recognize that distinct levels exist for which separate physical laws have their validity of operation. Having relativity valid and operative at one, autonomous localized level in no way vitiates higher-dimensional laws at a more implicate, nonlocal level. As physicist Sunny Auyang remarks:[24]

In physics, two isolated systems are idealizations. The world is an interactive system. We ideally carve out discrete entities by neglecting weak couplings. In

---

[23] In any event, Stenger appears not to be aware that superluminal travel is not expressly forbidden by general relativity. It is only precluded by the gravity-free flat space-time of special relativity. For more on this, see: Parsons: Science, (274), 202.
[24] Auyang,: *How Is Quantum Field Theory Possible?*, 120.

most cases, the neglected coupling is weak enough so that the approximation of discrete entities is good.

I would like to suggest that special relativity, which prohibits faster-than-light transfer, is a theory that ignores the weaker couplings of higher dimensionality that give rise to holism. In much the same way, Newtonian gravitation is perfectly valid and works well when the weaker couplings of general relativity are ignored, say by confining attention purely to satellites in Earth orbit.

Inevitably, problems arise when there is a conflation between two distinct regimes/couplings, and the relevant factors in each are ignored or omitted. This is bound to continue so long as the hyper-dimensional aspects of nonlocal quantum experiments remain unrecognized.

Stenger also quarrels with holists for deliberately choosing reality over locality:[25]

The results of the experimental violation of Bell's Inequality are clear and unequivocal: nature cannot be described in terms of physical variables, that are both local and real. Either Einsteinian locality, or certain commonsense notions of reality must be discarded. There is no third alternative. Most popular writers prefer to discard locality rather than reality.

Again, this is largely a contrived problem. Bell's Theorem, like the premise of 'interfering postulates', merely shows that two or more fundamental requirements cannot co-exist in the same quantum description (Bohr's Complementarity Principle). This applies, for example, to local and nonlocal descriptions, or modeling. While I can certainly invoke one or the other, I can't use both in the same model.

---

[25] Stenger: *op. cit.*, 232.

It also applies to locality and realism, in terms of defining an objective state of the system (i.e. saying a photon headed for an analyzer already possesses its orientation). One can therefore write, in accord with the premise of relative autonomy, using Poisson brackets:

$$[L, R] = (LR - RL) \neq 0$$

which is to say, locality (L) and reality (R) cannot be expressed in one and the same viewpoint. That doesn't mean different viewpoints cannot be held at *different* times, when it becomes necessary to do so. In all these examples of *complementarity*, there is a basic disjunction between our classical language and concepts (e.g. locality, reality) and the quantum context to which these are applied.

For example, when confined to classical language and logic, one is inevitably left with an 'either-or' choice. This is reflected precisely in one of Stenger's quotes[26]: *"Either Einsteinian locality or certain common sense notions of reality must be discarded."*

This is a perfect example of classical, either-or logic, but manifestly wrong. Neither one need be discarded so long as the respective domains of validity are recognized and used in their appropriate contexts. Euan Squires observes:[27]

Rather than running away from the problems by abandoning the search for realism, we should recognize that we will have to much cleverer. The real world is not as simple as we once thought.

The bottom line is elementary: One can obtain real knowledge, but it is never *simultaneously* complete and accurate (e.g. wave model of light to exclusion of particle/

26   *Ibid.*
27   Squires, *Conscious Mind in the Physical World*, 75

photon model).One has rather, a limited interplay between differing levels of an interwoven hierarchy of actions. This is more complex than naive realism's prioritizing classical Newtonian World views, with an exclusive emphasis on local reality.

The holomovement:

While Bohm's Quantum Mechanics is extremely interesting in and of itself, it is far beyond the scope of this book to even discuss its most rudimentary elements[28]. The only aspect I superficially describe is his quantum potential, which will be deferred to the next chapter. For now, I want to examine something that is more in the way of a conjecture—which follows directly from the Stochastic Interpretation of quantum theory. This is what Bohm calls *the holomovement.*

Translated, it means literally *moving holograph*. What is a holograph? Well, if two lasers are made to interact on special films a holographic image is produced, say a flower. If this flower image or hologram is examined closely it will be seen that each part of the image is itself a flower! In other words, the whole image is embedded within each tiny section. All the information is apportioned to each tiny element of the whole.

Now imagine the total image changing from instant to instant—but all the information continuously preserved in each tiny element. That is a very rough analog to the holomovement (it cannot be other than a crude analogy since the holomovement is hyper-dimensional). In Bohm's own words:[29]

---

[28] For a comprehensive treatment see: Bohm and Hiley: *The Undivided Universe: An Ontological Interpretation of Quantum Theory.*

[29] Bohm:: *op. cit.* 150.

> To generalize, so as to emphasize undivided wholeness, we shall say that what 'carries' an implicate order is the holomovement, which is an unbroken and undivided totality

From this we can see that the holomovement is an agency to convey the implicate order instantly throughout the universe. However, it is not possible to delve into the 'mechanics' of how this is done, as Bohm continues:[30]

> In certain areas, we can abstract particular aspects of the holomovement (e.g. light, electrons, sound etc.) but more generally all forms of the holomovement merge and are inseparable.

The preceding quote warns us implicitly that the desire to conjure up abstractions and interactions is a byproduct of the human brain—which has evolved to cope with a fragmentary environment. The very abstraction of the term holomovement is itself contrived and artificial and de facto separates the holomovement from all other concepts, ideas, words.

Bohm reinforces this, going on to assert that the holomovement is 'undefinable' and 'immeasurable'. For the mystic or holistic scientist, these words are sobering. For my own part, they flash an alert that one must be cognizant of the ever present 'mystic's paradox' in having to use fragmentary language structures. For example, to the erstwhile mystic the very use of a word, a noun, fragments his reality. Hence, he would not even say the word *holomovement* since it would abstract and divide it from the whole. But the problem is that one is then enjoined not to communicate anything! In this case, the non-communication—a form of isolation—is even more fragmentary and divisive than that which the mystic sought to avoid in the first place!

---

[30]   *ibid.*

There are two solutions to this quandary, passive and active. The passive solution is to minimize analysis or discussion of the holomovement. By recognizing that it is indeed undefinable and immeasurable we accept that severe language constraints exist in our ability to discuss or dissect it. It is 'wholeness'! Case closed.

However, any attempts to further illuminate it or amplify it will run into the limits and contradictions warned about in Kurt Godel's Incompleteness Theorem. That Theorem basically says that no logical formal system of axioms can be without contradictions. Hence, it must be incomplete. Since the holomovement already exists and is beyond all logical systems, we know we can't incorporate any meaningful description or definition which is not self-contradictory. Thus, one is advised not to even attempt to do so.

The Human Connection:

What is the significance of Bohmian quantum mechanics, and in particular the holomovement, for humanity? I believe its great use will be in subsuming our fragmentary perceptions within one of ultimate wholenes. The key is in the relation of Mind to the 'undivided whole' that the holomovement embodies. Can we equate it to a 'Universal Mind' in other words?

In Cartesian duality, championed by reductionist science and even modern psychology, the mind and body are totally separate entities. Indeed, the most recent research has attempted to dispense with mind entirely, either relegating it to the status of an epiphenomenon of the brain, or identified with the brain's own activity. The main point is that one does not conflate mind and body.

Bohm allows a radically different interpretation, based on his quantum potential and the paradigm of the implicate order. In his words[31]:

---

[31]   Bohm,: *op. cit.*, 209

> In the implicate order we have to say that mind
> enfolds matter in general and therefore the body
> in particular. Similarly, the body enfolds not only
> the mind but also in some sense the entire material
> universe.

The full implications of the above statement can easily be
undervalued amidst all the words. But when they are carried
to their ultimate conclusion they leave no doubt whatever that
we need to enact major changes in our lives.

First, mind and matter are no longer separate, but one
dynamic. One's mind is in one's body and other bodies (not
only human) as much as one's own. Second, one's mind is
also within inanimate nature: within the rocks, the stars and
the collective cosmos all around us—as is one's body. What
does this mean for us?

It means that we are enmeshed in one interconnected
whole. What I do to another, good or ill, I do to myself. In
addition, what I do to resources I do to myself and others.
And finally, what I do—for good or ill—to any animal,
affects all of humanity and nature for good or ill. There is
simply no way—within the Bohmian universe of undivided
wholeness, to compartmentalize Being or classify our duties,
or prioritize them—as we have been accustomed to doing so
long (i.e. 'humans first', then animals, then nature).

Consider comparing a piecemeal or reductionist cosmos
to a holistic one. The piecemeal one presumes separability
as a basic property, hence regions A and B one-hundred
light years apart are ineluctably isolated unless a signal can
propagate between them, or some field can affect both in
the same way (not likely). But in Bohm's model, the holistic
universe is already enfolded into a higher dimensional
implicate order so that A and B, are in reality connected at
that higher dimensionality. What appears to be separate really
isn't.

It is for this reason Bernard d'Espagnat refers to the latter, counterfactual universe as "far reality" in contrast to the reductionist's "near reality" which considers locality paramount. The question emerges: How are the two related, if related at all? And if not, how might we think of them within the context of scientific inquiry?

The *Principle of Complementarity* can be applied in a simplified form to our perceptions of reality. Call the near reality N and the far reality F, then what do we make of [N, F]? If it is analogous to the non-commutation operators of quantum mechanics, it must be true that:

$$[N, F] = K \text{ (constant)} = (N \times F) - (F \times N)$$

In other words, the near and far reality observables *do not commute*.[32] If they did, one would find:

$$(N \times F) - (F \times N) = 0$$

This would be the same as saying that both realities disclosed in measurement are equivalent or equally accessible. Another way to put this would be that for every element in the ground form reality, there corresponds exactly one member of the physical theory used to describe that reality.

We can expand on these ideas even further by letting 'N' be the theory embodying near reality or that identical with Newtonian physics (as revealed by Isaac Newton in his Newtonian laws of motion), and let 'F' be the theory embodying 'far reality' (e.g. the nonlocal reality) implicit in present day Bohmian-Bell quantum mechanics.

Use of an example for comparison will quickly show that one-to-one correspondence between theory and reality does

---

[32] Commute (def.): Subtraction of their products (with factors juxtaposed) yields zero. Thus: $xy - yx = 0$.

not exist for both N and F. Consider the description of motion, using 'N' for the motion of a ball thrown at a wall, and 'F' for the motion of an electron released from an electron'gun and heading for a screen.

For the case A: using 'N' to describe a ball's motion, we will see:

```
*----*----*----*-------*
x1---x2---x3---x4----x5
```

In this case, each theoretical position of the ball, x1, x2 etc.is perfectly matched to its actual position as unfolded in its motion. There are 5 'real' positions singled out from the motion here, and there are exactly 5 theoretical positions which correspond to them and could in fact be predicted using the right Newtonian equations of motion. Now, consider the quantum mechanical example of the electron in its motion:

```
     .      .       .
X1---X2----X3-----X4----X5
```

Here, each X position is theoretical, but only 3 of them correspond one—to—one with the actual electron motion No information exists for either end position X1 or X5, and therefore all objects of the theory do not correspond to all objects of reality. There is what we call a "mismatch". In fact, the motion as captured in velocity and position cannot be simultaneously attained to the same threshold of accuracy.

Then the disjunction we arrive at is exactly the same we saw earlier with the locality vs. reality controversy. Using Poisson brackets, as we did with N, F:

$$[L, R] = (LR - RL) \neq 0$$

which is to say, locality (L) and reality (R) cannot be expressed in one and the same viewpoint. But it does not mean that locality is in error, say if we reject locality to embrace reality. What we're actually doing *is embracing far reality over near*.

The physical justification is none other than Bell's theorem and its validation via the Aspect experiment.

On account of the brain's predisposition to N-reality models, it is extremely difficult for it to surmount latent reductionist tendencies and accept an F-reality vision such as a holistic cosmos requires. Add to this the fact that nearly all F-reality models are non-visualizable (such as the superpositions of quantum mechanics) and the daunting nature of the task becomes clear. To fix ideas, the task is to see that the concept of a holistic cosmic reality is valid, even though it is not describable in an N-reality format or formalism.

Aside: Is the Universe a Virtual Simulation?

While a holistic cosmos may be difficult to comprehend, it is possible to put the footing on a different level to encourage greater appreciation. That said, consider the question of whether the universe we inhabit might really be a virtual simulation, and the repercussions that arise from it.

In a conjecture published some ten years ago[33], Nick Bostrom considered whether the universe and everything within it (including stars, galaxies, planets and human beings.) is one massive simulation—a vast and intricate hyper quantum computer program being run from outside—perhaps by an extraordinary intelligence.

Note here that the basis for a quantum computable universe has already been well explicated in books such as: *Programming the Universe* by Seth Lloyd. In addition, given all entities are mostly empty space anyway, ultimately

---

[33]   Bostrom: *Philosophical Quarterly*. (53), 243.

predicated on quantum wave forms or wave functions, one can easily see how the ability to manipulate quantum units at will could lead to a simulation of an entire universe. In fact, if one builds consistently on quantum mechanics one can theoretically arrive at all the macroscopic laws of nature that we see govern our universe. For example, in the limit of the quantum number n $\rightarrow \infty$, quantum mechanics converges to Newtonian mechanics.

In a sense, if the universe is simulated, then we and all other life forms within it are *avatars.* But how would one know it or prove it? First things first: Is this equivalence of physical body and cyber-body (avatar) going too far? I don't believe so. The cyber-body is ultimately composed of moving electrons and quanta (photons) that cause multiple pixels on the monitor screen to vary in intensity, producing the illusion of motion. By the same token, the physical body is ultimately constituted of electrons, and can receive and process photons, e.g. by the optic nerve. On a quantum mechanical level the two bodies are very nearly the same. The differences appear at the gross or macroscopic levels, where the physical body displays a 3-dimensional solidity and differentiation of organs, tissues and cells. But are these fundamental? Who can say? It depends on the constructions, doesn't it?

Assuming clever enough simulations, say using quadrillions of quantum spin system gates operating in tandem, arguably no one would know the difference. In 1982, the Nobel-winning physicist Richard Feynman made a notable (and as it turns out, prescient) observation concerning a "universal quantum simulator". Feynman conjectured that to obtain 300 nuclear spins, the quantum simulator would need only 300 quantum bits or qubits. So long as one could program the interactions between qubits so that they emulated the interactions between the 300 nuclear spins, the dynamics would be simulated.

Was Feynman off his rocker? Not really! As it turns out one of the best ways to generate simulations via a quantum computer is to use nuclear spins. To see how this could work, study the accompanying diagram with three versions of nuclear spin—to which each is assigned a wave state vector in bracket form. In this case, the nuclear spin down state corresponds to 1>, the spin up state to 0> and there is a combined state: 0 > + 1 >. (The last is a state of spin along the axis perpendicular to the spin-axis).

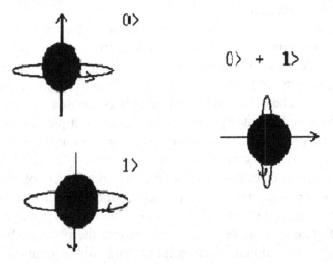

NUCLEAR SPINS IN QUANTUM COMPUTING

More to the point, the latter superposition illustrates the property of quantum parallelism: the ability to compute or register two states simultaneously, which is impossible for normal computers (which register 0 OR 1, never both at one time—unless they are in glitch mode!) Thus, a quantum computer can manipulate two bits (qubits) at one time. If there are a trillion such qubits, each can potentially register 1 and 0 in combined wave bracket states, simultaneously. It should also be easily seen that this combined wave state is the analog of the superposition of states seen in the electron double slit experiment, e.g. for

$$\psi = \psi 1 + \psi 2$$

Any qubit in a state (0) can be placed in the double-qubit state by rotating it one fourth of a turn (as evident from inspection of the diagram) Much more fascinating (and to the point) is that if another qubit is introduced into the scene—say with the same wave state 0> its presence can "flip" the original qubit, effectively producing a quantum-controlled NOT operation which acts like a classical NOT gate. It is billions and billions of such logic gates which form the basis of computing. Given that qubits also hold much more information than ordinary bits, it is easy to see that if such nuclear spins can be used in the sort of logic gate manner described, one can have the basis for a quantum computer.

If one can have such an entity, then one could simulate just about anything. To use the words of Seth Lloyd[34] :

A quantum computer that simulated the universe would have exactly as many qubits as there are in the universe, and the logic operations on those qubits would exactly simulate the dynamics of the universe.

And further[35]:

Because the behavior of elementary particles can be mapped directly onto the behavior of qubits acting via logic operations, a simulation of the universe on a quantum computer is indistinguishable from the universe itself

This is a profound statement! It implies that if the universe were indeed a mammoth simulation we'd likely never be able to prove it or see outside of it. To us, locked inside as individual quantum simulations—interacting dynamically with millions of other such simulations—it all

---

[34]   Lloyd: *Programming the Universe*, 154.
[35]   *Ibid.*

appears quite real. But what is real? We think we know, but in fact not. Most people aren't even remotely aware that they're mostly empty space. They may have heard that said before, but the fact they can press a hand to their arm and not see it go right through (because of the repulsive electro-magnetic forces acting at the surfaces) means they don't take it literally. How could they?

From this example, I maintain that such a simulated universe is in many respects analogous to the holistic universe, and further, it's unequivocally a *"FAR reality"*. Let's use an example to try to pursue this point and elaborate it further, in a kind of thought experiment.

Imagine yourself sitting in front of a computer monitor on which a virtual game (like the popular SIMS) is being run. Now, without touching anything on the keyboard, imagine yourself *actually inside the display*, interacting directly with the various virtual denizens. Actively project yourself into that virtual reconstruction What would you see? Hear? Feel? Think?

You experience this virtual world. You can be pursued by its various beasts, confronted by its more obstreperous human inhabitants, hear them screeching or bleating and you can get hurt by them as well. You are inside the virtual world! You are also subject to its laws and unwritten imperatives. This obtains unless you experience a liberating revelation allowing you to master its influences and control others' perceptions as well.

It is the thought of active participation that infinitely regresses you from outside the display to the inside. To accomplish that, the following words might be used: *I am thinking of myself, in the display—thinking of myself in a display within the display; thinking of myself within a display of the display of the display . . . . etc. ad infinitum*

A crucial point, in this regard, has been noted by Alex Comfort[36]:

---

[36] Comfort: *Reality and Empathy: Physics, Mind & Science in the 21st Century*, 41.

In treating mind, though virtual, as a separate explicate, Buddhist and many Hindu philosophers tend to share a radical view of reality which asserts that since all conventional phenomena are illusory, anyone who adequately masters his own illusion of the phenomenal can manipulate it and other people's experience practically at will.

In other words, if one can see the simulation of the universe as the artifact it is, and thereby *master his or her own perceptions* (misperceptions?) then it is possible to manipulate it at will using one's mind. Lloyd in his perceptive book notes that the backdrop to all the super-quantum computer calculations is the quantum fluctuation. As one manifestly masters his perceptions, and sees that indeed all conventional phenomena are illusory then he can induce his own quantum fluctuations at will, and thereby manipulate (re-program) "reality".

Here's the paradox: why would one wish to do that, except to attain or use power which the nonlocal philosophy militates against? Well, one plausible answer is to show the hard-nosed skeptics like Victor Stenger that you have the capacity to control their lives via this virtual display!

Other Simulations: Ω Points of Teilhard and Tipler—

The concept of the Omega Point was first conceived by Teilhard de Chardin, a French mystic-priest, banished to China for his avant-garde speculations. In his books[37], Teilhard developed the basis for the Omega Point through a number of distinct laws or principles. These may be summarized as follows:

---

[37]   These include: *The Phenomenon of Man, The Divine Milieu,* and *The Future of Man.*

1.   *There is both a within and a without of everything in the universe.*
2.   *A law of complexity/consciousness obtains by which increasingly complex structure corresponds to increasing consciousness.*
3.   *Evolution is not merely due to pure chance but is directed.*
4.   *Though the universe appears constituted of diverse objects, it is fundamentally a unity.*

Perhaps the best description of the Omega Point is given in *The Future of Man:*[38]

> . . . in the heart of a universe prolonged along its axis of complexity, there exists a divine center of convergence. Let us call it the point Omega. Let us suppose that from this universal center, this Omega Point, there constantly emanate radiations hitherto only perceptible to those persons we call 'mystics.' Let us further imagine that, as the sensibility or response to mysticism of the human race increases with planetisation, the awareness of Omega becomes so widespread as to warm the Earth psychically while physically it is growing cold.

This passage describes a unitary cosmos in metaphorical terms. The Omega Point refers to a grand unification of all explicate forms in the cosmos, i.e. into a single *implicate* form. Ultimately, it represents a threefold synthesis: the material world with consciousness, the past with the future, and variety with unity.

This is exactly opposite to the vision of resurrection at a putative Omega Point as proposed by Frank J. Tipler. He sees

---

[38]   de Chardin: *The Future of Man*, 127.

a convergence of all representations to one single mode.[39] In this single mode at some real instant of time, all humans experience an eternity as "simulations" in subjective time. However, from a Metacosmic view, one common subjective instant cannot be isolated from another. In fact, the implicit topology allows an infinite array of subjective times and real times in an infinity of permutations. If anything, Tipler's vision is much too confined.

In addition, he simplistically limits his Omega Point to a closed universe[40] as opposed to an open (infinite) one. His reasoning is[41]:

. . . open universes expand so fast in the far future that it becomes impossible for structures to form of sufficiently larger size and larger size to store a diverging amount of information.

However, information divergence is not an exclusive function of macroscopic structures (i.e. brains, machines) to enfold it. Indeed, the Nonlocal Omega Point has a fundamental feature of non-conservation of quantum probabilities. Here resident structure size provides no impediment. This gets around the objection that protons may decay and introduce information losses. My point is that this is neither here nor there, since what we call 'proton' is only the limit of observation to a particular scale size. The information is still there—say in quarks, after proton decay.

One of the most problematic aspects of Tipler's version of the Omega Point, is how it supposedly 'resurrects' all human beings who have ever lived as simulations.[42] As we

---

[39] Tipler: *The Physics of Immortality*,. 241.

[40] Tipler:, *op. cit.*, 140.

[41] *Ibid.*

[42] Tipler,: *op.cit.*,. 206.

saw earlier, the use of the term simulation is appropriate in a virtual reality context.

For example, in *MOOs*,[43] the avatars used are iconized simulations of people. Perhaps the ultimate virtual reality scenario entails Tipler's use of the *Bekenstein Bound*.[44]

According to Tipler, [45] every being that's ever lived will be resurrected in an infinitely advanced virtual reality. In the subjective time frame, all those inhabiting that last instant (in proper time) will experience a reasonable (virtual) facsimile of eternity. It is important to note that all these resurrected beings are *simulations*, not beings in solid material form (i.e. human bodies). Nonetheless, these simulations, much like those in a high-level virtual reality computer program, can interact.

One problem with Tipler's simulation scenario is the fact that the Bekenstein Bound has been proven to apply exclusively to flat space-time. The geometry of the putative unitary cosmos is curved, and complex, i.e. hyper—toroid.

Another major problem involves the use of informational replicating machines, or von Neumann machines[46], to spread

---

[43]   MOO = Multiple User Dungeon, Object Oriented. This is the specially created space in which avatars interact with each other.

[44]   This is defined as the number of possible quantum states in a bounded region, or as the number of bits (i.e. of information) that can be coded in a bounded region. In other words, an upper limit on the rate of information processing.

[45]   I employ quotes here since—according to Tipler—this actually occurs in subjective time, not proper time. That is, for all those experiencing it in the framework of subjective time an instant appears to last forever, even though in proper time it amount to no more than an instant.

[46]   See, e.g.: Tipler,: *Frontiers of Modern Physics*, 160. The von Neumann machine is here taken as the machine equivalent of a human. Tipler's argument—in both this article and *The*

humanity (and presumably intelligence) to all corners of the cosmos. Indeed, this is a pivotal assumption on which Tipler's Omega Point depends. If von Neumann machines cannot exist, or they cannot achieve these grandiose objectives (replicating themselves and spreading throughout the universe), then Tipler's simulation-resurrecting cosmos cannot come into being.

As I see it, the postulate of self-replication violates two basic principles: *Gödel's Incompleteness Theorem(1)*, and the Principle of Information Entropy. I examined the Incompleteness Theorem earlier. Basically, it asserts that in a sufficiently rich logical system there exist propositions that may be true, but cannot be proven. There also exist other propositions that are undecidable.

One such structured logical system might be the computing code for a von Neumann machine. This may comprise some N formal statements—that are used to specify the behavioral and other limits for the machine. The key question is whether these N coded statements, comprising the entire matrix of machine information, can successfully be replicated in another machine. This is possible if E, the entropy (in bits/second) of the message/information source (von Neumann machine), is less than the capacity of the information channel[47] (in bits per symbol).

Physics of Immortality—is that if the Bekenstein Bound applies to humans, they are also finite state machines—like 'von Neumann machines'. This, however, can only be true if humans are localized. In the Bohmian QM view, humans are nonlocal and can access an infinite frequency domain. Hence, the finite state description, via the Bekenstein Bound, is only applicable at the entropic level.

[47]   Information channel: the medium through which information can pass in bits per second. The information capacity is the proportion of genuine information I (in bits per second) to wasted information or entropy (H). Thus, roughly: I-H.

For the sake of argument, let 10^{10} bits be associated with each statement in a von Neumann code (program). Each machine processes an entropy $E = N \times 10^{10}$ bits/second. In addition, we have: $E = (N +1) \times 10^{10}$ bits/second. Here is the problem: all the statements in the code concern the behavior per se: what the von Neumann machine is to do. They include nothing about replicating itself! This replicative statement therefore exists *outside the code*—it is a meta-statement! One requires at minimum an entropy E:

$$E = (N+1) \times 10^{10} \text{ bits/second}$$

We can see E exceeds this threshold, so the message cannot be transferred! The entropy exceeds the bounds of the information channel capacity. Phrased another way, the statement for replication arises from outside the system of code, not from within its instructions. In other words, the command 'Replicate!' may be true but it is unprovable within the Gödelian loop to which all logical systems are constrained. And, so long as it is unprovable, it will not be executed by any von Neumann machine! In effect, there can be no 'self-reproducing universal constructor with human level intelligence'. The Omega Point, at least as conceived by Tipler, cannot be a reality now or in the future.

I already noted the geometrical aspect of the problem with Tipler's assumption of a flat space-time. Related to it is the fact that any resurrections *must occur in the past not the future*! In other words, humans existing here and now are exactly the simulations (processed information) manifest in a distant future signal that has been propagated from the Alpha-Omega point of the Tipler cosmos.

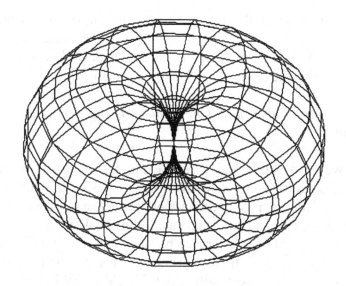

Note that the (V-point) intersection is for all times as depicted above. Tipler's error is postulating the Omega Point as an exclusive endpoint, when it is *both* end *and* beginning! He further errs by concentrating all subjective existence in that single, future instant. In fact, it is diffused to all past instants. In short, Tipler's major oversight is using an entropic-based arrow of time rather than a negentropic view.

The last feature exposes Tipler's conception to be a grandiose extension of a near reality (type N) as opposed to far. In a near reality we demand a distinct arrow of time, for example, to support Newtonian mechanics. (Technically, time reversibility is feasible in classical mechanics but it's always understood to be a computational device, not a verifiable reality!)

If one thinks about it, this makes eminent sense. If information processing is confined to a lockstep, say the immutable progression from past to future, there will be inevitable losses of order due to entropy. This derives from the fact physical states generally evolve from order to disorder as time progresses from past to future. In effect, Tipler's simulations are compromised from the outset because they suffer from the inevitable loss of information which entropy inflicts.[48] But entropy is itself a fundamental property of a local realism, or N-reality, i.e. the applicable law states that it only tends to increase in closed systems.

Heisenberg States and Quantum Ontology—The Optimal Solution?

We have considered several examples of virtual cosmic manifestations, none of which works very well to confirm a truly holistic cosmos. In the case of the nuclear-spin generated (or other quantum spin—generated) universal simulation, the problem is that of interference by select conscious units who somehow "master" their perceptions. The problem is that if such an entity genuinely existed we'd behold numerous instances this mastery is evident. But it isn't. Events in our world are more a case of random chance confluences than planned or mastered outcomes.

Teilhard's Omega Point is far too metaphysical to be much use, and isn't based sufficiently on physics. Nonetheless, the underlying concept of cosmic unity is enticing. In the case of physicist Frank Tipler's Omega Point numerous problems and contradictions abound. A primary one is being hostage to classical physics, e.g. the 2nd law of thermodynamics, so it remains firmly in the near (N-) reality domain. This applies when trying to describe an "infinite return".

Is there then a solution? Is there some path that can lead to a holistic universe without all the problems? The model of David Bohm has already been articulated but it hasn't been accepted, primarily because a key discriminating experiment hasn't been performed up until now. This experiment has

---

[48] This is particularly true in the context of a closed universe, which becomes infinitely hot and dense in the future. A cold, open universe would be far more conducive to open-ended information processing of the type required by Tipler.

become known as the Gozzini experiment and was originally to have been conducted near Pisa, Italy ca. 1995. If it had been successful, real de Broglie waves would have been detected and assorted skeptical harangues and critiques regarding "quantum quackery" quashed. Even Bohm, before he died, admitted the plausible acceptance of his holomovement depended upon the Gozzini experiment being done and succeeding. Minus that, there is little basis to claim a quantum-based Overmind or Universal Mind, but we can retain Bohm's concept as an inspirational tool.

So, what other path might there be? Henry Stapp has elucidated an option in his book, *Mind, Matter and Quantum Mechanics*. Stapp's solution of the problem is novel and perhaps best presented in his own words[49]:

> In Heisenberg's picture . . . the classical world of material particles, evolving in accordance with locally deterministic mathematical laws, is replaced by the Heisenberg state of the universe. This state can be pictured as a complicated wave which like its classical counterpart, evolves in accordance with local, deterministic laws of motion.

Below, I show a graphic which blends a possible geometry of the cosmos with the wave function of Stapp's Heisenberg state:

---

[49]   Stapp. *op. cit.*, 148

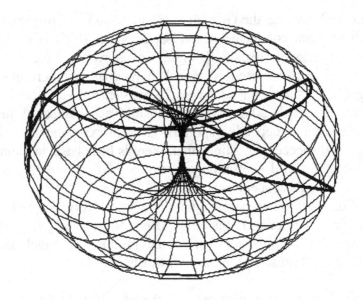

Note the wave is visualized in three-dimensions and its evolution is captured at one particular time, T_o. In a next instant this configuration can be expected to change according to local deterministic laws. In this sense the wave state behaves in an analogous fashion to the B-wave in relation to its controlling pilot wave. Stapp goes on to clarify[50]:

> However, this Heisenberg state represents not the actual universe itself but merely a set of objective tendencies or propensities connected to the impending actual event.

Stapp notes the actual event is just an abrupt change in the Heisenberg state, sometimes called the *collapse of the wave function.*

In other words, Stapp resurrects the Copenhagen Interpretation, but now fleshed out with an actual form, as

---

[50]   *Ibid.*

opposed to merely a quantum cookbook of recipes. As he puts it[51]:

> By introducing in this way a quantum ontology, and thus departing from the purely epistemological stance of the strictly orthodox Copenhagen Interpretation, one can remove the subjective human observer from the quantum description of the physical world and speak directly about the actual dispositions of the measuring devices rather than the knowledge of an observer.

The positive consequences of this are formidable. Not only do we escape the quirky controversies that had plagued the Copenhagen interpretation, i.e. the wave function can be collapsed by a cat but not by an amoeba, but as Stapp notes, the Moon really is there when nobody looks and Schrodinger's cat actually is dead or alive.

In other words, we have a dramatic simplification while at the same time gaining realism from a nonlocal purview. Stapp points out that his ontology has both local and global aspects, the first wherein an event is triggered over a defined macroscopic domain, say the firing of a Geiger counter, but the second global, so an action extends to distant parts of the universe.

In effect, changing to a localized quantum operator, such as that for momentum:

$$i\hbar\, \partial / \partial x$$

produces a global change in the tendencies for the next actual event.

---

[51]   Stapp: *op. cit.*, 149.

Stapp's ontology is therefore entirely in line with Bell's Theorem and the Aspect experiment. Indeed, in one paper Stapp shows Bell's theorem to be a nonlocality property of quantum mechanics[52].

It's interesting that despite all of Victor Stenger's objections to quantum nonlocality, i.e. in his latest book, he insists it's *"all in the minds of the authors"*[53]—he hasn't challenged any of Stapp's substantive claims. One suspects a possible reason for this is that he labors under a misconception of nonlocality. In Stenger's mind it's the same as superluminal signal transfer, so it violates special relativity. According to Einstein's theory, nothing travels faster than light.

For example, consider the mass relation in special relativity:

$$m = m_0 / [(1 - v^2/c^2)^{1/2}]$$

where m is the mass moving at velocity v, m_0 is the rest mass, and c the speed of light. If the mass were to move at the speed of light, c:

$$m = m_0 / [(1 - c^2/c^2)^{1/2}] = m_0 / [(1 - 1)^{1/2}] = m_0 / 0 = \infty$$

In other words, the mass would have to be infinite, i.e. have infinite inertia in which case it would be impossible to move. If this applies at the velocity of light threshold, it rules out faster than light masses too, hence superluminal transfer of information. But this is *not* what quantum nonlocality means! In Aspect's experiment it means[54] *causally-bound photons connected by causal action at a distance* which is different.

---

[52] Stapp: *Physical Review Letters*, (49) 1470.

[53] Stenger: *God and the Folly of Faith,* 162.

[54] Aspect, Grangier, and Roger,: *Physical Review Letters* (47), 460.

As Aspect et al put it[55];

No energy can be exchanged between the photons in Σo, so that *no causal anomaly results* from this particular action at a distance.

This is known as *causal covariant action at a distance* and can be represented in the following way:

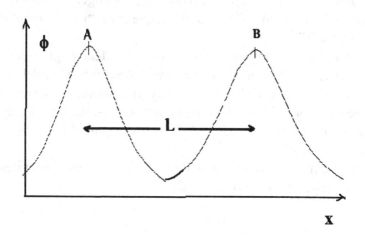

Here, two photons A and B are apparently displaced from each other by some distance, L, measured between their maxima, are actually connected at low levels of field intensity, φ. It is only at high levels of this intensity we observe them as separate (singlet) photons. It is in that displaced condition Stenger is considering superluminal transfers but in reality it's not needed because the two photons are already bound. Lastly, physicist Bernard d'Espagnat's words are certainly worth a look[56]:

---

[55] Aspect et al, *ibid.*
[56] d'Espagnat.:*op. cit.*,143.

The experimental corroboration of nonseparability (i.e. nonlocality) quite obviously constitutes a strong argument against the hypothesis of objective realism as applied to microscopic objects, and even . . . . against that of objectivist realism applied to macroscopic objects only.

d'Espagnat further concedes that for anyone *"believing in both locality and realism"*—as Stenger does—the observed violation of the Bell inequalities *"would remain inexplicable"*[57].

One last remarkable side note: Evidently physicists associated with Canada's National Research Council in Ottawa have succeeded in actually measuring a quantum wave function (hitherto believed impossible since it was only said to be statistical in nature.). This was reported in the June 9, 2011 issue of *Nature*.

Something to consider when hard core Copenhagenites insist the wave function isn't real.

---

57   *Ibid.*

IX. SOME PROBLEMS OF NONLOCALITY

The ultimate test for acceptance of a concept or theory is whether there is a sufficient base of verifiable observations and empirical documentation. This is what separates scientific speculation from scientific fact. This is also what separates theology from the harsh world of scientific accountability. While the notion of a nonlocal, interactive cosmos is exciting, we must tread carefully, always aware zealots are ready to pounce and make metaphysical hay of any remote support for ideas that seem to confirm their supernaturalism.

What must be avoided at all costs is the impetus to make quantum theory the handmaiden of some newfangled metaphysics. Already there have been disturbing steps in that direction with the publication of a number of popular books which mix quantum physics and mysticism. The temptation to "theologize" arises given there are *some* results of quantum physics, especially that of an unanalyzable whole, which seem to be supportive of a mystical type of cosmos. Unfortunately, the would-be quantum mystic forgets that 99.9 percent of human daily lives are made up of encounters with large (macroscopic) bodies, for which the Heisenberg

Principle should not apply. We do not precipitate the wave packet collapse of a table or chair when we observe them, for example.[1]

Having said that, I think the previous chapter merits more examination, from a more skeptical point of view. This is done, firstly, to assure atheists that I haven't gone totally bonkers, and secondly to discuss the very real limitations one faces in attempting to model or even theorize a coherent holistic model.

In the previous chapter, we looked at Bohm's holomovement and at Henry Stapp's Heisenberg wave state and ontology. The first lacked a defined experiment to support its contentions, including existence of hidden variables and how a quantum potential would really work. In the case of Stapp's concept, and his reconfiguring the Copenhagen interpretation, we see that if consciousness is capable of altering the Heisenberg states, humans become much more than passive spectators to the cosmic drama. They become actual participants, re-shaping every scene with their observations. As participants, humans contribute to the evolutionary unfolding of the universe and give meaning to this unfolding. Henry Stapp states[2]:

> Reinstatement of human freedom by appeal to quantum theory resurrects human responsibility . . . this approach to the mind-body problem creates a quantum mechanical conception of man and his role in nature. He is no longer a passive observer of a

---

[1]   At the same time, some new investigations do disclose evident macroscopic links. For one example of superposition of macroscopically different states, see:: Gider et al, in *Science*, Vol. 268 (1995), p. 77.

[2]   Stapp: *Consciousness and Values in the Quantum Universe*, in *Foundations of Physics*, (15), 35.

cataclysmic initial act of creation, but rather an active participant in the process of creation

This is heady stuff, but one must be temperate in how it's applied. While it's tempting to embrace the holistic universe as a humanist substitute to the (now) untenable universe of spirits and the supernatural, one needs to proceed cautiously. For one thing, there are few experiments that reveal the universe as a holistic entity. The 1982 Aspect experiments do appear to show instantaneous connections between widely separated particles,[3] along with more recent photon experiments. Also, there are alternative interpretations which can apply,[4] but these have not received the same attention of the holistic interpretation, for obvious reasons.

Physicist Roger Penrose has expressed his own concerns regarding the possibility of consciousness-created reality[5]:

(This is a) . . . very lopsided and disturbing view of the reality of the world. Those corners of the universe where consciousness resides may be rather few and far between. On this view, only in those corners would the complex quantum level superpositions be resolved . . .

Stephen Hawking is even more direct, calling it *"absolute rubbish"*.[6] Peter Coveney and Roger Highfield identify the paramount difficulty in quantum measurement, which has led to the naive notion that quantum theory *"is proving mysticism true"*:[7]

---

[3]   Aspect, Grangier, and Roger*: Physical Review Letters*, (49), 91.
[4]   Faster Than What? *in Newsweek*, June 19, 1995, p. 67.
[5]   Penrose: *The Emperor's New Mind—Concerning Computers, Minds and the Laws of Physics*, 295.
[6]   See:Boslaugh,: *Stephen Hawking's Universe*, 114.
[7]   Coveney and Highfield: *The Arrow of Time*, 134.

One may be appalled at these vehement reactions, but when one beholds what some authors have attempted, it might be understandable. Author Michael Talbot, for example, would seem to be a victim of quantum holism's compelling allure. In a 1991 book he invoked many tentative results to arrive at holographic theories for miracles, NDE's, Virgin Mary apparitions, ESP and telekinesis.[8] These comprise intriguing speculations, but nothing more, all of David Bohm's theories notwithstanding. The danger is that the unwary, seeing the references to scientists, could be tempted into thinking Talbot's holographic conjectures are established scientific facts. This is simply not so. Bohm's quantum potential[9], for example, is still regarded very skeptically by most physicists who adhere to the standard Copenhagen Interpretation of quantum theory. Their position may change, but not until further experiments are done to show that Bohm's interpretation is superior. This is certainly not to dismiss a holographic universe out of hand. One simply has to exercise caution and resist the temptation to jump to a foregone conclusion.

Mysticism also carries the seeds of paradox within itself, and to this degree is self-refuting. For example, mystics are enjoined not to talk about their meditations of cosmic unity because the latter transcends the power of words. At the same time, mystics recognize that if words are eschewed, their experiences can't be shared with the rest of humankind. In effect, they become self-absorbed hermits and effectively

---

[8]   Talbot: *The Holographic Universe,*.

[9]   Assume the total set of one's thoughts contains waves of frequencies ranging from f' (highest) to f, then the quantum potential φ can be expressed: $\varphi = \mathbf{h}(f' - f)$ where h is Planck's constant. Thus, φ has units of energy as the other potential functions in physics, e.g. gravitational and electrostatic. On average, the greater the number of possible states, the greater the difference $(f' - f)$ and the greater the quantum potential.

ignored by the rest of the world. Conversely, if and when the mystic does attempt to communicate his experiences, he ends up in self-contradictory statements because language is predicated upon a fundamental separation of subject and object, exactly the antithesis of the holistic mystical experience!

For my own part, I'm content to admit that a Universal Mind or holomovement *could* abide in the universe. I also concede that such an entity could possess attributes associated with a deity, albeit **natural** rather than *supernatural*. However, I don't think there will be a way for physics to establish its existence, any more than the bible can be used to prove the existence of the traditional "God". The reason is simple: if science operates on the basis of logic and analysis, there is no way it can make sense of an irreducible whole. Gödel's Incompleteness Theorem insures that physics and astronomy can never comprehend the universe in its entirety, with its infinite diversity and size. If that is true, there is certainly no way to comprehend a (presumably) vastly more complex Universal Mind![10]

Rudy Rucker makes exactly the same point, but he uses the term *Mindscape* instead of Universal Mind[11] :

> If the Mindscape is a One, then it is a member of itself and this can only be known through a flash of mystical vision. No rational thought is a member of itself, so no rational thought could tie the Mindscape into a One.

Does this mean that the Mindscape or Universal Mind (or holomovement) doesn't exist? No, only that science can

---

[10] However, as mystics are quick to point out, the object isn't to comprehend such a Mind but to intuit it by meditation.

[11] Rucker: *Infinity and the Mind—the Science and Philosophy of the Infinite,*. 51.

189

Philip A. Stahl

find no way of articulating postulates or laws that would establish the necessary and sufficient conditions for existence of a "Universal Mind". And perhaps this barrier is just as well. If science could reduce such an entity to a mere recipe of differential equations, how mundane it would become in the end! As Ken Wilber notes, it would become no more interesting than an electric or gravitational field.[12]

We are left, in the end, with an aura of indeterminacy about whether we inhabit a holistic universe, and whether it is permeated by a Universal Mind.[13] The absence of verifiable absolutes is evidently a fundamental property of a truly holistic universe, possibly because it's inherently indeterminate. This includes the absence of any absolute knowledge that the universe is holistic! Ironically, the holistic universe emerges as a concept that implicitly transcends any attempt to define it, and hence establish its empirical validity.

Given these limitations, I still believe it is feasible to arrive at a wholly Materialist (e.g. Physicalist) model of mind or consciousness that can incorporate holistic properties within itself—such as Bohm's quantum potential, and Stapp's Heisenberg states. The effort would show not so much that some independent "transcendent" exists which can be isolated or operationally defined, but rather that cognizant humans acting with awareness can incept an interaction which might be more than the sum of parts. In this case, we would have a putative emergence from the basis of a wholly physical world structure.

This ought to make everyone happy, atheists and religious believers alike. For atheists, it would make their discourse meaningful again so they'd no longer appear to

---

12 Wilber: *The Holographic Paradigm.*
13 Note that I emphatically would not view such a Mind as anything supernatural, even though it's indescribable to physics. Both universe and "Universal Mind" are, to me, wholly physical ideas.

be metaphysical hypocrites: arguing against the God meme on the one hand, then insisting the brain can't parse any "aboutness" on the other. Well that would include atheist brains too! Of course, these are the consequences one inherits when carrying the reductionist imperative to its logical end: the elimination of useful introspection.

For religious believers, it would at least show that although some (former) atheists like me aren't being converted, i.e. to a personal God-based religion, we're at least willing to go beyond standard reductionism to consider an emergent consciousness in a nonlocal universe. At the very minimum this step ought to be one that any reasonable religionist would applaud.

What isn't warranted is doubling down on aggressive Christian proselytizing as recently suggested in the press[14]. Therein, the Rev. Albert J. Mohler warned that unless people changed on their own the *"evangelical movement is going to be forced back into the Book of Acts."* He made reference to the ancient world of Acts wherein hyper-zealous witnessing and ferocious proselytizing dominated with the single goal of making converts.

If such a tragic step is taken, you can be sure atheists will display even more hyperbolic, doctrinaire reactions. We will then be headed toward a fractious world wherein fundamentalist Christians square off against fundamentalist atheists over nearly every issue. The tragedy is in fact likely understated given the Book of Acts is replete with abundant errors as well as the hands of forgers[15].

If we all just admit the noun "God" is an artificial symbol and what we're fighting over carries no existential weight as portrayed, perhaps we can collectively seek a better way.

---

[14]   TIME, March 25, 2012, 46.

[15]   Ehrman: *Forged: Writing in the Name of God—Why the Bible's Authors Are Not Who We Think They Are*, 206.

X. A MATERIALIST MODEL OF CONSCIOUSNESS

If, as Henry Stapp claims, humans can't be reduced to the laws of classical determinism and Newtonian mechanics, then we must be something more. I warrant that we're beings whose consciousness is emergent as opposed to epiphenomenal, so capable of at least partially controlling our reality. This means that a model of human consciousness must be forthcoming that takes this into account. In this chapter, I lay out the essential outline for such a Materialist holistic model of mind-consciousness.

I do this by integrating aspects of Stapp's Heisenberg states model with Bohm's implicate-explicate order paradigm. While neither physicist might believe this warranted I do think there's a case for integration in terms of the nonlocal properties peculiar to each.

What is energy? And in particular, what is energy at its most fundamental level? Is there scope for Mind to operate or be the core driver?

These are questions I've considered on and off for the past thirty years, even after becoming an avowed atheist ca. 1984. The problem? As I pursued aggressive atheism and scientific

Materialism—even writing a book[1] on the latter—I found the proposition of a mindless, purely mechanical cosmos less and less plausible. This didn't mean I'd acquiesced to any god meme so much as realized that the relation between matter and mind might be more subtle than I first believed. Matter wasn't merely inert globs or aggregations of particles, but was itself conscious! If this was true, it meant that consciousness as we understand it wouldn't be confined to the interior of a human brain. Rather, any mechanical, electro-mechanical or even purely material (non-mechanical) system could possess it!

Looking back now, the seed of change already lay within Chapter Five of my first atheist book, dealing with *Consciousness and Modern Materialism.* In that chapter I'd constructed a completely mechanistic consciousness (using aggregates of NOR, NAND etc. gates), but felt this first draft was suspect. It appeared way too artificial and contrived.

At that point I integrated quantum mechanics into the viewpoint via a number of quantum concepts I'd originally excluded for fear it might compromise my atheist credentials. Indeed, one noted atheist-materialist cited in my book, Daniel Dennett, had made it clear there was no place for quantum physics in any description of quantum mechanics.[2]

In a chapter entitled, *The Phantom Quantum-Gravity Computer: Lessons from Lapland,* in his book, *Darwin's Dangerous Idea,* Dennett expresses a serious distrust of quantum models applied to the brain or consciousness. This is very common among atheists who are painfully aware of how quantum theory has been abused and misapplied to try to account for miracles, and a whole range of alleged supernatural manifestations.

I rebutted Dennett's objections, showing how the synaptic cleft of the brain is of the ideal dimension for the Heisenberg

[1]   Stahl: *The Atheist's Handbook to Modern Materialism,* 131.
[2]   Henry Stapp also presents a devastating argument against Dennett's Multiple Drafts model. (Stapp: *op. cit.,* 23)

Indeterminacy Principle to apply, and this necessarily implies quantum mechanics. I also referenced the work of Henry Stapp, who showed that indeterminacy principle limitations apply to calcium ion (Ca $^{++}$) capture near synapses and disclosed they had to be represented by a probability function.[3]

In another radical change, I represented the classical Boolean NOT gate with what is called a unitary matrix, or Pauli spin matrix-operator σ_x[4]. This basically acts to flip the Boolean state of a single bit. So, it's a bit like a NOT gate, but much more subtle, allowing for greater flexibility. The Pauli spin matrices also have real eigenvalues[5] within a confined range. This meets a primary application requirement for *feed forward networks*, in describing synapse functions.[6]

Did this open the treatment of the brain and consciousness to supernatural influence via quantum nonlocality? I considered this question at some length and eventually decided it did not, all the worries of various atheists notwithstanding.

---

[3]   Stapp: *op. cit.*, 42.

[4]   Pauli spin matrices are: $\sigma_x = (0,1 \mid 1,0)$; $\sigma_y = (0, -i \mid i, 0)$; $\sigma_z = (1, 0 \mid 0, -1)$. (Note each left pair is a matrix 'top' and each right pair a matrix 'bottom'—since they are usually written in a rectangular array form.

[5]   In general, if M is a square matrix of (n x n) rows, columns and **x** is a column vector, then M*x = mx denotes a matrix eigenvalue equation. One solution, x= 0, is a null vector for all finite x. In general, for any M one can obtain n homogeneous linear equations in x. These have non-trivial solutions if the characteristic determinant is zero, viz. Det(M − x**I**) = 0 where **I** is the matrix identity element. Any such determinant can be expanded, i.e. by minors and cofactors, to give a polynomial of nth degree in x. When one solves the polynomial equation, the n roots are the *eigenvalues*.

[6]   Bar-Yam: *Dynamics of Complex Systems*, 298.

The inclusion of the Pauli spin matrices, along with Stapp's superpositions for Ca $^{++}$ ions, dramatically enhanced brain function and flexibility, since incorporation of quantum mechanics led to the much more effective basis of a quantum computer. That meant more options and more genuinely human creative responses, as opposed to purely mechanical reactions. (One reason why my numerous NAND and NOR gate examples were ridiculously simplified and the furthest thing from remotely approaching consciousness).

What I'd actually described in my chapter was a ridiculously absurd automaton. Thankfully, in the wake of publication, no one seemed to realize I'd foisted a caricature of a consciousness on them! But, as I realized later, this is exactly the point to which a too rigid interpretation of scientific Materialism leads. It can permit no role at all for anything of an insubstantial nature, but which nevertheless is *wholly physical*. I'd reached the point of counterfactual nonseparability so well articulated by physicist Bernard d'Espagnat.

As I later learned, when one integrates the latest quantum physics aspects into consciousness one arrives at something analogous to physicist David Bohm's holomovement. This is no longer strict physicalist-Materialism but something else, probably more in the realm of *panpsychism*, or at least *emergent Materialism*[7]. In other words, one arrives at a unitary construct which features attributes of both mind and matter, as opposed to a permanent dichotomy.

My point is that I no longer believe physical entities in the brain (axions, neurons, molecules etc.) are reducible *to pure physical interactions*. Another way of putting this is to

---

[7]   It seems odd that many reductionists and especially self-proclaimed Materialists, aren't aware of the many forms Materialism assumes. I examined a number of these in my previous book, see: Stahl: *Atheism: A Beginner's Handbook*, 52.

Philip A. Stahl

say that nuts and bolts biology can only take you so far in understanding consciousness.

One example appeared in my chapter *Consciousness and Modern Materialism*: that of the superposition applied to (Ca^{2+}) ion uptake.

$$\psi(n \in A, B) = \sum_{ijklm} \{\psi \, (Ca^{+2}) \, [n_i \, (A), n_j \, (B \ldots n_m \, (E)]\}$$

The main thrust of the above equation is that the position (and hence influence) of the calcium ion (Ca^{+2}) is totally indeterminate, since it can't be reduced to simple Newtonian motion. If indeterminate, then its action—and interaction with biological structures—is also indeterminate. This drives atheist reductionists crazy, and has them looking for "quantum ghosts" but their fear is unwarranted. The picture remains wholly physical, albeit *emergent*, which is not the same as supernatural!

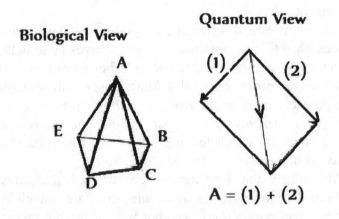

Biological View **Quantum View**

$A = (1) + (2)$

Development of Neuronal Assemblies

Consider (above) only the superposition of *the sub-assemblies for A and B*. Then an immediate

196

indeterminacy enters as a result of the wave properties associated with the calcium ions in A, B. Adopting the Heisenberg wave state of Stapp (see previous chapter) we can represent the situation in terms of a superposition of states for these relevant sub-assemblies of neurons.

Here the abscissa (x) identifies a Newtonian fixed position for the ion. However, the wave properties ensure it will *actually oscillate to positions* (+ x) and (–x), the exact difference depending on the amplitude of the waves.

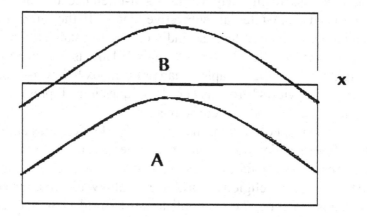

By inspection of the superposed wave states, it's clear that since position x is not possible to fix to any indefinite accuracy, then the attendant biological action cannot be fixed. Thus, the wave properties associated with matter (demonstrated by Louis de Broglie) disclose that there is *incomplete reduction.* The only way to eliminate this incomplete reduction would be to eliminate the wave properties of matter.

The disturbing conclusion of all this, certainly to hardcore atheists, is that the field of consciousness must exceed the locality of its apparent biological source. Or, to recite the words of one mystic that my now deceased father-in-law once quoted (who shall remain nameless):

All of the body is in the mind, but not all of the mind is in the body.

This short quote probably embodies most succinctly what I intend to show in my model of Mind.

What Exactly IS Consciousness?

What is human consciousness? Is there a way to define it which does not invoke unwanted dualities (such as the Cartesian *res cogitans* and *res extensa*). If so, to what extent can it access reality, say without self-reference or "noise" introduced from internal, subjective states? If the latter are inevitable, is there at least an indirect way to establish that a construct exists—for the outer "reality"? How is the scientist to rightly regard the metaphysician or orthodox believer—and their world views? To answer these questions I present a quantum-based model of consciousness.

The concept of Weltanschauung or 'world view' lies at the root of one's belief systems and to a large measure determines relations to one's fellows, as well to ethical and religious systems. While religious world views allow for emergence and transcendence, the materialist/realist world view doesn't nor do its contemporary derivatives: physicalism, causal materialism or peripheralism. In the case of Materialism (crude, atomistic form), the exclusion of emergent properties has been attained by virtue of adopting a strictly reductionist view wherein the entire universe can be reduced to hard, material particles. This view originally appeared at the time of the Greek atomists Leucippus and Demokritos, who used it as a basis for the philosophy of Epicureanism. It may rightly be said, therefore, that this was the precursor of the reductionist/materialist/realist school of thought.

At the other end of the spectrum, the Greek Stoics countered the Epicurean and atomist philosophy by postulating more to the cosmos than the mere sum of its parts. Scope thereby existed in the Stoic universe for *emergence*.

Indeed, the Stoics conceived of the cosmos *as an organic whole*, not unlike the view of the Tao espoused by many Eastern philosophies today. The Stoics set the stage for the Platonic idealists wherein the shadows in the cave metaphor for reality came to the fore. This was the precursor for the school of idealist philosophies, all of which questioned the validity of the existence of an external reality

In either case: realism/materialism or idealism, it must be understood that a context for truth is being defined. Clearly, one's affinity for scientific lines of thought will depend on where one stands in the spectrum of realism/materialism to idealism. That affinity will be greater the more one embraces the former emphasis—to the essential exclusion of the latter. Of course, before issues of truth can be approached there must be some comprehension of what consciousness is—at least in terms of operational definitions.

For their part, transcendent world-views tend to take the position that the human person is tri-partite in character: a "soul", a body and a "mind". Rene Descartes, starting from a "divine" conception—developed his dualistic conception of *res co*gitans (thinking thing) and *res extensa* (extended thing). In the first category he included the concepts of "mind"—the central thinking thing—and "soul", which ultimately governed the mind like a rider guides a horse. In the second category, he included all corporeal or physical things, including the body.

At the same time, Descartes postulated a *"center of consciousness"* or thought within the brain—in the pineal gland. This notion of a center of thought or conscious mind has—at least in the West—been adopted as almost axiomatic. Indeed, it does appear that each of us possesses a center point to thought—or through which outside things enter and are perceived uniquely inside ourselves. From this original "center of thought" notion, the soul concept was elaborated beyond mere theological conjectures.

Philip A. Stahl

In the West, this Cartesian dualism or mind-body split, inevitably brought with it a metaphysical elitism or preference—with the "body" being given short shrift to the "mind-soul" or res cogitans. Platonic idealists—particularly within Christianity—were motivated to debase and devalue the physical/material realm while giving priority to the mental. Christianity, which extracted many of its doctrines from (Persian) Mithraism—splitting the cosmos into "forces of light and darkness", and Manicheanism—which viewed all flesh as an "evil" creation, was ripe for an ontological hijacking by Cartesian dualism, aided and abetted by schools of idealism. The hijacking was evident in the writing of many post-reformation theologians who took up the decided anti-flesh, anti-world cant of earlier Fathers such as St. Augustine and Tertullian. It culminated in the elaboration of more than 2600 Canon laws, more than half proscriptions against fleshly acts.

It soon became plain that the religious proscriptions were offshoots of an idealist world view which sought to exclude all corporeal relations from what it regarded as the "exalted realm of the mind". This view also upheld "reason" and the action of the mind to be of far greater import than any mechanical activities, or desires of the body. Moreover, this exaltation, with no evidence to support it (neural network research hadn't yet been invented!) made them believe that reasoning could only be done from a "high platform" of soul or God. Thus, in their limited imagination, no reasoning was feasible if soul or God were foreclosed.

In effect, it was a tacit effort to relegate the body (flesh) to the realm of the ob-scene (off-scene, or off the stage of life as it were). It is arguable from a number of points of view that this extreme idealism—already in place at the start of the scientific revolution in the early 17th century called forth an uncompromising realism/materialism mindset as a corrective. This mindset, naturally, became entrenched within the epistemological arena of science. The so-called "battle between science and religion" is therefore, none other than a conflict between their larger philosophical contexts: idealism and realism/materialism.

Confronting Divergent Systems of Thought:

1. Idealism:

As noted by Euan Squires[8]:

Idealism is.the simple observation that all knowledge comes from sensations in the conscious mind. Thus, since everything I know, I know through my mind, it follows that in some way my mind is the only certain reality

Moreover, a soul must operate the mind or enable its function much like the Wizard of Oz operated the Great Oz from behind a curtain. To the idealist, it is inconceivable a brain could reason and function perfectly well in the absence of a soul, or by extension . . . God.

Perhaps the most damning critique of idealism has been offered by Squires who notes that[9] *the most useful argument against all such philosophies is that they discourage any endeavor to understand the sensations of the conscious mind.* This is certainly true in so far as understanding is contingent on a reductionist approach—and idealism rejects reductionism in favor of holism (or the new euphemism nonlocality) as the Greek Stoics once did. Certainly a holistic theory of consciousness would reject the notion of conscious sensations as disjunctive and reductionist. To that extent, such a theory would be opposed to any endeavor to understand them!

We see that idealist philosophies, which invest a primacy in the mind and enact a putative soul governor, have only

---

[8]   Squires: *Conscious Mind and the Physical World*, 74

[9]   Squires.: *op. cit.*, 74.

disdain for scientific techniques applied to uncovering dynamics of consciousness. Clearly then, any workable or testable theory of consciousness can't come from idealism but rather its alter ego: realism.

2. *Realism*

In contrast to idealism, realism is the underlying philosophy of science. It asserts that human consciousness receives experiences from an external world, quite distinct from that consciousness. As Squires notes[10]: *The images we obtain, involving for example eyes, ears, telescopes, etc. are images of a genuinely existing reality whose existence is not dependent on our being aware of the images.* Squires notes that in quantum mechanics, for example, there is an observer disturbance of the system, but *just because we observe and disturb it is not to say we create it.*

According to Flew[11] realism is the belief that physical objects exist independently of being perceived. (Or to paraphrase physicist N. David Mermin: *The Moon is really there when nobody looks!*) Arguably, therefore the notion of an "observation" only has significance in the context of a realistic philosophy, just as the question "What exists?" In order to even think of asking the latter, the implicit inference must be that there is a real, externally persistent world.

In the realist purview, the very existence of a brain with over ten billion neurons and trillions of synapses means that reason is enabled. No other outside agents are needed.

3. *Materialism.*

Crude materialism is a direct antecedent of today's *naive realism.* It is the simple re-statement of position for the

---

[10]   *Ibid*

[11]   Flew: *A Dictionary of Philosophy*

ancient Greek atomist school that whatever exists is either matter or entirely dependent on matter for its existence[12]. A more modern re-wording would substitute the phrase *laws of physics* for matter.

In physicalism, it is ultimately energy and fields which exhaust the universal set of constructs in the universe with nothing left over. We need not concern ourselves with umpteen particles or sub-particles (quarks, leptons, muons, etc.) since ultimately all are subsumed under the umbrella of energy by virtue of Einstein's mass-energy equivalence relation ($E = mc^2$). Taken to its ultimate conclusion, physicalism allows a theory of everything, for example, a grand unified field.

A physicalist model of consciousness allows a wholly physical explanation of mind minus any distracting supernatural agents. Such a model shows how a fleshly brain composed of billions of neurons can reason, without any assistance whatsoever from a supernatural controller or assumed law author. Some religionists claim reason is impossible without a supreme lawgiver having made the processes for it to be possible in the first place. But this is the classical argument from ignorance. It commits the *ignotum per ignotius* fallacy: postulating an unknown agent or cause to account for a not well understood process, e.g. consciousness or rational thought within it.

In what follows, I'll present a theory of consciousness which adopts a far realism context. By *far realism* I mean that elements of inquiry are required beyond the immediately material or mechanical—determinist. Thus we can't hope to explain consciousness using blood, cells or even plain neurons themselves. We must go to the deeper level of quantum phenomena. One indicator that we must do so is offered by the scale size of separation between neurons, e.g. in the synapse. Thus, the synaptic cleft dimension (of about

---

[12]   Flew, *op. cit.*

200-300 nm)is exactly the scale at which the Heisenberg Indeterminacy Principle would be expected to operate. That necessarily implies quantum mechanics. We will see then that by invoking the appropriate processes that we can show the brain operates as a quantum transducer: converting quantum wave forms to signals embodied as thoughts. No other creators are needed!

A Model for Nonlocal-Quantum Action of Mind:

In my hybrid Bohmian-Stapp / Heisenberg wave state model, activation of conscious observation occurs via engagement of the microtubules in the brain. Though Stapp and Bohm approach nonlocality from differing positions: Stapp via the Heisenberg Ontology applied to the Copenhagen Interpretation of Quantum Mechanics (CIQM), and Bohm via the deterministic de Broglie wave concept in his Stochastic Interpretation of Quantum Mechanics (SIQM) both use the Heisenberg Indeterminacy Principle as a starting point.

In Bohm's case, the Heisenberg relations are embodied in his theory as a limiting case *over a certain level of intervals of space and time*. However, the potential exists for the fields to be averaged over smaller intervals and hence, *subject to a greater degree of self-determination than is consistent with the Heisenberg principle*. As Bohm concludes[13]:

> From this, it follows that our new theory is able to reproduce, in essence at least, one of the essential features of the quantum theory, i.e. Heisenberg's principle, and yet have a different content in new levels

Bohm is primarily concerned with the canonically conjugate field momentum, for which the associated

---

[13] Bohm, *op. cit.,*. 91.

coordinates, i.e. Δt, $\Delta\varphi_k$ fluctuate at random. Thus, we have, according to Bohm:

$$\pi_k = a\,(\Delta\varphi_k / \Delta t)$$

Where k is a constant of proportionality, and $\Delta\varphi_k$ is the fluctuation of the field coordinate. If then the field fluctuates in a random way the region over which it fluctuates is;

$$(\delta\,\Delta\varphi_k)^2 = b\,(\Delta t)$$

Taking the square root of both sides yields:

$$(\delta\,\Delta\varphi_k) = b^{1/2}\,(\Delta t)^{1/2}$$

Bohm notes that π_k also fluctuates at random over the given range so:

$$\delta\,\pi_k = a\,b^{1/2} / (\Delta t)^{1/2}$$

Combining all the preceding results one finally gets a relation reflective of the Heisenberg principle, but time independent:

$$\delta\,\pi_k\,(\delta\,\Delta\varphi_k) = ab$$

This is analogous to Heisenberg's principle, cf.

$$\delta p\,\delta q \leq \hbar$$

Where the product *ab* plays the same role as $\hbar$

Given the preceding, my conjecture is that the brain is a quantum wave receiver/generator, with the tuning governed by the topology of toroidal space-time which itself undergoes quantum fluctuations. It makes little sense to suppose it evolved to such a stage within an environment which was not also accessible in terms of quantum waves. In other words, the human brain evolved to its quantum processor/receiver stage, precisely because the universe was already at that processing/transmitting stage.

The corollary is that the universe is quantum wave mechanical at the most fundamental level. What we call cosmos is the aggregate of all quantum wave forms in a state of ongoing interaction, via the Bohmian quantum potential. This means that the brain, in its current evolutionary state, can interact quantum mechanically with any of the objects in the cosmos. It also means that these objects must share in the conscious attribute.

This aspect conforms to Stapp's Heisenberg ontology form of the CIQM, whereby an observational choice *actualizes as a whole* and injects into the quantum universe an integrative aspect.[14]

How does this transpire, and how exactly does it trigger the fluctuations Bohm designates as $\delta \pi_k$ ($\delta \Delta\varphi_k$)?

My proposal, following on from John G. Cramer's quantum transaction concept[15], is that waveguide action in microtubules, incited by an observational choice or effect, generates a coherent signal. This is a standing wave composed of one wave from the future($-\tau$), and one from the past (τ). The basic idea is depicted below:

[14] Stapp: *op. cit .* , 149.
[15] Cramer: *Reviews of Modern Physics,* (58), 647.

MICROTUBULE

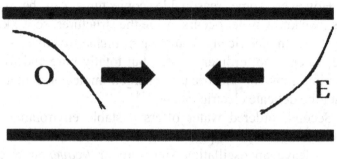

From the Past   **From the Future**

Some estimates place the maximal rate of operations per second at 10^{24}, for the prospect of microtubule computing.[16]

Where do these changes occur? Not through the whole body but in highly localized structures within brain neurons. These structures, cylindrical in shape, are called *microtubules*. If one examines them on the inside, thin strips called tubulins are observed, and within them smaller sections called dimers.[17] The micro-tubules play the same role in the brain that microchips play in modern computers.

More importantly, their structure emulates a cavity resonator, which other bones in the body don't. In computers, information persists through the storage of bits, the 1s and 0s in the registers. In the brain, information persists through a phenomenon called quantum coherence. This means that a multitude of quantum wave states are stored in a multitude of microtubules. Precisely how this is done remains a topic on the frontier of current research. Research into the microtubule

---

16   Penrose: *Shadows of the Mind,* 366.
17   *Op. cit.,* 361.

connection to human consciousness is, after all, still in its infancy.

However, some reasonable conjectures can be made. First, we know water occurs inside the structures, so we know they have an electrically insulating or *dielectric* environment. The water is not ordinary water, but totally pure and free of roaming ions, or electrically charged molecules, that can upset the delicate electric balance.[18]

Second, ordered water offers a stable environment for quantum states[19], via quantum waves, within it. Indeed, the waves leave an oscillating signature or *frequency.* Such a frequency has been observed at 5×10^{10} per second.[20] This suggests that the tiny micro-tubule cylinders act as *wave guides.*[21]

---

[18] Hameroff,: *Ultimate Computing: Bio-Molecular Consciousness and Nanotechnology.*

[19] By ordered quantum states, I mean states acting collectively as one. (Similar to what is called a Bose-Einstein condensate). In this case, some set of n states in the microtubules, e.g. {s1, s2, s3 . . . . sN} act as one single quantum state ρ. A system such as this, for biological systems, was proposed as much as 30 years ago by Prof. Herbert Fröhlich. (See: Fröhlich: *International Journal of Quantum Chemistry*, Vol. II.) It must be emphasized, however, that all such models remained largely conjectures until the Bose-Einstein condensate was actually physically observed in a system in which all its properties were accessible. For more on this discovery see: *'A New Form of Matter Unveiled'*, in Science, Vol. 270, December 22, 1995, p. 1902. Hence, my own serious interest did not begin until after this watershed discovery, and after I learned of the nature of 'Goldstone bosons' as suitable members of the condensate.

[20] Penrose,: *op. cit.,* 374.

[21] In general physics terms, a waveguide is any device that guides waves propagating through it. Generally, the term has been reserved for EM, or electro-magnetic waves, such as

In the diagram shown below, (O) and (E) denote respectively real offer and echo waves, as described earlier. The first comes from the past, the second from the future.[22] Their combination in the microtubule wave guide[23] yields a standing wave that has coherence and information. In the diagram below, a real coherent standing wave is shown, inside a typical microtubule:

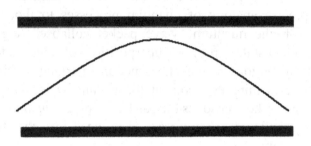

O And E Combined

This is a quantum wave function, now combined. The peak of the wave (near the center) could be regarded as the probability peak for the given state, within the microtubule.

---

microwaves or radio waves. However, if a waveguide has the same scale of size as the waves it is conducting, this definition need not be so restricted. In the case of the microtubules, their scale would seem to indicate that quantum waves are the waves to be guided through them, hence that is the way to picture them in this model.

[22] The combination can be written: $\psi(O) + \psi(E) = \psi(2/\pi)$
$e^{\omega\tau} + \sqrt{(2/\pi)}\, e^{-\omega\tau}$

[23] Wave guide is actually a general term in physics to describe a variety of devices the guide waves transmitted through them. The transmission properties are often reckoned in terms of the angular function ω ($= 2\pi f$) where f is the frequency we already have given for microtubules (5×10^{10} /s). Remember that $\tau = it$.

So long as the wave pattern holds, information is in a potential or storage mode. This peak also correlates with the Bohm peak for the local field intensity and in Stapp's parlance, would be exactly that situation that "injects into the quantum universe an integrative aspect". In other words, this putatively micro event *extends to different parts of the universe.*

It was physicist David Bohm who first pointed out the very precise analogy of quantum processes to thought. In particular, the quantum "wave packet collapse" (e.g. to a single eigenstate, from a superposition of eigenstates) is exactly analogous to the phenomenon of trying to pinpoint what one is thinking about at the instant he is doing such thinking[24]. When one does this, as Bohm notes, *uncontrollable and unpredictable changes* are introduced into the thought process or train.

People are often heard to say: *Sorry, I've lost my train of thought.*

What they really mean is the thought coherence they'd earlier enjoyed has been obliterated, so that they have to commence the thought process anew. The coherent state has collapsed into a single state which they no longer recognize. In this way, as Bohm pointed out, the *instantaneous state of a thought* can be compared to the instantaneous position of a particle (say associated with a B-wave in a brain neuron). Similarly, the general direction of change of a thought is analogous to the general direction of change in time for the particle's momentum (or by extension, its phase function).

Now, let's get into more details.

Assume the total set of one's thoughts contains waves of frequencies ranging from f' (highest) to f, then the quantum potential V_Q can be expressed:

---

[24] Bohm: *Quantum Theory*, 169.

$V_Q = h(f' - f)$, where h is Planck's constant.

Thus, Bohm's quantum potential, V_Q has units of energy as the other potential functions in physics, e.g. gravitational and electrostatic. On average, the greater the number of possible states, the greater the difference $(f'-f)$ and the greater the quantum potential.

In general, $V_Q = \{-\hbar^2 / 2m\} [\nabla R]^2 / R$

Of course, in a real human brain, we have a many-particle field (especially since we're looking at neuronal complexes) so that the quantum potential must be taken over a sum such that:

$V_Q = \{-\hbar^2 / 2m\} \sum_i [\nabla R_i]^2 / R$

The velocity of an individual B-wave is expressed by:

$v_{(B)} = \nabla S / m$

Here m is the mass of the particle associated with the B-wave, and *S* is a phase function obtained by using Bohm's relation:

$U = R \exp(iS/\hbar)$

Where R, S are real. So thought occurs with the collapse of the wave function U and the onset of a new phase function S' as a result, such that the B-waves in an original P-wave packet can become dislodged and arrange as a modulated waveform. This modulated waveform is also driven in part by the quantum potential, and is represented below in relation to the original P-wave ensemble and packet:

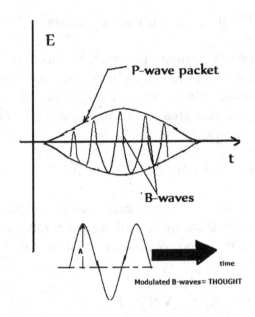

Again, in the many—particle realistic situation of the brain, a change in momentum (P) of each particle (x_i, x_2, x_3 .... x_n) must be referenced. So we need:

$$P_i = dS(x_{(i)}, x_2, x_3 .... x_n) / dx_i$$

Now, we reference the figure in the diagram which shows the situation for one such particle (x1) in the wave train, at the onset of an initial thought. The B-waves are initially enfolded in a wave packet we call *the P-wave* (for pilot wave) packet as neurons (and their B-waves) interact with each other, the associated quantum potentials are activated and fluctuations occur in the synapses—associated with the Heisenberg Indeterminacy Principle.

Thus, action within proximity of synapses discloses why exactly microtubules function differently from say, "bones in the big toe" which Stenger makes facetious reference to[25],

---

25   Stenger,:*op. cit.*, 270.

inquiring why they don't also display such unique quantum effects. The point is it is precisely the choice of thought that activates the fluctuation in field intensity $\Delta\varphi_k$ and the canonical momentum to which Bohm's hidden variables are related and which also paves the way for the nonlocal action via Stapp's Heisenberg ontology.

Ultimately, the fluctuations become large enough in amplitude to allow the trapped B-waves to break from their respective P-wave packets and form their own modulated sets or wave trains (bottom of diagram). This mental condition associated with this is what I call a *"primordial thought"*. I emphasize here, the nature is of a proto-thought and certainly nothing like thinking of a new way to solve cubic equations, or challenge special relativity! But it marks the start!

In general, more complex thought will occur when Heisenberg—type fluctuations apply, of the form:

$$(\delta p)(\delta q) \geq h/ 2\pi \approx \hbar$$

And these fluctuations don't exceed the amplitude (A) of the modulated wave form, as shown in the bottom of the diagram. Scope is limited for a more mathematical development here, but I show this in Appendix D.

The origin of logical or rational thought would arise when *numerous modulated wave trains* of the form shown reinforce each other in a process we call "constructive interference". The logical nature of the thought is validated so long as the momentum shift (see arrow direction in diagram) of the total wave train is not disturbed or disrupted. Since quantum superpositions can also link fields, e.g. electrical in the brain, then it is possible for these fields to also exist outside the brain's immediate physical dominion.

The sketch below is intended to show this, based on a cartoon depiction of what Bohm has referred to as *Einstein's Non-linear field approach*. The upper image-graphic shows a particle in the wave limit, with the particulate localized near the maximum, A. The particle is defined more clearly (i.e. localized) given the field intensity φ falls quickly as the distance x increases from the maximum. It is non-linear equations such as invoked by Einstein which allows such a pulse to remain coherent over protracted times. Indeed, it can move through space with a certain overall momentum, π. A particle thereby arises as a nonlocal form in the field.

It is also possible to have two such particles which are nonlocally connected (as per Stapp's Heisenberg ontology) because the field intensities of the individuals, say φ (A) and φ(B) never fall to zero, so at low levels of the fields A and B merge in one continuous field which has 2 maxima. This is what I believe Stapp meant when he referred to each actual event (i.e. particle materialization by pair production) not being confined to any local region.

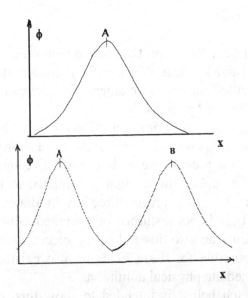

Clearly then, if the initiation of thought has the same attributes, it also cannot be localized so we can image above—instead of ordinary particles—modulated B-waves that are capable of making interconnection with proximate or even distant parts of the universe.

Physicist Henry Stapp notes:[26]

> In the present quantum-theoretical approach, consciousness is considered built from conscious acts. The conscious act that selects a course of action is represented naturally in physical theory as the act of reduction (collapse) that selects the course of action.

There is no arbitrary or ad hoc correspondence that has to be cooked up . . . This conception of nature gives to Man the role in nature he has always intuitively felt was his, and places the deterministic (mechanical) physical laws in their proper perspective as representations of certain statistical properties of the collection of free acts that constitute the process of creation.

So that, again, it is the conscious act or thought selection that entrains coherence of B-waves within the brain's microtubules and leads to the sort of manifestation (of those choices) that Stapp describes as constituting a "process of creation". In other words, we create by our thoughts. The above description allows two types of thought to be distinguished: pure and processed. In pure thought, all quantum states co-exist as *possibilities* of some final, expressed outcome. For example, pure thought occurs in the original, primitive approach to wherein I may entertain 10 or 15 different visions—going from one to the other.

In processed thought, one image structure is selected and amplified (focused) to that exclusion of others. At this stage, my conscious intent selects from among the vast set of

---

[26]   Stapp: *Foundations of Physics*, (15), 35-40.

possibilities. In effect, processed thought determines in which universe my thought will be made manifest. In mathematical language, pure (unprocessed) thought is:

$$\Psi = \Psi 1 + \Psi 2 + \Psi 3 + \ldots + \Psi N$$

where the terms on the right hand side represent the full set of possibilities available for selection. There are two crucial points to make. First, if thought is described by a quantum wavefunction then it must be a *physical wave*, not merely a statistical artifact. Second, the associated energy is amplified upon conviction or belief.

This energy comes from the source predicted by David Bohm, called the 'quantum potential'.[27] It can be thought of as an energy driver. A powerful means to get the quantum waves accumulated in the brain microtubules to propagate and affect external reality! It is written in elementary form:[28]

$$QP = M_0 F_0 - m_0 f$$

(Again, bear in mind, QP is just V_Q as defined earlier.)

With further 'massaging' it can be written in the simpler form:

$$QP = h(\delta f)/2$$

in the limit as m_0, the mass of a *Goldstone boson*[29], goes to zero. In this case, $\delta f = (F_0 - f)$ is the bandwidth of superposed

---

[27] Bohm,:(1980) *op. cit*, 77.
[28] completely: •R/R = $c^2/h^2 [M_0^2 - m_0^2]$, with F_0 = the zero order frequency of $M_0 c^2/h^2$, and f = the microtubule frequency = $m_0 c^2/h^2$. In most quantum physics papers, it is written this way:
[29] The Goldstone boson may be one of the two key ingredients for highly coherent thought. The other being B-waves (or

frequencies. It should not be surprising here, that as one approaches the bandwidth limit also approaches a "Super Frequency", e.g. $\delta f \rightarrow F (\infty)$. And for the quantum potential at this level of thought:

$$QP \rightarrow \infty$$

so that we expect instantaneous influence over an essentially infinite region of space and time—coupled with infinite magnitude of influence

Where is the vast energy to drive the quantum potential coming from? Bohm names the source as *the Dirac Ether*, the vacuum energy resident in empty space. According to Bohm[30]:

> If one computes the amount of energy that would be in one cubic centimeter, with this shortest possible wavelength, it turns out to be far beyond the total energy of all the matter in the universe . . . what is implied by this proposal is that what we call empty space contains an immense background of energy and that matter as we know it is a small, quantized wavelike excitation on the top of this background, like a ripple on a vast sea

---

deBroglie electron waves). Also called Nambu-Goldstone bosons, they are creatures of broken symmetries which always have zero mass and spin. This renders them excellent candidates for the processing of consciousness. For more about them, see: Weinberg: *The Quantum Theory of Fields*, 167.

[30]   Bohm: *op. cit.*,191.

Spencer-Brown operators are also useful to show the recursive action of consciousness in nonlocal access. We can write, for example[31]:

$$\Xi \rightarrow O \mid \sim O$$

Here O is *that which observes*, and $\sim$ O is *the totality of that which O operates upon*. By Henry Stapp's Heisenberg Ontology formulation of the CIQM, this necessarily means the whole cosmos. In this operation, the latter is acted upon by a recursive mode (called Mind) given by the first term, and a non-recursive part[32]

One might say the preceding operator equation encompasses the whole of what some may call "quantum mind" but which I more specifically refer to as the operational function of the brain under a quantum mechanical dynamic that indicates nonlocality.

---

[31] Comfort: *Reality & Empathy-Physics, Mind and Science in the 21st Century,* 164.

[32] By definition, the recursive part can be completed in a finite number of steps, while the non-recursive part requires an infinite number of calculation steps for completion. For more on this, see Comfort: *Reality and Empathy: Physics, Mind and Science in the 21st Century*

XI. MY PATH TOWARD EMERGENT MATERIALISM

As in the case of academic advancement, multiple matriculations can be considered normal and expected over the course of one's life. Thus one matriculates from high school, then from senior year of university, then from grad school. One could say it's in the nature of things to advance, even beyond the formal educational setting.

Thus, in terms of philosophy and beliefs, I advanced and 'matriculated' from Catholicism by the time I was 22, having—as I told my mother—*"to escape the suit of Catholicism which had become far too tight for me, so I can no longer wear it"*. Their doctrines, especially in fantastic events such as the Immaculate Conception and trinity caused my growing rational mind to rebel. Certainly, once one had taken courses in rigorous logic and philosophy one would be a fool not to exercise those learned skills. That included questioning authority, especial papal authority and the very notion of infallibility.

It had also been encouraging for me to find agreement within the Catholic hierarchy itself, as I pursued my quest apart from the Church's grasp. Theologian Hans Kung, for example, observed the following[1]:

> ... no one, neither Vatican I, nor Vatican II, nor the textbook theologians, has shown that the Church—its leadership or its theology—is able to put forward propositions which inherently cannot be erroneous.

The preceding actually reinforces a point I made earlier in this book (Chapter I) in terms of God-concepts, and how they emerge from limited human brains. If our brains are limited, prone to error, then their products are incapable of being absolute certainties or perennial truths. They can only be relative and accurate only for a time, if at all. With such inherent limits there is no way any brain, even a pope's, can formulate a perfect or error-free doctrine no matter how much he may wish to believe it so.

The most a limited brain can do, with any reliability, is make limited, *negative* declarations i.e., of what our brains cannot do, especially in a domain of essential untestability.

I searched beyond Catholicism for other spiritual systems that resonated more with the real world, and found only two: *Mahayana Buddhism* and *Science of Mind*. The first appeared to have more in common with atheism, and its end point of nothingness, It was only years later, on reading Alan Watts' marvelous books, that this perception changed.

Meanwhile, Ernest Holmes' *Science of Mind* caught my attention and I attended several discussion sessions on its principles while living in Barbados. At the time, I was also taking a graduate Quantum Mechanics course, so I could see how many of Holmes' teachings—such as inseparability and wholeness—could be valid.

I soon became disenchanted when, as Hurricane David approached Barbados in late July of 1980, assorted Science

---

[1]   Kung: *Infallible? An Inquiry,* 143.

of Mind followers insisted that they had "used their imaging properties of mind to steer the hurricane away". The question I posed was: *Why did you not also steer it away from the island of Dominica to open sea, and spare those people a lot of suffering?*

So, at that point, I began my next matriculation on to hard atheism, and by 1990 had openly declared it while lecturing in physics at Harrison College, Barbados. By then I'd also joined the American Atheists, and had published the article *My Path to Atheism* in the organization's magazine The American Atheist. Supported by the resources of the most aggressive atheist organization in the country, by 1992-93 I was on the AOL religion boards having no-holds barred arguments and debates with assorted theists. The positions taken were always hard line with absolutely no compromise. I essentially insisted my opponents either provide at least indirect empirical evidence for their claims, e.g. analogous to spectroscopic analysis showing chemical elements in the stars, or shut up. I continually pounded them on this and often referred to Sir A.J. Ayer's thresholds for acceptance, i.e. that if a language reference didn't incorporate at least some kind of empirical component, then it was meaningless[2].

Tired of the inability of assorted religionists and godists to address my core arguments on AOL, I moved to the (more than 15-years defunct) *Mensa Atheist Advocate* by 1994-95. This was a special publication of the *Mensa* Special Interest Group, A-SIG, from about 1993 until it became defunct in 1995. Often chucked with incisive arguments, it ultimately met its demise with the SIG sometime in late August, 1995, after much internecine squabbling. Many of the issues, and arguments—I admit—were initiated by me, since I brought up the dichotomy of *"real" atheists* as opposed to pretenders or poseur atheists. Many of the letters exchanged highlight the differences in stance, mostly between me and the majority

---

[2]   Ayer: *Language, Logic and Truth.*

group of moderates belonging to the SIG. The bulk of those moderates believed Madalyn Murray O'Hair and American Atheists were "extremists" who gave atheists a bad name instead of advancing the cause. I disagreed, and often did so vehemently.

By the fall of 1995 I'd taken on all the Mensa atheist moderates in the A-SIG Newsletter. My robust responses often occupied eighty percent or more of the publication, since at any given time I was fending off attacks by six or more opponents. By October, the Editor wrote me an email asserting she'd had enough, and basically couldn't deal with my intensity. I left that group and went on to continue working on my book manuscript.

The manuscript was left a de facto orphan after the disappearance of Robyn Murray-O'Hair, the Editor of American Atheist Press. She'd been found dead, September 29, 1995, with her mother and brother Jon Garth Murray. Devastated by the news, since she'd taken a special interest in my book, I worried the timeline might be adversely affected. Still, I'd hoped the new editor, Frank Zindler, would expedite its release in order that it could appear under an official book publisher's imprint.

In reviewing the manuscript, however, Zindler kept finding numerous problems, each of which I addressed in comprehensive, updated revisions. One example concerned a point made in Chapter Three of the book, regarding chaos and the prediction of planetary positions using celestial mechanics. Zindler seemed to believe such future predictions couldn't be made because chaos prevented it. In my response, and also in the book, I took pains to explain that relatively near term forecasts, such as Jupiter's position in the year 2050, could be forecast without major errors. This is because the equations of celestial mechanics, used to make the predictions, were not majorly affected by chaos over short intervals. I added, however, that if one sought to achieve a forecast one million years in the future it would be futile since chaos *would play havoc with the result.*

By late 1998, I'd had enough of this back and forth with the inevitable delays[3] and my long time friend Dr. Richard Stahl suggested that we publish the book on our own as a joint exercise and a Vicar V Project[4]. Thus, it came out in the fall of 2000, under the Professional Press imprint, as I had originally laid it out, though I did incorporate a number of Mr. Zindler's more useful editing suggestions.

I also repeatedly invoked David Hume's Miracle test[5]:

No testimony is sufficient to establish a miracle, unless the testimony be of such a kind that its falsehood would be more miraculous than the fact which it endeavours to establish.

In other words, which is the more likely: that a miracle really did occur—say when Christ was recorded to have walked on water—or that someone (even a zealous transcriptionist) just added a few words to change them and make the event a miracle? For example, Prof. Hugh Schonfeld (*The Passover Plot*) has a simple explanation for the claim of Jesus walking on water: a mistranslation of the Hebrew word *al* which can mean *by* or on. So, when a scribe wrote *walking*

---

3   To be fair, Mr. Zindler also had the magazine (*The American Atheist*) to get out mostly on his own so couldn't devote all the time he needed to for my book's release. Hence, it made sense other books took higher priority, which weren't so scientifically complex. Nonetheless, I don't regret the decision to go with independent publication.

4   *Vicar V* was intended to be the imprint for a series of atheist books.

5   Hume: *An Enquiry Concerning Human Understanding,* 104.

by the water (use of the Hebrew al) it was actually translated *walking on the water*.

By the Hume test: Is the Schonfeld claim of mistranslation more or less miraculous than a man actually violating the law of gravity and walking on water? It doesn't require a lot of thought or effort to see that the mistranslation of a passage of the New Testament is less miraculous (or if you prefer, less improbable) than that a man actually, literally walked on water.

The miracle at Fatima is another example. So which is more miraculous? That the Sun actually moved before a crowd of 70,000—which would have meant that its feat would have to be visible to all the observatories around the world (it wasn't) or that the entire crowd experienced a mass hallucination? From a strictly rationalist viewpoint, the former has to be deemed more miraculous, so that the latter—no matter how much one's temperament and instinct may rebel—has to be accepted as closer to the explanation!

One can also reframe the Hume test this way: Which is more miraculous, that miracles can occur in an actual, real cosmos strictly governed by physical laws, or in a *simulated universe in which the laws can be temporarily suspended* if a glitch (e.g. run time error) occurs? The answer—which ought to be self-evident from what we've articulated—is that the miracles would more likely occur in a simulated cosmos. Thus, the person who accepts miracles but rejects a simulated universe is out on a limb . . . and no small one at that! He then has to explain or justify how clear physical laws—like entropy or conservation of mass-energy, can be willy-nilly suspended at some times, but not others.

I generally framed my own arguments in terms of *necessary and sufficient conditions* which I had introduced earlier. Robert Baum correctly observes[6] that n-s conditions are *practical replacements* for causes. In other words, instead

---

[6]   Baum, *op. cit.,* 469

of saying or asserting x caused y, one stipulates that a, b are *necessary conditions* for x to exist at all, and c, d are *sufficient conditions* for y to have been the sole effect of cause x.

Baum's reasoning is clear[7]: Because a cause (generic) can be interpreted as proximate or remote, or even as *the goal or aim of an action* it is therefore too open-ended, ambiguous and construed in too many different ways. Thus, cause is too embedded in most people's minds with only one of several meanings, leaving most causality discussions unproductive and confused. If my cause and your cause in a given argument diverge, then we will not get very far. This also simplifies debates by removing the need to posit first Causes since if one does he becomes entrapped in a labyrinth of causal regression.

Because of this one uses the more neutral term *condition* and distinguishes between necessary and sufficient ones. These are specifically meaningful in the context of determining causal conditions, and hence, causes. If one eschews them, then one concedes he is incapable of logical argument incorporating the most basic affiliation with cause or causation.

In my more refined arguments invoking n-s conditions it appeared that no Christian could counter arrive at such for his claimed deity. Attributing omniscience, omnipotence, and omnipresence to the deity? Fine! Then also please provide the necessary and sufficient conditions for such an Omni-Being to exist!

Moreover, the capacity to provide such conditions is not trivial. If the believer is unable to do this basic exercise, then we can't know if his posited deity is substantially different from all other claimed deities, say as embodied in the Hindu Brahman, the Islamic Allah, or the Jewish Yahweh. Thus, the ability to provide n-s conditions for a putative deity is no mere

---

[7]   *Ibid.*

cosmetic or semantic exercise. It is essential in providing a discriminatory basis for identifying a God-concept as unique!

After perhaps hundreds of arguments and debates, a fraction of which I documented in *Dialectical Atheism,* I wanted to probe more deeply into loose ends related to atheistic ontology. So I read Alex Rosenberg's *The Atheist's Guide to Reality.* The book, predicated on an ultra-atheist perspective, sought to show why a meaningful conscious experience of reality couldn't work.

In its most extreme form, Rosenberg claimed that just as there can be no cosmic purpose there can be no *aboutness.* In other words, our brains—despite the appearance of an ability to generate meaning—did no such thing. In the end words meant nothing. The brain didn't interpret reality and couldn't assign any dimension of interpretation, whether to history, psychology, physics, astronomy or whatever. So if equations such as in celestial mechanics have no interpretative dimensions, how did we manage to use them to send spacecraft to Mars, Mercury, Venus?

In the most recent demonstration, how did we manage to get texts, descriptions and equations which meant nothing to land a one ton Rover Curiosity on Mars? Indeed, how did we manage to construct such a complex piece of engineering which descended from a Martian altitude of two kilometers—using parachutes and reverse rocket thrusts—so it could make a picture perfect landing exactly in the pre-selected landing site of Gale Crater? How did we manage this using instructions and words that, according to Rosenberg, exist no where in the brain's neurons and hence are non-interpretable? It didn't add up. (Rosenberg for his part argues that his book, which must also be meaningless by extension, didn't intend to actually transmit meaningful information to the reader but to alter the reader's brain using his own memes. Fine, but if the words are meaningless and can't be interpreted, this is as useless as claiming you can use ESP to alter a reader's brain.

Rosenberg bases his claims on documented experiments, such as those by Lüder Deecke and Hans Helmut Kornhuber in 1964, showing that all human actions *precede* conscious decisions to perform them. For example, Rosenberg argues, in his discussion concerning neural time delays, that a simple action like flexing a wrist can't be done at the instant one consciously thinks of doing so[8]. Instead, there's an inevitable time delay of about 200 milliseconds from conscious willing to wrist flexing and finger pressing[9]. He adds that the cortical processes responsible commence 500 ms before that! The obvious implication: *Consciously deciding to do something is not the cause of doing it.*

Or: If there is no real will, there can be no willpower. Rosenberg adopts this as a grounding for his notion that we are beings entirely governed by *blind sight*[10]. In other words, all our sensory outputs are based on ex post facto—conducted neural process corrections to much earlier sensory inputs.

The point is humans aren't equipped to gain real time access to anything in their world! What actually happens in vision, for example, is that the brain must perform tricks to first erect an image that appears inverted on the retina. The process takes time and processing via the optic nerve is also needed. Thus, in Rosenberg's parlance, *vision turns out to be hindsight not foresight*. Rosenberg's inescapable conclusion is that because of this we are victims of a monumental illusion condemned to live our lives through rear sight, not foresight or will. This transfers to his Chapter Eight, in which we are shown *The Brain Does Everything Without Thinking About It At All.*

There can be no aboutness for introspection or description of any meaning, according to Rosenberg's perspective, since

---

[8] Rosenberg: *The Atheist's Guide to Reality—Enjoying Life Without Illusions,* 152

[9] *Ibid.*

[10] *Op.cit.,* 155.

introspection is an illusion given the fact our brain doesn't really think. We only think it thinks.

All these words I'm writing? Meaningless gibberish! Shakespeare's work, *The Tempest*? Doggerel and drivel! Einstein's original paper on special relativity? A product of human imagination run riot. Jean-Paul Sartre's *Being and Nothingness*? A delusional, solipsistic voyage that could as well have been produced from LSD ingestion! Basically, all our fine cogitating, ruminating and writing translates to a torrent of meaningless effluent. All our millions and billions of volumes of books, e-books and scientific or other journals amount to culminations of massive forest destruction or wasted bytes. With no introspection, the products of human thought have no interpretative dimensions. They're merely elaborate chemical-physical automatons operating under the illusion of genuine personhood.

Human history follows suit, reduced to the simple retelling of all our accidents, and nonsense. Philosophy is reduced to nothing more than assemblies of chaotically processed, random signals input to our neurons, then output. A group of monkeys using typewriters could generate as much sense or worth but at least monkeys don't take their doggerel seriously!

I cite all the above to show the state to which current, radical atheism has evolved: a parody of skeptical extremism, or skepticism run amuck. So radical that atheist authors like Alex Rosenberg appear not to have realized they've effectively reduced their own works to indecipherable babble and meaningless rubbish. Clearly, if there's no capacity for introspection, then symbols on a page can't mean anything, so they could as well be nonsense.

This is how I encountered *What Is God?*, by Jacob Needleman. Needleman offers a personal journey from his own hard core atheism, to a moderated stance open to an emergent entity which, for lack of a better term, he calls God.

Most intriguing is Needleman's encounter with Buddhist scholar D.T. Suzuki. Needleman as brash, arrogant youth confronts Suzuki with the question: *What is the self?* Suzuki calmly replies: Who is asking the question? This effectively unnerves the young atheist and sends him off in near despair because he realizes he can't provide any intelligible answer. Thus begins his quest for Self and a deeper spiritual path.

His involvement with the writings of G.I. Gurdjieff follows, and is more illuminating than his Suzuki exchange, or non-exchange. He observes that certain elements of Gnostic writings remind him of the terminology and underlying messages in Gurdjieff's works[11]. Chief among these is that *"the human condition is a state of waking sleep in which the whole of man's life is mechanically ruled by the impersonal forces of world which itself is lost in meaninglessness and illusion"*[12]. Gurdjieff therefore considered nearly all humans to be puppets, incapable of acting as truly autonomous agents

Even so-called atheists became hollow puppets incited to react predictably to whatever believers wrote, thought or expressed. Believers emerged as reciprocating puppets, trapped within pre-conditioned reactions to atheists as well as rigid concepts of rightness, salvation and knowledge. So long as both sides remained chained to their archaic notions, false logic and concepts they remained puppets in life, endlessly reacting to each others' memes, never acting as autonomous agents.

In some ways, this take on atheists and ultra-believers echoed one by author James Byrne in referring to *"the idea of God as the creation of the philosophical gaze"*.[13] In other words, Byrne interpreted the philosophical gaze as a reaction to an artificial, symbolic ideation, hence a precursor for human puppethood. If humans don't transcend that gaze,

---

[11]   Needleman, *WHAT is God?*, 75.

[12]   *Ibid.*

[13]   Byrne, *GOD.*, 151.

they remain trapped in an endless cycle of blind response. Needleman next introduces us to the work of Kant, in his Critique of Pure Reason., He explains how merely reading its first pages made such an impact it brought tears to his eyes. As Needleman puts it :[14]

> The general message of Kant's book is clear. Just as what seemed to be the movement of the heavenly bodies about the Earth was actually an 'appearance' created by the Earth itself, so also what seemed to be the real world that presented itself to the human mind was actually not the real world at all.

One of Kant's most remarkable comments is:[15]

> The transcendental object that grounds both outer appearances and inner intuition is neither matter nor a thinking being in itself, but rather an unknown ground of those appearances that supply us with our empirical concepts of the former as well as of the latter

In other words, Kant proposed that objective reality is never directly and uniquely apprehended. What we actually observe is a confection synthesized from secondary sense stimuli and/or or derivative measurements. It is not the system in itself. Thus, *"the indisputable knowledge we have of the world is indisputable only because we have projected our logic upon it. In knowing the world we actually create it in its most fundamental structure.[16] "*
The problem is this fundamental structure is really a secondary fabrication. This exposé of human knowledge shocked the world at the time and still does, though the

---

[14]   *Ibid.*
[15]   Kant,: *Critique of Pure Reason,* Cambridge, 431.
[16]   *Ibid.*

mental fabrication aspect didn't become evident until hundreds of years later. Then experiments using brain imagery confirmed outer reality had been reduced to a virtual display with which our minds could engage.

What does this all mean, and what does it have to do with Jacob Needleman's central question: *What Is God?*

Only this: that the *illusion of knowledge and its false reality* creates an illusion of self which is ego-dominated. This illusion perceives itself as an atomistic individual separate from others in the universe and supposes all its actions are independent. This goes back to the issue of D.T. Suzuki asking the younger Needleman: *Who is asking the question?* Needleman in turn asked him: *What is the self?*

Suzuki wanted to know if Needleman knew whether his artificial or constructed self was asking the question, or the SELF! The latter being an infused Über-Being, endowed with the essential energy and identity of a transcending Reality. It was, in effect, the difference between being the puppet and being an Awakened Active Agent of the Universe. The puppet has a 'self' (small, ego-ized) but the Awakened Active Agent is THE SELF, i.e. the Ground of Objective Being—possessing aseity! In other words, a fundamental conscious Being that existed and was not external to humans but an energy-abundant energy connection available if we accepted it and don't impede it. In this sense, it bears some resemblance to Bernard Haisch's pantheistic—activation entity where he observes that *an Infinite Intelligence turns potential into experience, actualizes the merely possible, lets things happen that otherwise would not, lets novelty arise.*

The novelty to which Haisch refers is what differentiates the puppet self from the authentic SELF. Expressing novelty means shunning all automatic responses, or automatic prescriptions for one's life. Once one adopts special prescriptions he reverts to puppethood and novelty is abandoned. This means one can't run one's life chained to any simple formula or authoritative artifact, whether the latter be a bible, a dogma, a Pope's

Philip A. Stahl

Encyclical, a statue, a prayer, an implement (e.g. rosary) or some other presumed ironclad coda.

Of course, this conception ("I AM GOD") is not new, and has been around for as long as the perennial philosophy, and popularized in such books as U.S. Andersen's *Three Magic Words*. The difference is that Needleman's explorations and conclusions are totally committed to his own self-discovery and hence more meaningful to the reader based on deep, internal reflection and experience.

What about the issue of human evil and how it can co-exist with this God-conception? Needleman notes that evil in whatever guise is the direct result of the puppet-self acting in its own self-interest, with inattention and automation. By contrast if the über-SELF acted, e.g. manifesting the ultimate consciousness (directed by *attention*) the negative words and actions would cease. People kill others because they're auto-directed puppets, not embodiments of THE SELF. If their consciousness configured the latter then they'd act in accord with it and be unable to inflict evil on others. This makes sense! Thus, what I will call *the ALL* is not responsible for human evil. It abates evil provided humans act beyond the limits of chemical assemblies. Only puppets are responsible for evil, that is beings *mechanically ruled by the impersonal forces of world which itself is lost in meaninglessness and illusion* in the terminology of Gurdjieff.

Most stirring was Needleman's defined place for Atheism, or at least the atheistic mindset in this pursuit of the groundform of Being or SELF (his emphasis). That is, in order to more ably seek and find this SELF it is essential to first *tear down all pretense, all religious self-deception, as an essential purgation of the human mind and heart.* In other words, we can regard the atheist mindset as a mental disinfectant preparing the mind to be receptive to the great SELF. As Needleman so brilliantly puts it[17]:

---

[17]   Neeldeman, *WHAT Is God?*, 223.

232

That bittersweet absence of illusion and self-deception, that empty space swept clean by astringent skepticism and purgatorial self-honesty: here perhaps is the truly sacred space in our otherwise self-deceived, chaotic world.

In that sacred space, within the individual and within a civilization, and only in such a space, can the new birth be seeded from source higher than we know, a source searching for us even more than we are searching for it. I will call it, if I may, God.

By the time I finished both Rosenberg's and Needleman's books, I realized that I'd outgrown my earlier take no prisoners stance and hence, the reductionism on which it's based. In retrospect I perceived profound sterility in the meme I'd labored under for more than thirty years.

I'd finally understood that the religious targets with which I'd been obsessed amounted to artificial projections of the human imagination. The subject also differed from the ultimate ground of Being that pervades and animates us. Again, to even refer to it as an independent object or entity was an illusion since one can no more do that than separate a wave from the ocean. We are part and parcel of it already, in current time and our consciousness shares Its own consciousness.

Philosopher Alan Watts puts it brilliantly :[18]

A universe containing self-conscious beings must have a cause sufficient to produce such beings, a cause which at least must have the property of self-consciousness. This property cannot simply evolve from protoplasm or stellar energy because this

---

[18]   Watts: *Behold the Spirit,* 180.

would mean that more consciousness is the result of less consciousness and no consciousness.

This probably provided the spark to write the present book, after I realized extreme atheism represented a dead end. If one author's exercise in literary *reductio ad absurdum* can highlight the extermination of aboutness, decimating all history, literature and philosophy in its wake, then it has gone too far. What point is there for a man to be free if he's shorn of brain, will, emotion and meaning?

A second important dynamic that prompted my book has been an increasing wariness of the "us vs. them" divisions within the ranks of atheists. Indeed, I myself had been guilty of this marking of *real* atheists vs. pseudo-atheists. This had been in *The Atheist Advocate*, a special publication of the *Mensa* Special Interest Group, A-SIG, from about 1993 until it became defunct in 1995.

I displayed a highly aggressive atheist stance while I lived in Barbados, especially after I'd made contact with a number of American Atheists visiting there ca. 1990-91. From those early contacts, and as revealed in my assorted letters in the Barbados newspapers[19], I'd been in synch with the thinking of Madalyn Murray O-Hair and American Atheists, Inc. Indeed, my book manuscript, *The Atheist's Handbook to Modern Materialism*, had recently been conveyed to Robyn Murray-O'Hair, the then Editor of American Atheist Press.

On leaving Barbados I found I needed some kind of atheist connection or network, so sought them in Mensa's Ath-SIG. I had only joined Mensa a couple years earlier and now wanted to participate at a deeper level and a special interest group seemed the obvious outlet. In many respects, I thought the Ath-SIG would be a perfect fit for me, but I grew increasingly aggressive at the degree of namby-pambyism. One of my early shots at the Mensa atheists appeared in a

---

[19]   Stahl: *Dialectical Atheism:* 5.

short note published in their Newsletter in which I insinuated real atheists had no use for Christmas. To bolster my viewpoint I cited an article by Thomas Flynn who observed that[20]:

> Ultimately any festive observance at the end of the year, whether winter solstice or Chanukah, strikes mainstream Christians as acquiescence in the holiday as they perceive it. Our careful silences are drowned out once we join in the common shout.

> We infidels have a stirring message: of an undersigned, unintended and unmanaged universe. Yet who will listen to us if we appear as hypocrites because we cannot muster the will to forego a holiday whose history and principles we would reject in any other setting.

To say that this missive stirred up a hornet's nest would be putting it mildly! I was blistered from every angle as an out of touch purist, or dogmatic. How dare I tell Mensa Ath-SIG members they can't do Christmas or darken church doors, and that they're hypocrites if they do! After enduring several issues of this abuse, as I thought of it, I let loose in one long published comment, observing that real atheism as opposed to the faux imitation, was a path for the very few not the many. Further, only the most rigorous intellects that didn't require fantasy embellishments and wish fulfillment ideations were up to it.

This final over-the-top indulgence exhausted the long suffering Editor, who had to call it quits, as the internecine division had been too much for her. Looking back now, I understand that I'd almost single-handedly fomented this discord in what Chris Stedman named as toxic atheism or a

---

[20] Flynn, *Free Inquiry,* (Fall, 1993), 26.

rigid atheistic anti-pluralism. It's as if we are poised to fight against anything remotely evocative of divinity or worship.

In an article published in Salon.com[21], Stedman recalled a conversation with a person he took to be a fellow atheist. The conversation turned to the contributions of well-known people and Stedman mentioned Mahatma Gandhi and the Rev. Martin Luther King, Jr. At the mention of putatively religious names, the fellow atheist responded with a sneer: "Oh, I get it! You're one of *those* atheists."

Stedman was dumbfounded when the guy clarified and declared Stedman to be a *"Faithiest"* instead of an atheist. This perfectly echoed my own early separation of mock atheists from real ones. As if to underscore the unsavory aspects in his opponent, Stedman went on to note:

> I fear that some atheists are doing what I used to do in my antireligious days: engaging in monologue instead of dialogue. After years of dismissing religious people outright, I realized that I was so busy talking that I wasn't listening. I was treating religion as a concept instead of talking to people who actually lived religious lives. When I started listening, something interesting happened:
>
> I saw that my approach to religion had been distorted. I'd been thinking narrowly about the texts, not about some of their positive applications

In my own case, I finally perceived that much of my atheism was antagonistic and reactionary to what I'd endured during decades of Catholic school education and my parents foisting their doctrines on me. Seeing that allowed me to grasp that my dogmatically held positions and arguments

---

[21] Stedman: *Salon.com*, Oct. 21, 2012.

weren't objectively based but designed to rationalize my reactionary stance.

Stedman, in his Salon.com piece, makes a vigorous case for what he calls *engaged religious diversity, of intersecting religious difference* but I see it more in terms of *consciousness and God-concept diversity.* As I noted in the Introduction, religion is a vehicle for an artificial mediation by which organized constructs are supposed to translate God's nature to us lowly humans. They do this by interpreting their sacred scriptures for us, or their dogmas, doctrines and decrees. But in reality, they are unnecessary and they are the source of many of our problems because the hierarchical mediators will almost always demand things be done their way.

The enlightened atheist, while he can surely tolerate religious differences, is under no obligation to regard religion itself as the ultimate in how we can relate to one another. That, instead, depends on the God-concepts which we embrace and these concepts are not dependent on having a religion. This take was one of the first highlighted by me in a Colorado Springs Freethinker article, *On Memes and Mind Viruses*, appearing in a Colorado Springs independent newspaper[22]:

The subtext of the article, short though it was, is that humans need to aspire to a consciousness that transcends "infectious values" say in propagating like a disease. This means religions can't help us given they are based on memes. Instead we need to strive or aspire to a greater consciousness that is capable of accommodating something vaster than ourselves. Indeed, the problems we're faced with are so complex and the language so fraught with difficulty, that most of us aren't aware of them. Take the simple term "oneness" as embodied in quantum nonlocality. But according to philosopher Alan Watts[23]:

[22]   Stahl: *Colorado Springs Independent*, May 9-15, 2002, 5.
[23]   Watts,: *Op. cit.*, 141.

The very concept of one-ness is a term of duality, because it is inconceivable apart from the idea of two, or of many or even of none.

This alone bids us tread carefully when we seek to extend quantum nonlocality to being an objective property of a transcendent whole. At the same time, Watts is also (again) sounding the same sort of warning that I am against placing overmuch stock in religions as the arbiters of reality. This is because by their very nature—we have thousands of religions after all—duality is implicit within them! To put it another way: If there is only *one* God, then why isn't there one religion? The answer is that religious differences inhere in each one seeing itself as being closer to the truth than its competitors. For this reason one could say "religious diversity" is a non-starter, or what we call in Barbados a losing wicket. In like manner, any emphasis on religious diversity is an invitation to compound duality, leading to more fractious god-concepts that divide us, as opposed to those which can unite us.

As for atheism, another option must be found, one that doesn't exact memetic suicide on itself.

That option in a first iteration, showed atheism to be a step toward a more comprehensive perception, by acting as a purgative for superstitious nonsense. In other words, my time spent as a hard core atheist was not wasted, but rather enabled me—as I showed with assorted examples earlier in this chapter—to rebut and reject naïve religious nonsense and childish God-concepts.

Now, let me clarify for any orthodox Christians perusing my book for evidence I've been "saved": Not so! In addition, let me make it clear I am not rejecting atheism but rather embracing a less hard line atheistic stance. One that can accept emergence in the cosmos as opposed to remaining hostage to hyper-reductionism and scientism.

In effect, though I now more embrace and accept a transcendent ground form, which is nonlocal and hence "the ALL", this doesn't mean it possesses any supernatural or personal attributes. To the extent I still reject supernatural Macguffins and god-Men I remain firmly an atheist, since I don't accept those naïve fairy stories. After all, when one becomes a man one puts away childish things! I believe the saying had been first voiced by St. Paul and presume he will excuse it being used in "the wrong hands."

The ground form I accept, like David Bohm's holomovement, is entirely physical, though yes, it hinges on vast energy (in the Dirac Ether). Being entirely physical it obeys physical laws, some of which humans may not have uncovered yet. The point is, there are no entities that form any personal aspects, including for personal salvation.

Though physical, I 'd not describe it as pantheistic for the reason that—contrary to Alan Watts' take—the elimination of the physical realm via subtraction does leave something. The elimination of the physical realm doesn't affect the implicate order, only the explicate. Hence, the domain of temporary forms (analogous to ocean waves) is removed, but not the infinite substrate, analogous to the ocean. It follows that a multi-dimensional oceanic reality is not a synonym for physical reality, but rather: *physical reality + a transcendent groundform.*

My point is that to the extent one can find affinity with the transcendent ground of Being he can encompass ultimate reality and hence, "salvation". There is absolutely no need for intermediaries, special books, or any other artificial constructs.

What if one still insisted he needed a Christ? Then my advice would be not to think in personal Savior terms but rather in Bohm's sense of an implicate order in which you (as an explicate order form) *is expressed.* Thus, as an agent of conscious action and co-creator with the universe (in Stapp's phrase) you can be thought of as embodying that ground form within yourself—and indeed, all the energy that goes with it.

If one required a Christ then it would be of the Gnostic variety. Undoubtedly, the most daring, and threatening proposition of the Gnostics, was their belief in *gnosis*, or the 'de-localization' of Christhood. Why? Because if the (Institutionalized) Church accepted it, they'd have to surrender their coveted power wielded via intermediaries (priests, bishops, cardinals, etc.). St. Paul knew this full well, which is why he had to fight against the Gnostics' egalitarian Christhood with all his might.

What does *de-localization of Christhood* mean? It means that rather than waiting for one special being to "save" humanity, each human has the power to become a Christ. All that's needed is to consciously make the connection to the ALL (or Self) in Needleman's terms, and ditch the small s-self! One then taps into that vast source of energy in the Dirac Ether.

Religious scholar Elaine Pagels observes[24]:

Whoever achieves gnosis becomes no longer a Christian, but a Christ.

In effect, in the Gnostic teachings anyone could aspire to becoming a Christ. Pauline Catholicism, meanwhile, held there could be only one on which all lesser humans had to depend for salvation. This was the nexus for power and control over the masses, by way of Church hierarchy and patriarchy. Pauline Catholics clearly detested the Gnostics because they removed any role for mediators or middle men. For this reason, as Pagels notes, the Catholic orthodoxy and tradition saw fit to consistently denounce the Gnostics "while

---

[24]   Pagels: *The Gnostic Gospels,*.134

suppressing and virtually destroying the Gnostic writings themselves[25]."

Am I advocating that everyone become Christs? Not at all. I'm merely showing that in the context of an emergent physical but transcendent ground form (based on the Stapp-Bohm nonlocal ontology) it's feasible to consider this if one agrees an individual consciousness can link to a meta-Cosmic consciousness.

How might one effect such linkage? One way would be meditation. The beauty of this model of consciousness is that it can also be invoked to show or predict what happens in *meditation*, such as transcendental meditation. Recall the aim in TM is to still or so far as possible cease all thoughts. Generally, this is roughly accomplished by singing or thinking of a recycling word . . . . *OM* . . . . repeated over and over so all thoughts are blotted out.

How so? The image of the brain (actually its microtubules) as a parallel processor, is extremely useful. However, it also acts as a *transducer*. A transducer is a device which converts an input signal of one form, say electricity, into an output signal of another form, say light or sound. Various examples include: loudspeakers, photoelectric cells, microphones, doorbells, and automobile horns. In the case of the brain's marvelous microtubules, there is a two way transduction:

1) Dirac energy to localized physical energy
2) Time signals converted to frequency signals.

Both are essential to understanding the ultimate, creative goal of converting thought into physical reality—which is basically the work of a Christ. However, (2) is somewhat more straightforward, specifically, the connection underlying the time and frequency domains. For example, differing

---

[25] *Op. cit.*, 102.

cosmic objects (e.g. stars) manifest different frequencies: f1, f2 .... f_N, or subsets of frequencies (f1 .... f_{N-1}).[26] At the level of the nonlocal cosmos these would hyper-dimensionally be one Super-Frequency F.[27] The information of this Superfrequency F is unfolded (explicated) in each of its component frequencies, so the relationship is holographic.

What do we expect? As we saw earlier, assuming a varied and total set of one's thoughts initially, it will contain waves of frequencies ranging from f' (highest) to f, then the quantum potential V_Q can be expressed: h(f'—f) If the passage of all thoughts is "stilled" then the time t for the meditator becomes zero. In other words, meditation occurs in an approximately timeless (pure frequency) domain. In the case of $\Delta t \approx o$, then f = 1/ Δt and one expects: f = 1/0 = ∞.

A frequency of infinite magnitude means that for an instantaneous quantum measurement of the phase function (S) during meditation, he would obtain S = 0. Since: U = R exp(iS/ℏ), then if S = 0, the exponential factor is 1 and the quantum potential simply U = R. That is, a fixed relational value for all individual wave trains and particles, which is just what we'd expect.

---

[26]   Each cosmic object is made up of some N or (N-1) electrons. Each electron has associated with it a deBroglie wave with a wavelength (deBroglie) defined: λ_D = h/mv where h is the Planck constant, m is the mass and v the velocity of the particle/wave. Similarly, a particular (deBroglie) frequency can be identified such that, for each λ_D: f = v/λ_D.

[27]   The Super Frequency is related to absolute Meta-cosmic time by F = η, where η = {Θ}. Mentation, as an action, can be expressed: $\Psi(\tau) = 1/\sqrt{\Theta_i} \, \Sigma_\tau \, | \, O, E>$. In terms of SuperFrequency this is: $\Psi(\tau) = 1/\sqrt{\eta} \, \Sigma_\tau \, | \, O, E>$ and finally, $\Psi(\tau) = F \Sigma_\tau \, | \, O, E>$. Special mathematical devices called Fourier transforms allow conversion between time and frequency representations.

The advantage of the above incorporation of quantum mechanics into brain function is important to scientific Materialism because it permits a demystification of the whole topic of consciousness, i.e. as some type of ghost in the machine. Without a quantum mechanical link to brain dynamics, the Materialist surrenders the explanatory advantage to the supernaturalist since the classical Cartesian mind-brain dichotomy persists. This dichotomy is what invites soul postulation and the nonsense that *soul* (or God or spirit) is needed for a brain to operate or engage in logical thought.

In conclusion, the model of consciousness provided here is not empirically proven. However, it is based on an (intuitional) extension of one interpretation of quantum theory that has at least succeeded in accurately reproducing the verifiable predictions of quantum theory. This is without introducing dualistic constructs.

The above cautionary note is conveyed because I know the atheists criticized herein may come back and accuse me of hand waving, obscurantism, or wholesale "quantum quackery". I assure them that I haven't and moreover, I'm certainly not offering a general prescription for all to adopt. I merely offer the basis for why I found extreme atheism to be self-defeating. This prompted my quest for what I refer to as "transcendent Being". Note also I deliberately eschew any reference to "a Being"! Since BE-ING is an integral, holistic whole it can't be compartmentalized, so to isolate a "Being" is redundant. We are all part and parcel of Being and can't be separated from it any more than any transcendent form that may also be identified with it. This is also why attempting to isolate a superlative part of it, say as "God" is absurd. Hence, "Beyond God" in the sense words which fragment one part from the whole end up useless, unproductive. "Beyond Atheism" because it's just as absurd to tilt at an artificially sequestered fragment!

Many will also be tempted to say this Being is synonymous to Bohm's holomovement, and that's okay. It does bear many similarities. But because I interjected aspects of Henry Stapp's ontology it isn't quite the same and what I call Being is more open-ended. It may share properties of the holomovement, and again it may not.

There is also a lot more that can be elucidated from this model, say by making the assumption we inhabit a multiverse, as opposed to singular universe. I leave most of these extreme speculations for Appendix F.

XII. TYING UP LOOSE ENDS: THE PROBLEM OF EVIL

No book of this type, certainly which conjectures a transcendent ground form, would be complete without at least attempting to address the problem of evil. In some cases atheists have argued that theodicy and the encounter of evil in the world (natural or human) is so formidable that it *excludes the existence of a deity* (and by extension a conscious, nonlocal ground form such as I proposed in the last chapter). I don't want to go that far and will explain why subsequently. For now I will only say that it's feasible to square the circle regarding God, the attributes of God and evil, so long as one *loosens the conditions for the putative divine attributes!*

The naturalist-atheist's premise can basically be summed up thusly:

If pervasive evil (natural or human) exists in the world and is allowed to continue unabated despite a claim for an infinite God, then either:

a) God is powerless to stop it, in which case God is not omnipotent or infinite, *or*

b) God chooses not to stop or limit it, in which case God is a sadist or evil himself

Some religionists in order to counter one or both points have tried to interject free will but this doesn't work for the following reason: if one person's (e.g. victim's will) is not operative, then it is only a one-sided will, so what was done to help the person of passive will or other incapacity?

For example, one of the most horrific crimes on record saw intruders break into a Connecticut family's home, tie their daughters (ages 11 and 17) to their beds, before raping them and setting them on fire[1]. The intruders also killed the girls' mother, while they left the father bound in the basement. This incident marked human evil manifest in its most malignant form.

A truly beneficent deity would not have allowed this to occur, but arguably would have acted at least to the minimal standard of a decent human parent[2]. Thus, if a human parent were to observe (e.g. using a remote monitor) a baby sitter about to assault his or her baby, he or she would intervene forthwith and not wait for the baby to make up its mind whether it wanted to be assaulted or not! In like manner, a true beneficent or just deity would intervene to prevent the rape of Michaela and Hayley Petit, perhaps by causing the perpetrators to stumble and break their legs, or whatever. Anything but inaction!

Yet in the world as it is we behold inaction even when the most vulnerable are victimized. So the central question of theodicy is: How can this be reconciled to the claim for an omnipotent and omniscient deity? We behold here the

---

[1]   Fernandez and Cowan, *The New York Times*, Aug. 7, 2007, 1.
[2]   Neilsen, *Ethics Without God*, 70.

paradox of an assumed infinite and all-powerful Being unable to do one small thing to stop an impending evil, say like the recent Newtown massacre in which twenty first graders were mowed down with a Bushmaster .223 assault rifle. The parents of the slaughtered children admirably came to terms with the horrific event, not by blaming their deity for their loss, but rather blaming the manufacturers of high capacity magazines and the assault weapons. This is justified, of course, but if one *does believe in an active and powerful deity*, It cannot be let off the hook either! Consider:

1) If God is omniscient then He knows about all events, including attacks by human predators, well in advance.

2) If His response is inaction, despite the fact a mass murderer is coming to a school, then either: *a) he declines to act, or b) can't affect it anyway!*

3) If 2(a) is true one must question any attribute of goodness, and if 2(b) is the case, then one must question any attribute of omnipotence.

If either 2(a) or 2(b) is true, then why worship this God? What is the purpose in even acknowledging a Being that either won't act, or can't? One could as well believe in nothing.

I once had occasion to bring this up in an argument with a Christian friend in Barbados, some five years ago. The example I presented to him was based on the case of an 11-year old Florida girl who had been abducted by a known sex offender, then repeatedly raped and buried alive. I asked my Christian friend how or why any truly just and merciful deity would countenance such an evil act by standing by and doing nothing.

He was intelligent enough to grasp that the free will argument wouldn't cut it since the girl was snatched at a mall, bound and gagged with rope and duct tape and effectively had no free will. However, his response remains to this day one of the most bizarre and chilling I've ever heard.

He said (and I copied this word for word):

"God, since he is all-knowing, could probably see in advance to what she would become in ten years. Perhaps he saw that she would become a prostitute and go to Hell. So, in his wisdom He intervened and allowed her to be killed while still young and before her sexuality developed. So from our limited vantage point it was a horrific crime, but for her it meant dying in innocence and seeing God!"

I immediately raked him over the coals for this vicious answer, first noting he'd provided the perfect excuse (intentional or not) for any child predator! Second, the maniac didn't just kill the girl. According to then press reports he raped her repeatedly before burying her *alive*. If my Christian friend's answer had any remote ring of plausibility then the predator would've simply killed her. No raping or burying alive! Third, it begs the question and confects a hypothetical *future* evil, i.e. assuming she'd become a prostitute, to justify God's inaction in *the present to spare the girl a real evil!* There is no proof, after all, the girl would have veered into prostitution, so the justification for God passively allowing her murder and torture in the present *is the far worse evil.* Thus, God plays the role of a diabolical, evil parent.

This interjects even more severe problems for the orthodox theist. For example, if God is indeed all-knowing, He had to know before all time what would befall this innocent. He foresaw the evil deed, but despite this foreknowledge (which few earthly parents have the benefit of) God allowed it to unfold. He allowed the girl to be abducted then taken away by this sex predator to be defiled and killed in a brutal, horrifying manner.

Let's go beyond even this, to the nature of an alleged omnipotent designer who could even fashion (or enable to be fashioned-created) such horrific people as the sex offender, or for that matter Pol Pot, Attila the Hun, Hitler or Charles Manson and Jeffrey Dahmer. Note here again that free will can't be the universal answer since it begs the question.

Now, if a proposed intelligent designer could manufacture (create) human beings with such deformed brains or pathological tendencies, and also knew in advance they would lead to evil acts, is he not also responsible? After all, we hold car makers fully accountable for making cars that don't respond to the brake pedal, and suddenly accelerate, posing a hazard on the highways. Should not God also be held accountable if we posit he has the capability of an über—Designer? One would think so! Why would an alleged, beneficent, good God allow such a thing to happen?

How can one even assign the quality of goodness to God if the entity isn't even held to the standards of a decent human parent? It's therefore a cop-out to insist humans *can't understand the ways of the Lord.* This is merely an excuse that refuses to address the core issue of human evil in theodicy problems and what it says about the alleged divinity.

The ancient Greek Materialist, Epicurus, first enunciated the core problem concerning the apparent limitations of divine power:[3] *"God either wishes to take away evil and is unable, or He is able and unwilling, or He is neither able nor willing, or He is both willing and able."*

Mathematician John Paulos draws the key logical inferences[4]:

---

3   Paulos, *Irreligion*, 125.

4   *Ibid.*

In the first three cases He is not very God-like, which prompts you to wonder about the prevalence and persistence of evil. Or to make the situation even more concrete: imagine a serial child killer with his thirtieth victim tied before him. Prayers for the child are offered by many. If God is either unable or unwilling to stop the killer than what good is He? It seems the usual response is we don't understand His ways, but if this is so why introduce Him in the first place?

Indeed. If God refuses to act in the case of innocents, such as Hayley and Michaela Petit, or is incapable of effective action, then for all practical purposes He does not exist. It is therefore a useless exercise to introduce a deity at all. One could as well toughen his mind, admit there's nothing out there, and we're all on our own in a totally purposeless, amoral cosmos devoid of remorse or empathy. In fact, one major Torino scale-10 asteroid could obliterate our entire species and nobody would be the wiser.

As seemingly sealed as this case of human evil, I'm not going to prematurely foreclose its importance for Christian theodicy. The reason is that there is potentially a *God Theory* which can explain it, put forward by Bernard Haisch in his book by the same name. Haisch's premise is that we behold divine inaction because the divinity itself isn't fully knowledgeable, aware, or complete. This is because it's constrained to act via limited, finite conscious beings[5]. Along the same lines, the cosmos and world are still in a process of evolution, and that de facto incomplete process allows for what we call evil and human (as well as divine) misjudgments and mistakes. It was the philosopher N.M Wildiers who first observed[6]:

---

[5]   Haisch,: *The God Theory: Universes, Zero-Point Fields and What's Behind it All*, 43.

[6]   Wildiers : *An Introduction to Teilhard de Chardin*, 143.

Whatever is yet to be completed is of necessity imperfect, defective, unfinished. Evil is thus structurally part and parcel of a world in evolution. An evolving world and a perfect world—these are mutually contradictory ideas.

In other words, evil is inevitable in an imperfect world governed by evolution. If we know and have data to support we inhabit an evolving world, universe then it is irrational to expect it not to display evil. We must therefore not expect divine intervention because God himself is working things out amidst a sea of polarities in the relative domain of physical reality. Haisch argues this is the only way it can be, since the infinite can't simply manifest in the physical cosmos *as the infinite*. The only choice is to become *finite* then manifest at the dunned down level this dictates. This is *not the same* as the Socinian heresy, as I will later explain. In this frame let's now examine the problem of natural evil.

A few natural evil cases: seven years ago we beheld news of a massive earthquake that struck Kumming, China killing hundreds. Then, in January, 2009, a magnitude 7.0 earthquake struck Haiti killing over 200,000. Earlier, in December, 2004, a tsunami struck Indonesia and over 220,000 were killed. What gives?

For the atheist-reductionist or naturalist: nothing. These are simply normal events for a planet with a dynamic core and tectonic plates. There is no evil in any of the earthquakes since humans inhabit a disruptive planet. There are usually about seven earthquakes per year over magnitude 7.0 *all over the Earth*. We don't hear about most of them because they occur in inaccessible, far off regions like Siberia or Mongolia or in the sea. We do hear about them when they manifest in populated land centers, but this doesn't imply their frequency is increasing.

So how does natural evil enter? It enters only for the theist, and specifically one type whose world view hinges on a benevolent Creator or designer. Because at root, if humans inhabit a world subject to monster storms, hurricanes, tidal waves and earthquakes, it is the fault of the Creator *for designing such a world* in the first place when He knew he'd put humans at risk.

Religionists go round in circles trying to avoid this unsavory conclusion, but there it is! If you're going to posit that a Designer made it all, then logic demands that if we inhabit a world with large faults (no pun intended) it's the Designer's responsibility when natural tragedies occur! After all, He designed it! If an entity is deemed truly omnipotent then why not design a planet without defects that had to be known well in advance? If, as some religionists argue, He did it to teach us some moral lesson, then what exactly is it?[7] And does it require mass death to convey?

The evils (natural and human) in the world, lead us to conclude that either the world and cosmos by extension—is not the product of a designer at all or: the world and cosmos is the product of a putative, supra-physical agent that is likely incomplete and whose actions are constrained by being manifest in an incomplete, evolving universe. Since the perfection of such a universe, the *best of all possible worlds* (e.g. of the Many Worlds quantum theory) if you will, requires the greatest input of consciousness, we can't be surprised if the imperfect version—replete with limited consciousness—bears many defects. After all, a cosmos where limited consciousness is the rule is more likely to be one with many mistakes, deficiencies, or evils!

In this case, we'd side with Leibniz, who opined that natural disasters—say like the Haitian earthquake in January, 2010—aren't the result of any divine punishment for sin but simply the consequence of a regulated and overall

---

[7] Most religionists assert the lesson is that we help and care for each other. The problem is that many people won't step in, and so the victim is left to his or her own fate.

consistent system of natural laws. More importantly, Leibniz contended in an exchange of views with another philosopher, Malebranche, that: *"God permits evil for the sake of a higher value"*[8]. Hence, for God to intervene to halt suffering—say by child cancer victims, or those affected in the horrific Boston Marathon bombing, or killed in the Newtown massacre—would "require Him to violate superlative principles He put in place to govern the world[9]." In other words, humans shouldn't complain because this is the "best of all possible worlds". It has exactly the right amount admixture of evil, relative to good!

One professor from Notre Dame, writing about Leibniz and his philosophy, noted[10]:

> One unsettling consequence of Leibniz's view is that God's plans and purposes aren't as human-centered as we might have believed. It is oddly wonderful to think the whole cosmos, even natural disasters, revolves around us, but that belief may already be hard enough to sustain given what we already know about the history and size of the universe.

Indeed, and I might add it's the epitome of human arrogance and conceit to believe such given a cosmos sixty-six billion light years in diameter and teeming with trillions of galaxies each containing over a one hundred billion stars each on average. Only a totally ignorant or self-worshipping species could entertain such an incredibly egomaniacal fantasy!

So to believe any natural disaster or cosmic event is purely for human purposes and interpretations is to commit a ghastly

---

[8] Nadler: *The Best of All Possible Worlds: A Story of Philosopher, God and Evil,* 133.

[9] *Ibid.*

[10] Newland, *The Wall Street Journal*, April 7, 2010, A15.

mental crime that boggles the imagination. It rivals that of the egomaniac ant in one ancient Barbadian myth. According to that myth, an ant decided one today to pick up a small piece of straw in its mandibles and drive all humans from its land! Before it could move two inches it was squashed by a human foot—not intentionally—but merely because the ant's tracks were in the wrong place at the wrong time!

The whole history of the advance of modern science, especially astronomy, also provides a cautionary tale to anthropocentrism in showing how humanity has been repeatedly driven out of its preferred roosting perches: from Copernicus' revelation of the heliocentric theory of the solar system (showing the Sun, not the Earth was the center of the solar system), to the discovery that the solar system is not at the center of the Milky Way galaxy but two thirds to the edge, to the discovery that the Milky Way itself is not the center of the cosmos, but that all galaxies (in clusters) are moving away from each other in the expansion with no single geometric center.

Finally, in 1997-98, the discovery that the matter of which we are composed doesn't even comprise the predominant building blocks for the cosmos. It's only about 7 percent of the total. The other 93 percent is dark energy and dark matter![11]

We'd do well to bear all this in mind, next time we fancy a major earthquake or natural disaster is God's punishment. Or that multiple earthquakes or other natural disasters herald some "end times" event!

---

[11]   This is based on a wealth of data from multiple publications, referencing the Boomerang and MAXIMA UV measurements to do with type Ia supernovae. See e.g. Perlmutter, *Physics Today*, April, 2003, 53.

Haisch's God Theory And Problems:

Bernard Haisch is an astrophysicist and was formerly the Editor of the prestigious *Astrophysical Journal* for ten years. He was also Editor-in-chief of *The Journal for Scientific Exploration.* In other words, he's no intellectual flyweight, nor is he a long lost hippie from Woodstock still toking on his stash.

Haisch, in the course of his scientific work became increasingly fed up and impatient with the reductionism of his colleagues. Reductionism, as I noted earlier in the book, is the entire basis of empirical science as currently practiced, by which we analytically reduce a system or phenomenon to its components, then look closely at how those components function. Haisch grew up a Roman Catholic and even spent a year in minor seminary (I applied to the St. John Vianney Minor Seminary but was refused entry for being too introverted).

However, like me, he soon found that Catholicism didn't have all the answers and the deity it posited was too severely diminished and anthropomorphized. As he notes[12]: *Much of today's religious dogma concerning God and the nature and destiny of mankind is flawed and irrational. It fails to resolve basic paradoxes, like why bad things happen to good people.*

Now, as I have repeatedly noted, no serious God theory is worthy of even passing interest unless it can address the basic ontological questions, primarily by positing the necessary and sufficient conditions for proposed divinity to exist. I don't care how many bible quotes a person has memorized, or how often he reads his King James or whatever. If he's unable to nail down the ontology he could as well be a madman babbling on a street corner. In other words, he can't be taken seriously nor can the book from which he attempts to mine his reality.

---

[12] Haisch: *op. cit.* 1.

Philip A. Stahl

What do I mean by nailing down the ontology? Consider:

If *nothing* be the simplest state, in which an *already perfect*, infinite deity exists (e.g. as spirit) then why create an imperfect material addition? Why make such addition, especially if it would be fraught with violence, despair, sin, putative eternal torment and all the rest? Add to that a physical addition-creation that an omniscient God would have to know (if it was judgmental) that it would have to condemn billions *before he even created them*. This itself makes the act of creation an act of violence against those created who would not be able (for whatever reason, including where born) to live up to its standards.

Leibniz, as we saw, argued that horrific natural and human evils had to be part and parcel of the world as it existed "for the sake of a higher value"[13]. To be otherwise, or demand God halt such evils, would be to countermand the deity's design of a "superlative" system. However, Leibniz also erred by stating that *damnation* had to be part of this superlative, divinely-regulated system as well[14], which is nonsense.

If this were so, we'd have to question on an a *fortiori* basis any deity that created the cosmos with a putative good will. Benevolence couldn't be at its core, since it would know (via omniscience) its creative act consigned billions to eternal perdition.

As Leibniz also put it[15]:

The great principle of sufficient reason holds that nothing takes place without sufficient reason... a reason (or condition) to determine why it is thus and not otherwise

---

[13] Nadler, *ibid.*
[14] *Ibid.*
[15] Leibniz: *The Principles of Nature and Grace, Based on Reason.*

Thus, the principle having been laid down the first question one must ask is: Why is there something rather than nothing? Given that *nothing* is simpler, easier and less problematic than something, this ought to be a no-brainer. In pure nothingness there'd have been no need for pain, sacrifice, crucifixions, saviors, death, sin, horrors—and damnation. So why create something that in effect destroys an *already perfect* Being?

Unlike most religionists who dodge such questions, Haisch does address this one. His answer[16]: *Under the God Theory, an Infinite Intelligence turns potential into experience, actualizes the merely possible, lets things happen that otherwise would not, lets novelty arise.*

But why did God have to vacate nothingness to turn potential into experience? That had been the central fixation of Leibniz in arguing for the best of all possible worlds.

Haisch's solution is brilliant, though the concept isn't original but grounded in the Perennial philosophy known for eons. In a nutshell here's how it's explicated:

As nothing (*No-thing*) God was infinite but unknowing. He existed in all places but lacked any knowledge of himself or his potentialities because nothingness is devoid of experience. (In the same way a giant, uniform ball of wax has no features.) Consider the analogy of a highly sentient being placed into a sensory deprivation tank for a month, fed only with IVs. In such a vacuum one soon ceases to be aware of oneself.

In the same way, God had to vacate nothingness to jump start his road to potentiality and self-knowing. Haisch borrows the words from *Conversations with God*[17]:

All That Is could not know Itself because All That Is was All There Was—and there was NOTHING else.

---

[16] *Op. cit.*, p. 43.

[17] *Op. cit.*, 113. Note that all the emphases, capitals are as shown in Hasich's own book.

And so, ALL THAT IS was NOT. How did the primal escape from nothingness occur? It was rendered by a pure act of consciousness . . . the divine willing itself to be in a manifest rather than unmanifest form.

The mythical Genesis command *Let there be light* (creation) became God's command to himself to manifest as individualities in an evolving universe in order to make himself known to himself. As an infinite entity this was impossible, since all one has is one vast uniform Glop, changeless and featureless. In an evolving manifest universe, however, gazillions of forms including conscious sub-manifestations appear which embody quantums of the divine.

As Haisch notes[18]: "*In the God theory, consciousness is the primal stuff of reality. Consciousness is able to shape and direct matter. Consciousness, in fact, has created this universe.*"

And so[19]: "*The initiating consciousness (GOD) creates your whole world for its own evolution, its growth and perhaps its own amusement. This is the essence of the God Theory.*"

What it boils down to is that we're each incarnations of God, just like Jesus, Mohammed, or Buddha, though not to the same degree. In this way as manifest ideations we *essentially become his eyes, ears, hands etc. to know himself.*

Thus, we are the necessary agents at lower levels of consciousness that enable the infinite to manifest and experience itself in finite time. Why don't we know everything or why can't we do anything? Haisch argues it's because we are limited channels of flesh and consciousness. If the full force of infinity were allowed to "pour" into us

---

[18]   *Op. cit.*, p. 67.
[19]   *Ibid.*

unabated, we'd self destruct. Only a tiny quantum can be mediated and that only occurs very slowly at one time. Those of us more in tune and channeling that infinite see deeper—to deeper levels of reality (for example, to the stage that we are channels or media of divine consciousness).

It's up to each of us then to find his or her own way to God, or to that ultimate Conscious state with which we associate transcendence. As Haisch notes, we all channel or mediate the same infinite consciousness so there is no selectivity by It as to whom to choose and whom to ignore. We are all divine elements (just like roaches, ants, crickets, Komodo dragons, and Meer cats) so that to ignore one or more because it isn't following a specific creed, or book of revelation, or magic salvation formula, is tantamount to ignoring its own nature. As Haisch puts it[20]:

> We each experience the 'Godness' of our own being, since according to the God Theory, we are each individuated manifestations of divine consciousness

The divine potentiality plays out and manifests in each of us, according to this. It could not do so if it remained a vacuum of nothingness. (Also, as Haisch points out, whether one believes this or not is immaterial. Just as a person may not believe the pictures appearing on his TV are transformed from far off waves, but rather the person believes the picture is really "inside the tube" somewhere.)

In the course of his God Theory, Haisch implicitly nails down the necessary and sufficient conditions for the God of which he writes.

The necessary condition is that: *Consciousness, while originally infinite, cannot experience itself as infinite. It must be mediated in discrete elements.*

---

[20] *Op. cit.*, p. 33.

A good analogy from physics is the ultraviolet catastrophe which emerged just before German physicist Max Planck proposed the quantum. The "catastrophe" in a nutshell, showed that if an electron were allowed to continually circle an atomic nucleus, it would eventually reach an infinite acceleration and light would be emitted as an infinite quantity.

Planck's solution quantized the energy emitted by an atom, e.g. in bits of size: $E = hf$ where h is the Planck constant, and f the frequency of the radiation. In much the same way we humans elicit conscious energy in bits that are quantized and limited, not infinite. In a comparable fashion, an infinite divinity quantized consciousness in individual finite elements or units.

The sufficient condition is then: *The human brain is not itself the source of consciousness, but more like a receiver of it. Consciousness as a divine attribute exists independently of the human brain.*

If I one hundred percent bought into Haisch's theory, I'd have to jettison my Materialist Model for Mind proposed earlier. In that model I showed how consciousness arises exclusively from the brain. This is by an action involving deBroglie waves transduced into electromagnetic waves at particular frequencies. According to Haisch, this is all wrong and reductionist. The brain as three pounds of matter cannot incept consciousness, but it can mediate it like a radio or TV antenna mediates the waves coming from the broadcast station.

Summarizing the consequences for our daily lives, based on his God Theory, Haisch notes:

1. The God of the theory cannot require anything of us for Its own happiness.
2. The God of the theory cannot dislike, and certainly cannot hate, anything that we do or are.

3. The God of the theory will never punish us, because it would ultimately amount to self-punishment.
4. There is no literal heaven or hell.

Having read Haisch's book, I am prepared to critique it from an atheist's point of view. This will be divided into several parts, as pertains to the key or critical aspects of Haisch's thesis:

1. *The material brain is not the source of consciousness.*

This makes a good subjective argument based on Haisch's internal perceptions (and extending them generically to others), viz.[21]: *I know with absolute certainty, with an inner conviction that no amount of external logic can refute, that I am alive and conscious . . . . The fact that I am alive and conscious is a deep, direct experience that transcends all other rational acquired knowledge*

Of course, this may be so for Haisch, but not for strict Materialist rationalists! Yes, we can acknowledge the same perceptions as he does, but we'd not go so far as to parlay those into a God theory.

Haisch also offers a good analogical argument, e.g. comparing purely physical sourced-brain consciousness to a car on the highway lacking a driver. So the car will never get to its destination. All the gasoline, gauges, brakes etc. are purely peripheral to the task and not primary. Likewise the human brain is only peripheral to the activity of consciousness, not primary.

However, this comes perilously close to presuming the phantasm of a soul[22]. Thus, in this light, Haisch is surely

---

[21] *Op. cit.*, p. 57.

[22] Compare to the classic argument that a non-physical soul is needed to be the "captain" of the brain, or at least the active agent for its origin of thought

correct when he complains (p. 52) that "most scientists do not regard this topic (of a primary consciousness) as appropriate to discussion". He's also correct that they "cannot imagine any other model".

But here's the deal: Haisch as a practicing scientist ought to know that once models are offered they must be put on a testable basis, including offering tests to falsify them. He has offered a model of mind in which consciousness is a *sine qua non* non-physical agent, independent of the brain itself, despite the fact that when brains cease to exist (so far as we can discern) so does consciousness. After all, when EEG machines are attached to a dying brain they soon detect, at some point, no activity, hence brain death. The lack of activity is interpreted as a lack of recognizable consciousness.

If a mode of consciousness exists independently of detection by our machines then how do we establish that it exists? Where is it? *How* do we know it's really there? Hasich makes a few passing references to NDEs *or near death experiences* but like others who do so, doesn't flesh out his case[23]. The fact is: 1) NDEs are not *actual* death experiences, and 2) the manifestations that emerge can be explained by brain stressors and release of chemicals (e.g. dopamine, opioids etc.) that actually trigger hallucinations. The white light commonly reported, or even demons (in some cases) are likely just brain-incepted hallucinations and nothing else. In any case, it's the claimants' job to prove otherwise, not skeptics' job to prove they aren't! (Since proving a negative is logically impossible)

What Haisch needs to do is to make his conjecture *a bona fide theory* by detailing tests for its falsifiability. This might be something along the lines of what the late quantum physicist David Bohm did, in a series of papers on *real de Broglie waves*. That is, he postulated that if consciousness was nonlocal, there must exist real deBroglie waves that

---

[23] Haisch, *op.cit.*, 21.

can be associated with the ψ (*psi*) wave function of the Schrodinger equation.

The experiment he proposed was actually designed by Rapisarda and Gozzini and became known as the Gozzini experiment.[24] It was originally to be conducted near Pisa, Italy ca. 1995. Alas, up to now it hasn't been carried out. If it had, and real de Broglie waves had been detected, then this would be at least an indirect basis for Bohm's claim.

2. *Filtering the Infinite*:

A central contention of Haisch is that the infinite power and consciousness of the infinite Intelligence has to be *filtered through human brains*. Via this mechanism, the God Theory posits that the Infinite makes itself manifest in the world through evolution. It funnels its consciousness into its finite creatures, whose finite brains can bear only discrete fragments of the original consciousness, but no more. Our brains, in other words, are simply not structured to contain or process all of infinite consciousness, especially if we wish to live on this planet with finite dimensions and challenges. Because only limited consciousness of the divine is available to us, we're prone to making mistakes, or even committing crimes, since we don't or can't see the whole picture. This is part of the problem of inhabiting a world in evolution which at any given moment is incomplete and hence imperfect.

It would have been nice if Haisch had provided a process or basis for this to be understood. Instead he offers up anecdotal evidence citing autistic people and *idiot savants*[25], e.g. people that can multiply two ten digit numbers together in their heads and get the exact answer. These can, alas, be explained by other means and don't necessarily require the brain filtering hypothesis of Haisch. It is merely that he

---

[24] Tarozzi: *Lettere al Nuovo Cimento*, (42), 8, 1.

[25] Haisch, *op. cit*. 55-56.

personally believes this transduction of infinite into finite conscious elements sounds plausible.

What about using modern, nonlocal quantum mechanics to forge a more convincing basis? Haisch ought to be able to do this by invoking the Bohm quantum potential. Then again, from other aspects of his God Theory, it appears Haisch is convinced that a *supernatural* domain may well be the basis for his Infinite Intelligence, unlike Bohm's holomovement, which is wholly physical.

3. *Problems of Theodicy*:

I was most interested to see how Haisch dealt with the problem of human and natural evil. Unfortunately, what I read shows he's probably still working this out for himself. He seems, indeed, to be oscillating between two degrees of moral axis as manifest in the world:1) An axis based on *karma and reincarnation*, and 2) the Science of Mind position that one can control or at least exercise partial control over negative happenings via the use of mind[26].

Two key passages embody the author's theodicy issues and merit closer examination. This first introduces the aftermath of what happens if suicide bombers take lives from their insane action, and is relevant to (1) above. Haisch asks[27]: *Where will they find justice? Whether driven by pure malice or by the misguided view they were accomplishing some good, consequences will follow which may well be hellish.*

He then invokes the law of karma as the mediator of justice, since it is *built into the fabric of creation as surely as the conservation of momentum is built into the laws of physics.*

---

[26] Basically, if one obsesses over some evil act happening his thought + belief = creation, will bring it about. So, the moral is, don't think about such! Think positive!

[27] *Op. cit.*, p. 21

Haisch references this karma as: *re-education, rehabilitation, and inescapable balance.* One wonders how this would satisfy the victims' families, but since karma might imply rebirth to endure profound suffering, then who knows? Maybe justice is served! But the question remains: How do we know those suicide bombers will have come back as poor, Indian Untouchables who all eventually die horrible deaths from cholera? If we have no assurance that this is their end, how can the families of victims know that justice transpired? It is a difficult question but Haisch skirts it.

So, in this sense, the God Theory follows closely the teaching of reincarnation of eastern religions, though not necessarily exactly. For example, in Haisch's version, people would only come back as people, not as cows as Hinduism allows. His version has more in common with the metempsychosis doctrine of Origen, the early Church Father, before the Catholic Church declared such teachings anathema and formulated the tragic Heaven-Hell doctrine.

The reincarnation principle of karma and cosmic balance is okay so far as it goes, but some aspects don't sit well with serious skeptics or scientific Materialists. The reason is that the karmic basis often allows arguments and conclusions every bit as outrageous as the one spouted by my Christian friend in Barbados who argued that God allowed the 11-year old Florida girl to be killed to *preserve her innocence* and *get her into heaven before she could prostitute herself.* Thus, God's inaction enabled a measurably good outcome by allowing the girl to be abducted, raped and killed before she could mature and become a prostitute. In this way, which appears crude and brutal to us because we see it only from *a limited time dimension,* she surely made the heavenly short list! (Or so my friend argues!)

Similarly, when asked how to account for the Holocaust, I've been told by serious karmic espousers: *The Jews that died in those gas chambers and ovens were simply receiving karma for what they had done to many others in previous lives. They were just all collected in one place in this life and punished one time.*

Now, maybe in this so-called karmic cosmos that's really how it went down. But it comes over as brutish, totally insensitive and downright horrific! Something deep inside me yearns for a better, more empathetic explanation than that cold-blooded one based on a karmic calculus. In that line of thinking, I imagine that the 11—year old girl that was abducted, repeatedly raped and buried alive may also have undergone her just desserts, or karma. *But for what?*

This is what the karmic theodicy leaves unanswered. Because unless we humans living at the time of these abominations *know* the original infractions—say that the girl had been a serial killer in a previous life—we can't invoke karma as a moral justification or answer in this life. If we did, we'd allow the perpetrator to claim he'd simply fulfilled his karmic duties, keeping the universe in balance. Then there is the matter of the karmic causal chain. Where does it end? Or does it? Saying we can't know is no answer, and leaves us unimpressed. The Socinian deity is probably better, in these terms, implying an evolving God but one who isn't infinite or infinitely intelligent but simply reduced to no more than what the maximally enabled sentience allows. Not much!

Haisch goes on to cite evidence for *multiple existences* but mainly to do with near death experiences. I don't think this is adequate, for the reasons given earlier. How about instead finding people who make the claim, tracing them to their putative origins and then having them give detailed accounts of their past lives which can be checked against extant historical or public records?

In respect to (2) Haisch's answer is the golden rule: live by it, do right by it, and for all practical purposes, good will emerge. As he notes [28]:

---

[28] *Op. cit.*, p. 20

Under the God theory, the requirement that you treat
others with respect and compassion is for all practical
purposes, a moral absolute, since all beings participate
in the infinite consciousness that created them

But what about the suicide bombers mentioned earlier?
What about the savage beast that defiled and killed the
11-year old Florida girl? Are we to treat them with respect
and compassion after the fact? Did the Nazi S.S. deserve
compassion and respect after they saw to the extermination of
millions, or did they merit a dose of human justice based on
the Nuremberg trials?

Then we have this[29]:

But under the God theory, you never have to worry
about whether God himself is offended by your
behavior

Even after someone raped a child and buried her alive,
or bombed a market and killed hundreds? Or, flew jet planes
into trade towers believing the act earned them a visit with
seventy-two virgins?

Haisch, in my opinion, needs to do more to flesh out his
theory's theodicy aspects. Are we to expect karmic justice
in this life for the human evildoers, or is it only to come in
future lives? On what basis is there a difference? If God is
not offended by the horrific acts of his individuations or
conscious fragments can one say He is really good?

One is led to ask whether life is one big play for divine
amusement. No one *really* gets killed, or raped, or hurt. No
child really gets incurable cancer. It's all more or less like a
virtual game ultimately ending with everyone united in one
Being and Intelligence.

---

[29]   *Ibid.*

Perhaps in a future book by Haisch, we can learn further details. Right now, the jury is still out, at least for atheists and moral Materialists. Until Haisch firms up the metaphysical flab we will withhold belief in his deity like the others.

However, it's encouraging that at least his God theory takes major steps toward credibility, especially in terms of resolving the basic ontology. In this regard, I do believe mainstream Christians have much to learn by examining Haisch's hypothesis with an open mind.

Practical Reason and Human Evil:

One of the canards circulated about human evil over the years is that it's irrational. If the person only knew better, or reasoned properly, he'd arrive at the generic good. Fortunately, philosopher John Kekes disposes of this myth quite forcefully![30] As Kekes observes, abundant historical examples disclose that people often robustly justify their actions on the basis of a good perceived in their minds, but which in retrospect turns out to be evil. Therefore it's not the lack of reason or rationality that infuses their actions but instead the false beliefs that supported the reasoning!

Thus, Pope Innocent VIII summoned excellent theological reasons for issuing a Bull allowing for the wholesale pursuit and torture of witches, warlocks, familiars and others in the form of incubi or succubi. Much of this was formalized in the *Malleus Maleficarum* of Heinrich Kramer (Dean of Cologne University) and Jacob Sprenger (Dominican Inquisitor General of Germany). This book gave the prescriptions and methods for exposing those possessed, or under the influence of familiars and demons. In so doing, it provided a pretext to torture and murder just about anyone the general community found offensive or odd.

---

[30]   Kekes: *The Roots of Evil*, 156.

On account of the well-reasoned Bull, tens of thousands were subjected to vile tortures, including finally being crushed in the Iron Maiden or barbecued on large, heated griddles. Other unfortunates endured hanging upside down, after which torsos were sawed from pudendas to heads. Many more met their fates by having to sit nude on the *Judas Cradle*—a wooden pyramid with the sharp apex positioned below the scrotum or coccyx—then ever heavier weights slowly added to increase pressure. Most of these tortures are well-documented[31] with little excuse for debate by the Inquisition's sometime defenders, many of whom parrot the justifications of the torturers that they were *doing God's holy work.*

Meanwhile, an abundance of derivative evil manifested through the papal doctrine of *Ad Extirpanda.* This Bull permitted the seizure of property before a heretic was turned over to the Inquisitors[32]. If the unfortunate person broke under torture, Inquisitors interpreted it as being under the influence of Satan, so confiscated the victim's property. Thus, in the case of religion, torture, death and persecution *were institutionalized* as part and parcel of advancing its own memes, doctrines.

This is also why the skeptic rationalist must reject the suggestion that a foundational "goodness in humankind" is vested in the moral imperatives of religion, as another atheist author has claimed[33]. In fact, religion's moral imperatives are inevitably fashioned on the basis of how that religion perceives the world and the role of humans. As in the Catholic case, it means all manner of confounding moral deficiencies and violations can be countenanced provided it meets the

---

[31] Donnelly and Diehl: '*The Big Book of Pain: Torture and Punishment Through History,* 79.

[32] Lea, *The Inquisition of the Middle Ages,* 33

[33] Sheiman: *An Atheist Defends Religion—Why Humanity Is Better Off With Religion Than Without It,* 25.

religion's self-rationalizations. To fix ideas, recall again C.S. Lewis pardoning the witch burners for a "mistake of fact"[34].

As another example of evil no less widespread one can cite the rational justification for aggressive national policy, including military occupations of sovereign states, and the implementation of economic evil such as austerity policies.

A case in point for the first is George W. Bush's "war on terror", begun after 9/11. Launched after that horrific event nearly twelve years ago, it had been driven with all the best intentions to find and kill all those responsible for the deed that left nearly 3,000 dead in the World Trade Center. But in the aftermath what did we actually see? Well, an invasion of a sovereign state (Iraq) that had nothing to do with 9/11, and which left nearly 600,000 Iraqis dead according to World Health Organization statistics. Added to that, the widespread use of the most debasing torture methods (used by the CIA) to extract information including on bin Laden's hiding place. The combined American occupations, unpaid for in additional taxes, left the U.S. with nearly $4 trillion in deficits that have now come back to haunt us. These have the nation facing the specter of draconian cuts to the most vulnerable citizens under the specious rubric of "sequestration"[35].

Bush and his minions truly believed they were doing good at the time they demanded congress vote on *The Iraq War Resolution* in 2002, never mind what we later discovered[36]. Bush's aggressive foreign policies also exposed

---

[34]   Lewis: *Mere Christianity*, 14
[35]   Sequestration had been formalized in 2011 following the U.S. failure to raise its debt ceiling, and having its credit rating downgraded by Standard and Poor's. It provided for equal cuts ($600 b each) to defense and domestic programs if no agreement was secured within two years.
[36]   *We now know an Iraqi (codename 'curveball') made the whole WMD baloney up in order to trigger regime change to replace Saddam, oblivious to the human costs.*

unsavory aspects about the U.S. as a nation. For example, one willing to violate Nuremberg Article VI to actually launch a pre-emptive war by invasion as the Nazis did when they invaded Poland. The rich humor of it all is that at the time the Bushies actually compared Saddam to Hitler! Never mind that Saddam was the one being pounded by the most devastating shock and awe attack since the Blitzkrieg launched by Hitler on Poland in 1939.

But this sort of human evil had been strenuously reasoned and formally justified by Bushie Neocons like Paul Wolfowitz and Dick Cheney! In addition, the U.S. corporate media acted as a willing accomplice, fully complicit in spreading the hysteria that led to the Iraq invasion on March 15, 2003. Hence each and every one of these actors, agents share blame in manifesting human evil, including the devastating costs exacted on Iraqi civilians. Far from malignant human evil emerging without rationality or reason, it instead erupted as if from multiple cancerous cells becoming malignant. We the citizens also played along by being cowed, afraid to speak out lest we be deemed unpatriotic or even terrorist sympathizers. Many of us also allowed ourselves to be too uninformed, even ignorant of the issues, thereby allowing ourselves to be played. Susan Jacoby, for example, references "two thirds of us can't find Iraq on a map and many members of Congress don't know a Shiite from a Sunni[37]" In a nutshell, too many Americans have "become too lazy to learn what we need to know to make sound public decisions.[38]"

This is tragic, because if Americans can't or won't exercise their minds to think critically, especially concerning our national history, then we stand to be led into more reckless wars. Even now as I write the war hawks are screeching for us to interfere in Iran and Syria. Knowledgeable people, real citizens, can't allow this to happen—not again. John F.

---

[37]   Jacoby, *op. cit.*, 310.

[38]   *Ibid.*

Kennedy was correct in his American University speech on, June, 10, 1963 when he warned that reckless involvement using American weapons of war to impose a *Pax Americana* on the world, would never work.

In the case of the 9/11 attacks, a few courageous voices held forth, including Chalmers Johnson's. He saw the catastrophe coming in the form of blowback for our ill-conceived Middle East policies. A renowned Asia specialist and founder of the Japan Policy Research Institute, Johnson was the author of more than a dozen books about world politics. His 2000 book, *Blowback: The Costs and Consequences of American Empire*, argued that U.S. interventionist foreign policy and military overextension would lead to unintended and unpredictable consequences. A year later, his warning seemed eerily prescient.

In a September 13, 2001 interview with the magazine *In These Times*, Johnson pointedly noted in response to one question on whether what happened on September 11 was an example of blowback:

Of course it is. That's exactly what my book was written for: It was a warning to my fellow Americans, a year ago, that our foreign policy was going to produce something like this. It's important to stress, contrary to what people in Washington and the media are saying, that this was not an attack on the United States: This was an attack on American foreign policy. It was an example of the strategies of the weak against the overwhelmingly powerful.

Chalmers Johnson was clearly referring to American power plays and policy leading up to, September 11, 2001. That singular event had been preceded by multiple decades of interventions, brush wars and assistance to nefarious, iron-fisted rulers like Saddam Hussein, e.g. against Iran, after Ayatollah Khomeini came to power. These interventions later emerged to militate against U.S. interests, i.e. when Saddam invaded Kuwait in 1990. The U.S. then had to mount the Gulf War to beat him back. Little did they know then that they'd also soon have to face off with a ragtag group of Afghans, headed by one Osama bin Laden that they'd shipped high powered weapons to in the early 1980s to beat back the Soviets. But bin Laden was infuriated that the holiest land in Islam (Saudi Arabia) had been used as a staging arena and base for the Gulf War. What goes around comes around, and this human evil didn't just pop up out of the blue, it was years brewing and stewing, alas to most Americans' ignorance.

At another level, Kekes makes clear the distinction between *universal goods* and *diverse goods* in accounting for the presence of human evil[39]. Universal goods define those necessities for human survival: adequate food, clean water, clean air etc. If these necessities are lacking, say from the devastation wrought by war or occupation, then the victims will rise up against the invading group and try to kill them or oust them in order to secure their universal goods. In a sense then, this sort of evil is perfectly explainable, and it follows as a direct result of being deprived of the fundamental goods by which to survive.

However, the more subjective category of diverse goods must also be factored in. Diverse goods might include: having a decent paying job, the respect of others, stature in the community, recognition for work done, and basic dignity. However, none of these is essential for basic survival. I can plow away in obscurity at an undignified, low level job but that doesn't impact my survival. However, for some human temperaments it may well do so! One conjectures, therefore, that when Aurora mass murderer James Eagan Holmes failed one of his Ph.D. exams, and saw no way to recover the elite neuro-research status he'd envisaged, he adopted the fame

---

[39]   Kekes,: *op. cit.* 153-55.

achieved by savage slaughter as an acceptable alternative outcome.

Another powerful blow struck by Kekes is against what he calls *the secular optimism of the Enlightenment*[40]. This holds that human nature is basically good but can be thwarted or otherwise deformed, perhaps even by natural causes, say like disease (e.g. schizophrenia) or even a brain tumor, such as the one that evidently triggered Charles Whitman to kill fourteen at the University of Texas—Austin, on August 1, 1966.

Apart from his sound arguments, Kekes proposes a series of question that challenge any of the secular optimists to respond, and with cogent, credible answers. One of his best questions is: *What is the justification for secular optimism which sees history as the march—apart from some unfortunate detours—with human betterment as the outcome?*

Of course, the wholesale acceptance of an affirmative answer to the above enabled Francis Fukuyama's *The End of History* to be taken seriously and its memes sown far and wide. That is, until 9/11 erupted and blew Fukuyama's propositions to smithereens. But more pressing are the questions Kekes lists which the secular optimists (like Phylicia Foot—cited by Kekes) leave unanswered. Included among the most cogent[41]:

1) What is the difference between merely bad and truly evil actions?
2) Why is it some people do and other people do not, act on their evil-prompting motives?
3) What is the role in explaining evil of such external factors as circumstances favoring evil and weak limits?

---

[40] *Op. cit.*, p. 160.
[41] *Op. cit.*, p. 163.

4) If evil is a biologically determined natural defect, should evil-doers be held responsible?
5) Is the presence or absence of intention relevant to explaining evil?
6) Is evil merely what prompts an action or does it also depend on the harm inflicted on victims?

Kekes goes on to emphasize that a satisfactory answer to each of the above must provide defensible answers to each. He also emphasizes that the failure of the secular or religious optimism proposition, inherent in the notion of human perfectability and innate goodness, "does not mean *the explanation is committed to pessimism as a result of supposed human wickedness*" [42].

He is correct here, since to conclude basic human wickedness because of lack of evidence for basic human goodness, is to give in to black-white binary reasoning. Much more likely, the essence of human nature is gray or ambiguous. Kekes avers that "*humans are neither good or bad but ambivalent*—and adds that *reason favors uncertainty*".[43]

It may even be possible to show this sort of ambivalence via Hilbert space projections. Hence, we'd see good and evil as varying vector component lengths for the outcomes of all human actions. To the extent the evil vector dominates the action will be decidedly evil, and vice versa. One cannot have, in the real world, any arrangement which totally excludes the evil component from human actions, any more than one can have a one-sided coin. Even much admired people believed to be saints, like Mother Therese or Pope John Paul II, must display an evil component to their Hilbert space defined acts, but perhaps with the good vector dominating. This is also precisely what one Buddhist master meant when he declared:

---

[42]   *Op. cit.*, p. 183.
[43]   *Ibid.*

Your goodness must have an edge to it. Human displays of the good can therefore never be fully good, meaning beneficial to all who may be affected.

An even more powerful observation by Kekes, which relates to my showing human actions as composed of good and evil Hilbert space vectors is this[44]:

Good and evil propensities often conflict and motivate incompatible actions.

He adds:

Whether good prevails over evil depends on the particularities of the circumstances, the character and education of the subjects, the foreseeable consequences of the incompatible actions, the prevailing state of morality and so forth.

The issue of responsibility for the evil actions then depends on the ability to foresee their consequences. In the case of Aurora theater mass murderer James Eagan Holmes, he possessed the education and likely critical thinking skills to perceive the outcome of terrible actions. However, a plausible internal dynamic such as submerged personality disorder may have prevented him from fully appreciating them. This would have dominated after the consequences of his failing a Ph.D. exam sunk in. Then he'd see only that the diverse goods he'd accumulated over time were about to be dispelled. No more stature in academia, no jobs likely any better than flipping burgers. At this point, the submerged personality in order to cope, interjects an outward, violent and aggressive persona (the pseudo-ego) which in Holmes' case became "the Joker"—a ruthlessly violent imago dedicated

---

[44]   *Op. cit.*, p. 171.

to destruction[45]. Basically, the internal pressures creating this violent ego-imago achieved the perverse fame in life that Holmes' submerged personality could not. His violent outburst, killing twelve people in a cinema, resulted. Instead of killing himself like many other mass murderers, Holmes chose to live to at least partially enjoy his negative imago's notoriety.

What about incompatible actions? We can look no further here than President Obama. His "good vector" has led to propensities for peace in Afghanistan, expressing a willingness to draw down troops earlier than planned, but his "evil vector" has continued to support the use of drones to target assorted terrorists, often with dreadful civilian casualties. These latter deaths, whether numbering 20 or 2,000, cannot be deemed good or even acceptable *collateral damage* because of good intentions. As I pointed out, Bush Jr. and his neo-cons thought they launched a bloody occupation in Iraq with the best of intentions. But as seen in retrospect, that unwarranted and unlawful intervention claimed more Iraqi lives than if Saddam had been left alone[46]!

What about apparent, personally-inflicted evil such as computer whiz and RSS-Reddit founder Aaron Swartz taking his own life? Recall he'd been found guilty by an over-zealous Justice Department and faced thirty-five years for copying online journal files from the academic site JSTOR via an MIT server. In this case Swartz's act was perfectly

---

[45]　See, e.g. Alexander Wolf and Irwin L. Kutash, eds., *The Psychotherapy of the Submerged Personality.*

[46]　Interestingly, the Bushies are now trying again to exploit Americans' pathetically short memories using the Bush Presidential Library. A special interactive venue called "Decision Points" steers the participant toward making exactly the same forlorn decision to invade Iraq that Bush made. A Bush avatar even appears to lecture the non-conformist who opts for *Take no action!*

justified and his acts embodied much less evil than that of the prosecutors attempting the equivalent of eliminating a fly with a machine gun. (In the case, JSTOR dropped all the charges against Swartz but the main prosecutor in the Justice Dept. still intended to pursue them, comparing Swartz to "*a thief who breaks into a home using a crowbar.*" Hardly!)

Kekes in his end—of—book summary clarifies these moral conundrums and shows that what determines the evil propensity for a given action entails active and passive agents impinging on a human consciousness as well as the internal and external conditions. In Aaron Swartz' case, there were obviously terrible external and internal pressures to do what he did. But he reasoned, correctly, that having to spend thirty-five years in prison for basically copying files produced at taxpayer expense anyway wasn't worth it. There was no moral balance, or coherence.

In much the same way the Roman Catholic Church has exercised an analogous moral incoherence by condemning chronic masturbators to Hell, as they do a guy who kills 26 people with a Bushmaster .223. Such moral imbalance blows all moral values into a cocked hat so they are worthless for being inchoate. If I am unable to parse any balance or proportion within an ethical-moral system then it is essentially useless. Worse, the sex abuse scandal now known to have been deliberately concealed by the Vatican has undermined the Church's authority to pronounce on sexual mores anyway[47].

Obviously, as a humanist—Materialist I don't subscribe to the concept of basic human good or basic evil. Indeed, the fundamental moral principle operating might well be indeterminate. And since quantum principles such as indeterminacy must apply at the levels of the human brain and consciousness, it needs to be factored into human actions.

---

[47]　See, e.g. the superb documentary film: *Mea Maxima Culpa—Silence in the House of God*, from Alex Gibney.

This is also why I disagree with Dacher Keltner's take that the mere summoning of positive emotions can reinforce the basic good in all humans[48]. If then we are fundamentally risen apes with an ambivalent moral-ethical template, we will need more than a Duchenne smile to reach a coherent ethics.

Most textbook humanist-optimists like Dacher Keltner do subscribe to the myth of innate human goodness, so I'd warrant they've have a much more difficult time answering Keke's questions! But how would a humanist-Materialist respond? I provide my answers as follows, all of which I believe are defensible and credible:

1) The difference between merely bad and truly evil actions is whether there occurs a fundamental breach of human worth, that is irreparable. Thus, the gassing of 6 million Jews in the Holocaust was a truly evil action. Similarly, despite the rationalizations (the Nazis had them too for "International Jewry") Bush's invasion of Iraq and laying waste to that country was a truly evil action. It doesn't matter what 'good" intentions he had, or if he removed a madman, terrorist or whatever. The irreparable human harm that resulted can't be remotely made up. By contrast, a merely bad action is usually at the personal level, say a person cheating on his wife and causing his wife, children what is likely to be temporary harm. Similarly, any theft of another's goods, property or injuring another by slander, lies etc. constitutes a bad action.

2) Some people act on their evil doing motives while others may not because evil is not caused by one thing but rather a disjunctive plurality of causes. Hence, one person may have a much lower threshold for releasing evil on others perhaps by virtue of more serious abuse inflicted on him, or even brain damage or

brain tumor—such as Charles Whitman suffered. Just as people differ in nearly all personality or physical characteristics so also they will differ in propensity for evil. But ultimately, since we all have our breaking points, it merely is a matter of depriving any of us of enough universal or diverging goods before we act out evil.

3) Weak limits are more likely to occur in stressed or unstable societies (e.g. Pakistan, Jamaica, Salvador etc.) where external factors such as economic inequality, terror, ubiquity of violent gangs, drugs causes much more vicious retaliation, and even vigilantism. In all such societies more evil will inevitably be favored because there is no means of achieving relative stability or equilibrium.

4) If evil was *solely biologically determined* and hence *only* a natural defect, then logically evil-doers can't be held responsible. In this case, Alex Rosenberg's puppet model devoid of true free will enters, and the evil-doer is basically no more than a violence prone automaton. However, the truth, as I noted, is that evil has multiple causes, not just one. So long as this is valid, the evil-doer must be held responsible, and that includes whole nation-states.

5) The presence or absence of intention is irrelevant to explaining evil. As I noted earlier, both the Inquisition and George W. Bush's Neocons, believed they had the best intentions when they resorted to their respective evil deeds. That is not the point, as the "road to Hell is paved with good intentions". The issue is that the central perverse beliefs that drove the intentions were evil in themselves hence their alleged good intentions manifested in the evil committed.

6) Evil must also depend on the harm inflicted on victims as I observed in (1). But given this degree can vary, from the relatively reparable to the

irreparable then it follows this is how "merely bad" and truly evil actions can be distinguished. Had mass murderer James Eagan Holmes gone into the Aurora movie theater and screamed foul mouthed epithets and tossed rotten tomatoes at the audience that would have been bad but not truly evil, shooting twelve dead and wounding dozens of others with semi-automatic weapons.

All of the preceding constitute a preliminary basis for the application of practical reason which the superficial moralists or orthodox religionists lack. They also distinguish the humanist—Materialist who is prepared to take ownership for human evil rather than fob it off on an imaginary Satan or temporary breakdowns of human nature, otherwise basically deemed good.

Another View: Partial Socinian:

Perhaps a more palatable perspective on human evil (and possibly natural evil) is based on the *Real Self* proposition of Jacob Needleman that we examined in the previous chapter. To briefly recap. Needleman proposed that the abundance of human evil manifested in crimes, wars, genocides is on account of humans reduced to acting as reactionary puppets. They act this way because of identifying with an egoistic "small" self or small-s self as opposed to the much greater SELF manifest as the ultimate energy in the universe, or what I refer to as the emergent ground form. (And David Bohm calls the Implicate order or holomovement).

For the purposes of elucidation, let's change perspective here and try to see reality from the viewpoint of the presumed "ALL' or ground form. As in the previous chapter, and the one preceding it, we posit that quantum non-locality governs consciousness. The result is a transpersonal and super-conscious state that precludes localized classes, or manipulations of such. (Note: The existence of such a state is not to be confused with the claim that humans are basically good, i.e. in their current evolutionary brain state.)

In this super consciousness, all times become immediately accessible, the past as easily as the future. The reason is that in hyper-dimensional consciousness all times are linked. This consciousness is not locked into a serial manifestation of events that unfold one at a time. It sees everything at once. Ego-less, there's no small "I" to fret over in terms of gaining power, wealth or whatever. It's devoid of personal identity or self in the sense of asserting power/status, occupying territory or projecting hegemony over nature. In addition, language and logic—with their built-in fragmentation—are not comprehensible to this entity. The separation of subject from object, as well as logical categories, would be perceived as purely illusory artifacts.

Physicist Henry Margenau has compared reality perception for a small-s, finite being (such as a human) and a boundary-free Being (holistic ground form) on the basis of "time slits".[49] In particular, he notes the latter would *lack a time slit* and this absence is precisely what makes all times instantly accessible. Humans, meanwhile, are *constrained by a narrow slit in the time dimension*. This narrowness of temporal dimension creates our sense of isolation, along with our limited three-dimensional body and sense apparatus. This can be understood better by reference to the diagram below:

---

[49]   Margenau. *The Miracle of Existence,*. 121. Margenau's use of the term time slit is intended to represent the temporal analog of a spatial slit, e.g. what extent of a room is visible to you see if you observe it through a narrow slit, say a keyhole?

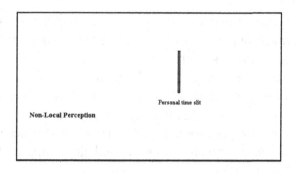

Each human goes through life as if constrained to peer through a narrow slit which gives the impression of personal isolation. This conditioning to separability is what feeds the continual power struggles, money grabs, murders and assorted evil . . . . because there is no perspective or consciousness of being affiliated with any greater vision. We see only our immediate security and will do any and everything to preserve it, as well as consolidate it. We are—to use the word of Jacob Needleman—Puppets! We react to everything but are never the authors of our reality. We simply rebound from whatever external forces impact us.

The holistic or non-local view (of the emergent ground or ground form) is much vaster and hence appears to connect all entities within its field of perception.

One is led to conclude that a transpersonal or emergent nonlocal entity with zero time constraints (consonant with an infinite, non-local nature) would be incapable of recognizing evil. The reason is that such an entity requires localized consciousness on the level of isolation or "separation" which is fundamentally incompatible with non-locality. Such a Being would be not be cognizant of finite beings' isolation unless their consciousness resonated with its own.

To make this more concrete, if such an entity (which is more or less analogous to Bohm's holomovement) existed, it would have to be literally blind to any transgressions against it, and certainly to puny human disbelief. This blindness arises not from overlooking human deficiency, but rather from its non-local nature that cannot at once be boundary—free and also localized in perceptions, including evil—which is by and large a local manifestation.

The key to escaping or avoiding human evil then amounts to expanding one's sense of identity to the level this emergent or nonlocal SELF. In other words, to escape the psychological confines of the ego-bound self. This means necessarily extending one's consciousness beyond the limits of human standards, expectations.

Let's examine the recent case of the Aurora, Colorado mass murderer, James Eagan Holmes. The evidence now available is that he left the University of Colorado, Anschutz campus after failing an oral examination. Thereby emotionally crushed, his human identity or self-worth was vanquished and he'd nothing left to live for in his mind. Overcome by grief at his loss of opportunity (after having been praised as a genius of sorts for his undergrad work and accomplishments) he redirected his misery and also hatred at the professors who flunked him, and at other outside parties, mainly at the Aurora cinema showing the latest Batman movie.

In other words, the evil that he manifested in slaying twelve innocents and wounding fifty-eight others was a direct result of being enmeshed in a limited purview that circumscribed his options. It also destroyed the life of his small self's mind. Because he perceived himself as an outcast and isolate, he perceived others the same way. There was no connection to them, no transcending consciousness bridging human elements, so why not eliminate them? They had become de-humanized in Holmes' mind and they would be dispensed with if seen as entities below him. This point of view is strongly supported in the work of David Livingstone Smith who dedicated an entire book to the process of de-humanization[50]. To the extent we remove others' humanity,

---

[50] Smith,: *Less than human: Why We Demean, Enslave and Exterminate Others*, 11.

they become expendable. This is an issue of the consciousness cultivated, not merely biology.

These are the wages when reductionism takes hold of a human's thinking and conspires to make him believe he's an island of inert molecular interactions with no connections or responsibility to others.

Of course, the reductionists will heartily disagree with this, but they really have little basis to make a stand! If they declare we're all ultimately assemblies of small molecules, compounds and components and our brains are identical with our minds, they can't be surprised that the result is pervasive isolation, manifested in personal-social fragmentation. Even worse, if they adopt Alex Rosenberg's sterile view, nothing they say or do has any meaning or significance either. It really is all hand waving in the end, including Victor Stenger's strenuous arguments against quantum brains. According to Rosenberg: Sorry! You can't have your reductionism and retain the ability to credibly criticize others too!

This is perhaps a primary reason for my pursuit of an emergent transcendent or simply holistic Being. A secondary reason is that I believe it solves (at least partially) the problem of theodicy as well. So perhaps, in a manner of speaking, the emergent ground form I've explicated is akin at some level to Socinus' God.

Basically the Socinian deity is limited by never knowing more than the most advanced consciousness existing in the universe at one time. Since the relationship is holographic, the manifestation in physical reality—for whatever acts or events there may be—hinges in the degree of connection to the individual conscious elements.

Physicist Freeman Dyson describes this entity as almost childlike[51]:

---

[51] Dyson: *Infinite in All Directions*, 119.

The main tenet of the Socinian heresy is that God is neither omniscient nor omnipotent. He learns and grows as the universe unfolds.

Dyson adds that the beauty of adopting this construct is that it *leaves room at the top for diversity.*[52] As this entity *grows to fill the universe it becomes as much a diversifier as a unifying force*[53]. The problem is *we* have to grow into its conscious shoes to make it happen!

An added benefit of the Socinian perspective is that it incorporates Carl Jung's view of evil as the polar opposite of good. If there were no evil, there would be no good which we might perceive. Perhaps then, an incomplete deity, not fully conscious of itself, enables evil to establish the human perspective of good—and more importantly, without seeing the evil in ourselves we will only see it in others. The latter is the basis for most of our collective ills, whether wars on terror, crusades, jihads, or world wars.

Is Evil Really in Decline or Only One form of it?

This is a key and very crucial question. If indeed the aggregate indices and totality of human-instigated evil have declined, it means nearly all the apocryphal tales of religious books and literature are wrong. It means in addition, that the entire meme of *Eschatological Messianism* is defunct and debunked. The latter, of course, refers to the period of glorious dominion presumed to follow the last period of world history, after Armageddon, when the "Antichrist" (the ultimate Evil-doer) is due to briefly reign, followed by a Second Coming of Christ. This is all according to evangelical-fundamentalist Christians in the U.S.

---

[52] Dyson: *op. cit.*, 120.
[53] *Ibid.*

Countering the Armageddon bafflegab is the strong evidence that violence in toto appears to have declined around the world relative to other eras. If this is valid, and not merely a statistical quirk, it means at least one element of human evil is in decline.

These propositions, or their derivatives, are implicit in Stephen Pinker's new book, *The Better Angels of Our Nature: Why Violence Has Declined.* I am here deliberately associating violence with manifest human evil as at least a proxy indicator of its extent. Pinker's arguments are essentially based on two propositions that he sets out to prove:

1) The past was far more beastly and vicious than presumed to be, and
2) The present is vastly more peaceful, contrary to appearances.

In a way these propositions are fairly sound. For example, in the immediate past rationalism was virtually non-existent or rare and when rationalists did emerge, they were rapidly eliminated. Not only their minds, but bodies too, as well as property and often offspring. Most of this was done via The Inquisition which lasted for nearly seven hundred years. Though they'd never admit it in a million years, the Vatican and Roman Catholic Church actually harbored one of the most malignant forms of human evil, in that same Inquisition.

In his excellent monograph *The Inquisition of the Middle Ages,* Henry Charles Lea, in his chapter *Subjection of the State* notes how papal bulls and direct threats were used to subvert and co-opt all state, civil authorities. This was to render them useless to oppose the will of the Inquisition. One such bull issued by Pope Innocent IV on May 15, 1252, is described as[54]: a *carefully considered and elaborate law . . . to*

---

[54] Lea,, *op. cit.* 33.

establish machinery for systematic persecution as an integral
part of the social edifice in every city and every state

Each ruler or magistrate thereby became the extension of the Church itself, and could apply bans, imprisonment, property confiscation or outright punishment to those deemed heretics and do it in the name of *the Holy Inquisition*. In this way, a civil metastasis of the physical evil embodied in the Inquisition could be spread far and wide.

Ad extirpanda ensured that the vicious violence perpetrated under the guise of protecting dogmatic or doctrinal purity was applied to a vastly larger population than it otherwise might have been. Because of its violent extent, especially in relation to seizure of property, it's estimated that by the middle—1300s half the population of then western civilization had been subjected to it, an unheard of proportion.

By comparison, the most recent mass outbreak of violence was World War II in which some 73 million are estimated to have been slain, either in direct combat, in brutal purges or exterminations such as the Nazis perpetrated in their concentration camps, including at Mauthausen, Treblinka and Auschwitz. Even so, 73 million dead would not even comprise 10% of then populated western civilization, say ca. 1944-45. Meanwhile, the proportion butchered or with property seized by the Vatican's Inquisition represented a far greater proportion than 10% of the then human population.

Thus, although modern era evil and violence appears more extensive and vile, it really isn't. It's a trick of our perception and historical selection bias. Pinker himself argues that murder rates in England peaked in 1300 and in New England in the late 17th century. Afterwards, both fell dramatically.

Pinker also accurately notes that in the modern era (from late 19th century through today) wars rather than tribal—religious wars or crimes, accounted for the lion's share of violence, and hence evil. But even given greater numbers killed in such conflicts, the curse of humanity since the ancient world has been in marked decline for the past two decades.

And while we may see genocides in these conflicts, such as in Rwanda in 1994, they pale beside the disproportionate genocides conducted by Israelite Tribalists. These were all.in the name of Yahweh, against the Canaanites, if Genesis is to be believed. Indeed, if those accounts are true, it means some 500-1000 times more humans were wiped out (as a proportion of then population), never mind the justification for it.

In this sense, Pinker's excellent graphs tell a lot of the story. For example, as expected, World Wars I and II show highly peaked points, then there's a bumpy but consistent trailing off following World War II. In terms of statistical frequency, the twentieth century naturally stands out for the sheer scale of the destruction of human life, including via atomic bomb, gas chambers and other devices.

However, when one normalizes the graphs to the actual populations present in the key eras, one finds that the past was actually far more vicious and the violent deaths—including being carved open by an Inquisitor with entrails removed and fed to the fires—more common than the 20th century or even present. Is dying by Zyklon B in a Nazi gas chamber worse than an inquisitor using his knife and pliers to extract your intestines while you're awake and cook them in front of you? I'm not sure I even want to go there. But the fact is, by proportion of the respective populations, many more humans were dispatched in the latter mode than the former.

Pinker also expatiates on the *neuro-plasticity of the human brain* and its ability to change in response to experience. He implies from this that people are less likely to resort to violence in their daily lives than their forbears, and that other behavioral changes and strategies work better. Of course, this assumes all factors are equal and they may not be. For example, verbal violence using computers (say on social network sites) now often takes the place of physical violence. However, the consequences can be just as terrible with the victims taking their own lives. Is this a retrenchment of evil? I would argue, no, only casting the evil in a different guise.

Then again, there's no assurance any current relative quiet epoch for evil will continue. As a case in point there is the catastrophic approach of Peak Oil. Indeed, one issue of *MONEY* magazine actually warned[55] that *"global oil supplies are near or past their peak*, while demand for energy product shows no signs of abating".

Even before the MONEY article appeared, warnings have been repeatedly sounded though one wonders how many have paid attention. For example, Peter Tertzakian[56] has used a somewhat different term—*the break point*—to describe an analogous phenomenon for which oil prices continue to rise as more efficient forms of oil (e.g. *light sweet crude*) continue to go down, forcing deep sea drilling, access to tar sands oil and oil shale fracking.

T. Boone Pickens, one of the most famous oilmen and the ultimate pragmatist, has asserted that[57]: *"We're now at the point where demand for oil is 87 billion barrels a day, while only 85 billion can be produced."* This is acknowledging Peak Oil by any other name. The Financial Times article further noted that the world's premier energy monitor was *"preparing a sharp downward revision of its oil supply forecasts"*[58]. The full formal report pointed to *"global oil supplies plateauing even as demand continues."*

The article also noted[59] that a growing number of people in the industry *"are endorsing a version of the 'peak oil' theory: that oil production will plateau in coming years, as suppliers fail to replace depleted fields with enough fresh ones to boost overall output."*

---

[55]   *MONEY* magazine (December, 2011) 'Making A Bet on Scarcity', 70.
[56]   Tertzakian, *A Thousand Barrels A Second*, 246-47.
[57]   Pickens,: *The Financial Times.* May 21, 2010, A1.
[58]   *Ibid.*
[59]   *Op. cit.* A12.

The drastic consequences of energy supply collapse in the face of exponentiating demand have been well described. The data show a disturbing gap by 2009 of nearly 2.1% between the total energy actually produced from around the world, and that consumed[60]. Much of this can be traced to the inability of fossil fuel production to keep up with population growth and energy demand[61]. Many experts, indeed, are convinced Peak Oil occurred in 2005.

Why the concern? Because we will face perhaps the most intensive external agent driving masses toward human evil in our history. Many may not buy this so we perhaps need to delve deeper. Richard Heinberg[62] has laid the case out in crystal clarity by using the primary quantifier of EROEI *or energy return on energy invested*. This is based on the actual chemical-energy of fuels, *none* of which even remotely approach that for oil!

Oil in the U.S. used to have an EROEI as high as 18 fifty years ago[63]. It only took one barrel of oil to extract eighteen barrels of oil. This was such a fantastic ratio that oil was practically free energy. But the latest data show this fallen to around 9 is still falling[64], a sure sign we are in energy trouble, since the minimum EROEI required for the basic functions of an industrial society is in the 5-9 range[65].

More critical is the food component of oil that's hardly mentioned except by the inner circle cognoscenti. To be blunt, oil = food given that it provides the primary bulk of fertilizer to support the green revolution or what's left of

---

[60]   *The World Almanac and Book of Facts: 2013*, 142.

[61]   See the site: *www.dieoff.org* which has a wealth of information, statistics for Peak Oil indiciators.

[62]   Heinberg: *The Party's Over: Oil, War and the Fate of Industrial Societies.*

[63]   Inman: *Scientific American*, (308), 59.

[64]   *Op. cit.*, 60. (chart)

[65]   *Op. cit.*, 61. (inset information)

it. Take away the oil fertilizers, not to mention the petrol to run famr machinery, and famine follows on a mass, global multi—billions level scale.

In his essay *Thoughts on Long-Term Energy Supplies: Scientists and the Silent Lie*, physicist Albert Bartlett pinpoints the failure to name human population growth as a major cause of our energy and resource problems[66]. Bartlett avers that scientists display a general reticence to speak out on this issue which stems from the fact that it is politically incorrect to argue for stabilization of population, at least in the U.S.

To put the numbers in more stark relief, Bartlett, in a follow-up extended letter in *Physics Today*[67], noted that *in the 1970s there were about 2.2 liters per person per day of oil*. Of this, one could estimate that just over half or nearly 1.3 liters went to food production, processing, preparation or distribution. This was in a world with nearly *2.7 billion fewer people*! Today, we are down to a production level of barely 1.6 liters per person per day while the *consumption level* approaches *4 liters per person per day*. After Peak Oil, the latter will continue to increase, while the former will diminish by about 2-3 percent per year.

It doesn't take a math genius to ascertain that this is a recipe for catastrophic crash of the human population![68]

---

[66] Bartlett: *Physics Today,*: 2004 (July), 53.

[67] Bartlett: *Physics Today*. 2004 (November),18.

[68] At the heart of these considerations is the net energy eqn. (cf. *Physics Today*, Weisz, July 2004, p. 51): $Q (net) = Q (PR) - [Q (op) + E/T]$. In effect, for break-even oil one would find $Q(net) = 0$ Thus, there is no net gain in energy given the quantity that must be used to obtain it. For the last 700 billion barrels, of hard to obtain oil (which we are fast approaching): $Q(net) =$ negative quantity $= -Q$. Since the rate of energy production ($Q (PR)$ must be debited by the energy consumed for its operation $Q(op)$, and the energy E invested during its "lifetime" T. Thus its $Q(PR)$ will be small in relation to the bracketed quantity.

Obviously, if the food supply is inadequate, we can expect violence will become commonplace as each person fights for whatever energy resources are available. The gist of it is that as the oil to support our energy-intense civilization ebbs, it will become harder to obtain water, affordable food as well as other amenities now deemed basic for living a civilized life. Power availability, say merely to stay cool in a scorching greenhouse world, will be scarce. Since power is also needed to preserve foodstuffs, and run furnaces or air conditioning the catastrophe isn't difficult to decipher.

When the old energy order finally breaks down, with power grids kaput because of excessive demand during global warming heat spells, and food in too short supply, it will literally be every man for himself. In such a brutish world, it's difficult to imagine brain neuroplasticity saving the day or spontaneously encouraging any better angels of our nature. The available useful energy will be too low to do such! More than likely, as the final food stores vanish, most of that brain neuroplasticity will be needed to mount defenses against marauding gangs, anarchists, cannibals and assorted other two-legged predators.

One must conclude then that given the cumulative harrowing facts and statistics, Pinker's concept of diminishing evil as violence, is more a pipedream than a credible continuing aspect for human affairs. The most generous take for Pinker's thesis is that he managed to capture a fraction of a cycle of human history within which violence did retreat from earlier epochs. However, he didn't factor the energy parameters far enough into the future to see that ultimately human civilization, predicated on moral order, requires ample energy for sustenance.

Thus, the problem in a nutshell is not "running out of oil' but running out of cheap, accessible oil. Bottom line, we need not run out of the stuff before the world economy runs into problems of untold, unspeakable proportions!

XIII. THE PROBLEM FOR HARD-CORE ATHEISM-REDUCTIONISM

Toward the deadline for completion of this book, I confess to having had serious reservations about going through with it. Never mind that I'd finished ninety-nine percent of it! I wondered if this was a door through which I genuinely wished to pass. All my atheist friends, including my best friend Rick Stahl, would be shocked and perhaps wonder what drug I'd taken. After all, Rick had been a mentor and investor in two earlier major atheist book projects. Meanwhile, Victor Stenger, whose work I've enormously respected, would never see me in the same way again, more likely ex post facto as a quantum bafflement architect! Most of the American Atheists, in retrospect, would breathe a sigh of relief that I'd left their organization.

But several further articles, papers with which I came into contact, convinced me this was the path to take, no matter how much heat it evoked. What I'd like to do is explore the main ones now and how they reinforced my perspective that intransigent, hard core atheism and reductionism cannot be a solution for our plant. The primary theme through the following threads: As much as atheists may fear and detest religion or spirituality they have to be big enough to allow it a place at the table and in the marketplace of ideas.

The Camus Conundrum—Where Most Atheists-Materialists Are Broken:

One way to expose the paucity of most atheistic stances is to examine the position of Alex Rosenberg, where humans are reduced to autonomous cogs lacking any sense of interpretative meaning for their actions. A much more severe test, however, is that discussed by Greg M. Epstein to do with Albert Camus' novel, *The Plague*[1]. The essence is embodied in a question Camus' character Jean Tarrou asks his friend, Rieux[2]:

Why do you show such devotion considering you don't believe in God?

Epstein puts this in a contemporary setting, referencing a 2006 book tour by Richard Dawkins for his *God Delusion*. According to Epstein[3], Dawkins was somewhat startled when a young man approached him and asked directly: *Dr. Dawkins, I am thinking of committing suicide, what do you have to say?*

Epstein relates that initially Dawkins was so nonplussed he could think of nothing to say then suggested the young man (a student at Harvard) could *go to the humanist chaplain* or—if he'd been at Oxford, he could *go to the Anglican chaplain.*

In understandable astonishment, Epstein observed[4]:

---

[1]   Epstein: *Good Without God*, 62.

[2]   Camus: *The Plague*, 126.

[3]   Epstein, *op. cit.*, 64.

[4]   *Ibid.*

Is that the best we can do? Rage, rage against the dying of the Enlightenment then shoo our troubled youth back to religion because we're too distracted or cerebral or both to spend a few minutes of our deep thoughts on being more loving and more helpful?

Indeed. But let's be clear the *Camus conundrum* highlighted in modern form by Epstein isn't just a problem for Dawkins! I am certain that in a similar situation, all the current hard core crop of atheists would be at a loss for words, but more out of diplomacy. If they were truly honest and forthright they'd likely answer along the lines of:

Well, you are just an assembly of molecules and atoms when all's said and done. Killing yourself is therefore nothing to worry over. You don't have to fear Hell since when you're dead, that's it! You are in the end a complex machine, but only a machine nonetheless, so killing yourself is no different from pulling your own plug.

What else could the reductionists say or do, if they have cast their lot with a remorseless meme that sees each human as merely an assemblage of trillions of inert component molecules? More to the point, they allocate no quantum mechanical dimension to any of those constituents, especially for the human brain!

As an emergent Materialist, on the other hand, I would have told Dawkins' questioner that emergence of a unified energy whole is more foundational than matter or apparent separation, as the professed realist-reductionists claim. I would have encouraged him to learn and become part of that emergent energy substrate or Being of which his consciousness was part. I'd then have added that this transcending consciousness conferred meaning and also abhorred extinction via its individual conscious units. In other words, killing oneself amounted to killing an expression of Being within oneself. It meant killing a unique expression of Being manifest in the cosmos, and hence extinguishing a light that might be there for others.

In Jacob Needleman's terminology, Dawkins' youthful questioner possessed *a real Self* that exists beyond the confines of his puny puppet-ego self. The response of the emergent Materialist has to point out it is the puppet self arguing for a license to self—extermination because it is blinded by locality. It is the duty of the respondent to insist the questioner lock on to his transcending Real Self, instead of being chained to the puppet self. This is critical since the latter is circumscribed by material proportions and needs taken to be real.

What would über-atheist Alex Rosenberg have to say? Well, he'd perhaps try to talk the student out of his plan using some misdirection ploy, but if he is consistent with the thesis in his book, he'd have to admit that a biological automaton (with no aboutness) has as much need to preserve his life as a hen has need for teeth. If no special brain centers or neurons exist that support meaning or any relation to reality, then why worry over offing oneself? Obviously, one can confect moral reasons in hindsight, as Rosenberg tries to do in the latter part of his book, but what is the point? One merely ends up with some judicious hand waving: *Oh look here! There really is some moral foundation that proscribes this act!* Well, actually there isn't if all philosophy, theology, ethics as well as science is reducible to meaningless drivel! I mean, does an i-pad exercise moral choices? I don't believe so!

Which Atheist You Gonna Believe?

Perhaps most reasonable people can agree that the Camus conundrum essentially precludes atheism as a rational response to the most serious questions, i.e. such as the one posed to Richard Dawkins. But let's concede that enough hard core atheists don't buy it and insist that, never mind—whether the kid decides to kill himself or not, the world overall would still be a better place if no one believed in God!

Not so fast! In his brilliant article *Atheism Wars*[5], the eminent economist John Gray, author of *False Dawn—The Delusions of Global Capitalism*, argues that *"evangelical atheism has so aligned itself with illiberal economic values that it's joined forces with the Christian fundamentalists in the Republican Tea Party."*

If this is so, why on Earth would I wish to make common cause, especially as I'm a 1960s-style *Kennedy liberal* who hasn't moved one iota toward any specious "center", especially since Kennedy's murder at the plausible hands of a rightist-based conspiracy[6]? Such affiliation, despite the much ballyhooed meme of "atheist diversity" is an insult to me. Indeed as Gray notes, it *would no more occur to Richard Dawkins that an atheist would reject liberal values than that he or she would take up witchcraft*. But the unsettling fact is too many do!

Be that as it may, millions have, and they sign on under the banner of Ayn Rand, and happily call themselves libertarians. As for a fire-breathing atheist and capitalist, there likely will never be one like Rand. In one of her polemics against religion she wrote[7]:

There is no greater delusion than to imagine one can render unto reason what is reason's and unto Faith what is Faith's . . . . Either reason is an absolute to a mind, or it is not—and if it is not, there is no place

---

[5] Gray: *Playboy* (60), 49.

[6] See, e.g. Douglass: *JFK And The Unspeakable—Why He Died and Why It Matters*. Coined by Monk Thomas Merton, *"the Unspeakable"* refers to an evil whose depth goes beyond the capacity of words to describe.

[7] Rand: *The Virtue of Selfishness*, 38.

to draw the line, no principle by which to draw it, no barrier faith cannot cross, no part of one's life faith cannot invade. Faith is a malignancy that NO system can tolerate with impunity, and the man who succumbs to it will call on it in precisely those issues where he needs reason the most.

Interestingly, perhaps 99 of 100 *explicit atheists*—say belonging to American Atheists—would concur with this statement. The question is whether, they'd also agree with Rand's other statements concerning Medicare such as:[8]

Out of context goals are those which have to be public because the costs are not to be earned but expropriated. 'Medicare' is an example of such a project.

Isn't it desirable the aged should have medical care in times of illness?

Considered out of context, the answer would be 'yes' it is desirable. Who would have reason to say no? But the fog hides such facts as the enslavement and therefore the destruction of medical science, the regimentation and disintegration of all medical practice and the sacrifice of professional integrity . . .

There would be no controversy about some young hoodlum who declared: 'Isn't it desirable to have a yacht, a penthouse, and to drink champagne?' And stubbornly refuse to consider that he robbed a bank and killed two guards to achieve that desirable goal.

---

[8]   *Op. cit.*, 82

There is no moral difference between these two examples: the number of the beneficiaries does not change the nature of the action, it merely increases the number of victims. In fact, the private hoodlum has a slight edge of moral superiority: he has no power to devastate an entire nation and his victims are not legally disarmed.

Well, thanks a hoot! Far fetched? No! As the 2012 political campaign revealed, the GOP budgetary doyen Paul Ryan (an ardent acolyte of Rand's) basically sought to adopt her views in his *Ryan Budget*. This would have replaced standard Medicare with vouchers with which the elderly would seek their own medical assistance each year, as opposed to depending on a government secured co-payment. I can just imagine how I'd have fared in my prostate cancer treatments if Ryan's vouchers were all the assistance available! With a $10,000 per year voucher allocation, I'd have ended up in major debt. Five figure debt!

Beyond this, according to Nobel Prize-winning economist Joseph Stiglitz[9], *"the upper 1 percent of Americans are now taking in nearly a quarter of the nation's income every year* and control 40 percent of the nation's total wealth". Conversely, the bottom 80 percent of Americans own just 7 percent of the nation's wealth. Stiglitz notes that *"while the top 1 percent have seen their incomes rise 18 percent over the past decade, those in the middle have actually seen their incomes fall"*[10]. By any measure this economic inequality is a corrosive, long term evil, given it reduces people's choices and indeed can incept criminal acts for economic self-preservation.

[9]   Stiglitz: *The Price of Inequality: How Today's Divided Society Threatens Our Future*, Chapter 1.
[10]   *Ibid.*

Charles Reich, in his magnificent book *Opposing the System,* explains[11]:

When society itself comes to be modeled on economic and organizational principles, all of the forces that bind people together are torn apart in the struggle for survival.

Community is destroyed because we are no longer 'in this together' because everyone is a threat to everyone else.

Indeed, an atmosphere of pervasive conflict encourages every form of racial, religious and class hatred as group is pitted against group; it encourages violence and crime and strips people of kindness and compassion as these qualities become disadvantageous in an ever more warlike atmosphere.

He goes on to show that it is economics upon which much of modern morality pivots. When people therefore must fight over a few scraps to keep their family together, they often are also more likely to turn to theft, prostitution, drugs, even murder. Economic health begets moral health, in other words. It follows that if a group of self-proclaimed atheists is opposed to this position, I can't stand with them in good conscience.

My point is that such gross economic inequality is the fruit of policy positions, i.e. as actively put forward by Paul Ryan in his *Ryan Budget*. Ryan isn't an atheist but a professed Catholic who just happens to love Ayn Rand's economics, but so do multitudes of market-worshipping atheists. The libertarian atheist essentially agrees with Ryan wholeheartedly and I've actually had the misfortune to meet

---

[11]   Reich: *Opposing the System*, 103.

a few of them at local Freethinker functions. The occasions for hot debate became so intense that I basically stopped attending Freethinker meetings in Colorado Springs. The final incident at a 2003 house party transpired after the devoted atheist Randite called Medicare recipients like my dad and mom "thieves" for *stealing his tax dollars*!

That incident got me thinking whether I really had anything in common with libertarian atheists, period. To what end? To make the world a more rational place, devoid of religious belief, but kowtowing to *their economic irrationalism* instead? It had become difficult enough to deal with these libertarians in the high I.Q. societies (Mensa and Intertel) to which I belonged. Their mindset appeared to have taken over and rendered the organizations less diverse.

Since I am also foursquare opposed to laissez-faire capitalism and especially the Neoliberal variety that worships the global free market, there is really nothing I have in common with the new breed of pro-free market atheists. I probably have much more in common with my evangelical brother than I do with them. Gray himself describes the extent of what modern, economically-contaminated atheism offers today[12]:

> Contemporary unbelief is a hollowed—out version
> of monotheism—a cult of human deliverance lacking
> the beauty and flashes of wisdom of traditional faiths.
> Defined properly, it is an entirely negative position.
> An atheist is anyone who has no use for the concepts
> and doctrines of theism

This is an honest take, and is also perhaps why Gray declares himself an atheist *in the proper meaning of the term*, as I do. That is, one who simply withholds belief. I provided the

---

[12]   Gray, *op. cit.*, 53.

original definition, of what later came to be known as implicit atheism, in a Mensa Bulletin letter. That definition read[13]:

> Let's be clear about what constitutes Atheism and what doesn't. The Atheist—to put it succinctly, absolutely withholds investing intellectual/emotional resources in any supernatural claim. Indeed the word Atheism itself embodies this definition"

> What is happening here is not active disbelief, i.e. making a statement *'There is no god'*, but rather simply passively withholding belief/acceptance in a statement already made. Hence, the deity believer has made the positive claim. The ontological atheist's is the absence of belief in it. No more—no less.

Interestingly, had I used and followed my own definition, I'd never have experienced any contretemps with Mensa's atheists. I had not realized it at the time, but the resulting brouhaha resulted from my holding an ardent position of *explicit atheism*, or outright rejection of deity and theism, rather than simple *withholding of belief.*

Reading John Gray's excellent essay in *Playboy* (yes, it is good for more than the photos!) showed me that my position is genuinely more *implicit atheism*, or what George Smith described as *agnostic atheism*, than the more hard-edged variety of Ayn Rand, or Madalyn Murray-O'Hair. In Smith's words[14]:

> The agnostic atheist maintains any supernatural realm is inherently unknowable by the human mind. And further—not only is the nature of any supernatural

---

13 Stahl, *Mensa Bulletin*, March (1994), 8.
14 Smith: *The Case Against God*, 9.

being unknowable, but the existence of any supernatural being is unknowable as well

Smith also did yeoman service in finally clarifying the agnostic position, which so many millions adopt but fail to grasp[15]:

Properly considered, agnosticism is not a third alternative to theism and atheism because it is concerned with a different aspect of religious belief. Theism and atheism refer to the presence or absence of belief in a god; agnosticism refers to the impossibility of knowledge with regard to a god or supernatural being.

These more refined definitions are crucial, especially in honing people's spiritual perspectives in their own minds, which in turn help to forge a coherent ethics. After all, if one cannot truly know anything supernatural, then how can one arrive at a supernaturally—based morality? It is preposterous. One then must work very hard to fashion a natural ethics, which features test markers and attributes based in the natural world. This, of course, is the heart of my Materialist ethics!

The problem is that a libertarian atheist's ethics aren't likely to agree with mine, any more than his definition of Materialism will agree with my own. I had warned about this division of interests and ethics in my first book[16]. I referenced a *Humanist Manifesto 2000*, originally put out in 1999, but questioned whether a majority of atheists would unite behind it. I also warned[17]:

---

[15] *Ibid.*
[16] Stahl: *The Atheist's Handbook to Modern Materialism*, 225.
[17] *Ibid.*

Atheists in various groups have also differed, sometimes vociferously, over other issues. Many of these relate to whether one advocates *weak atheism*, expressing disbelief in a god or gods, or *strong atheism*, wherein the objectives are ratcheted to a higher level. In the former, one simply withholds positive belief from the theistic assertion, the point being that the burden of proof rests on the believer. In the latter, the stance is more emphatic, and there is active rejection of the theist's concept.

Beyond even this is what has been called *aggressive atheism*. This is the adoption of an outright combative, in your face stance that brooks no compromise, and basically associates every ill on Earth with excesses of theism. This form is usually based on the strong Atheism viewpoint, but more energized and often via political and other avenues. The differing stances can lead to philosophical clashes as well as differing behaviors.

I went on to advocate that Materialism needed to become the singular umbrella to unite all free-thinkers, skeptics and unbelievers, but pointed out that no two atheists even agree on the meaning of Materialism! Obviously, if Daniel Dennett's or Victor Stenger's Materialism dispenses with any input for quantum wave functions, or even the Heisenberg indeterminacy principle, and mine requires it, then there is little we can agree on. In that case, I cannot be atheistic in the mold of Dennett or Stenger.

Nor can I justify sharing the atheist label with other prominent, high profile persons such as: Sam Harris, S.E. Cupp and Penn Jillette. The reasons dovetail with those proffered by Ian Murphy in a salon.com piece entitled

Atheists Who Ruin It for Everyone Else. As to Harris, Murphy observes[18]:

> Harris represents a disturbing anti-Muslim confluence between atheists and neoconservatives in this here post-9/11 'Murka

This also bugged me when I read Harris' first book, *The End of Faith*. I wondered why he had it in for Muslims so much more than Christians. As for Jillette, I disavow him as a fellow atheist as I would Ayn Rand, especially after an article he wrote for CNN in which he blabbered[19]:

> What makes me libertarian is what makes me an atheist. I don't know. If I don't know, I don't believe . . .

In the words of Murphy[20]: *OK . . . care to add any Cato Institute canards?* The point is that if one doesn't know, he emerges by definition as an agnostic, at the very least an agnostic atheist. Recall here George Smith's definition given earlier that the agnostic atheist *maintains any supernatural realm is inherently unknowable by the human mind.*

As for S.E. Cupp, I don't regard her as any bona fide atheist at all, but rather someone who's been able to parlay a purely nominal atheism into becoming a high profile media person. She basically found her special media niche by being the ultimate conservative, religion-friendly atheist! As Ian Murphy so aptly describes her shtick[21]:

---

[18] Murphy, Salon.com, August 4, 2012.

[19] Jillette, CNN.com, Aug. 17, 2011.

[20] Murphy, *ibid.*

[21] *Ibid.*

Cupp's self-loathing-token-atheist-in-the-conservative—
media routine seems so geared toward delegitimizing
atheism, and selling books to fundie Fox types, that it
strains credulity

She's also disqualified from being an atheist I'd ever
associate with by her comment[22]: *I would never vote for an
atheist president. Ever.*

To quote Murphy once more: *In an atheist integrity
contest, she loses to Stalin by a mustache.*

Again, all the preceding affords more reasons to disavow
atheism than to embrace it. This is especially so as atheism
has become more and more militant and akin to the very
extreme and dogmatic religions it seeks to criticize[23]!

Is it possible the aggressive memes of dogmatic religions
have called forth equally aggressive memes of non-belief to
combat it? This is possible, but sadly hasn't helped atheists win
the battle for hearts and minds. It seems most ordinary people
are as leery of doctrinaire unbelief as they are doctrinaire faith.

False Materialist Philosophies of Mind:

If it is true that not all Materialist philosophies are created
the same, and there is a subset that must be false, then it is
incumbent on us to expose the latter. Clearly, Victor Stenger's
non-quantum based Materialist philosophy of mind, and my
quantum—based version cannot both be true. If then, his
version is extolled as the one true philosophy to validate a
person as atheist, then I cannot be an atheist.

In a stirring article appearing in *Philosophy Now*,
Graham Smetham cogently argues that since formal quantum
mechanics dispenses with the fiction of a truly objective
observer (hence configurations of matter are dependent

---

[22]   *Ibid.*
[23]   De Waal, *Salon.com*, March 25, 2013.

on the observer and his apparatus) then the mind cannot be reduced to the brain[24]. Nor can mental processes be reduced to simple interactions of molecules in the brain. To show this, Smetham, as I have done, references the work of Henry Stapp and David Bohm.

Contrary to a physicalist model that incorporates quantum mechanics and mind, we have the hyper-reductionists *real locality* models which Smetham dismisses as false. These embody a false Materialism because they attempt to explain something as complex as thought and consciousness using simple bio-chemical interactions. As Smetham puts it[25]:

> In the most up-to date understanding of quantum theory, it is quite clear that *all* apparently material structures and processes, including the brain, are emergent from quantum insubstantial 'dream' stuff, to use a description by Wojciech Zurek.

I have no complaint with this description. It simply means there can't be an independent, material reality from which consciousness springs or is excited. That is what I call the Reductionist myth. Instead of the reductionists' nonsense, it must be true that *acts of consciousness produce reality from quantum potentiality*[26]. In other words, in the *valid theories* of Materialism, consciousness is not an *epiphenomenon* of material hardware but rather the author of the brain's running software. In other words: *the material of the brain is ultimately immaterial*[27].

Central to discriminating opposing Materialist models of mind are *qualia*. The term refers to subjective properties

---

[24]   Smetham, *Philosophy Now*, No. 93, 28. (Nov./Dec. 2012)
[25]   *Op.cit.*, 30. The author also cites from a dozen different works that bear out his position.
[26]   *Ibid.*
[27]   *Ibid.*

perceived in the material world, including colors, shapes and sounds (music). Arguably, none of these have objective existence but are tied to our neural processing and mode of consciousness. The qualia problem is often also called *the Mary problem* since it presents a hypothetical character ("Mary") who inhabits a black and white world, but knows everything about colors in physics terms. Still, though she knows what color signifies—a particular wavelength in the electromagnetic spectrum—she has never experienced it. The qualia problem helps to distinguish between what many call *monistic physicalism* and what I refer to as *quantum physicalism*. Monistic physicalism in its most rudimentary form can be summarized by Victor Stenger's comment[28]:

> It does not matter whether you are trying to measure a particle property or a wave property. You always measure particles. Here is the point that most people fail to understand: Quantum mechanics is just a statistical theory like statistical mechanics, *fundamentally reducible to particle behavior*

And the biggest contradiction to Stenger's interpretation is[29]:

> Although Ψ is a real field it does not show up immediately in the results of a 'single measurement', but only in the statistics of many such results. *It is the de Broglie—Bohm variable X that shows up immediately each time.*

On account of the latter position, physicist Henry Stapp has correctly noted[30]:

28 Stenger, *God and the Folly of Faith*, 155
29 Bell,: *Foundations of Physics*, (12,) .989
30 Stapp, H. *op. cit.*, p. 152

Brain processes involve chemical processes which must, in principle, be treated quantum mechanically. In particular, the transmission process occurring at a synaptic junction is apparently triggered by the capture of a small number of calcium ions at an appropriate release site. In a quantum mechanical treatment, the locations of these calcium ions must be treated quantum mechanically

In Stenger's monistic physicalism, reality is structured around locality (predicated on particles), and quantum wave mechanics and its inherent potentiality never enters the field Ψ to the extent of overturning particle dominance. In this way, emergence and holism are kept at bay. Conversely, J.S. Bell's awareness of the hidden variable X enables quantum waves to supersede particles and in turn, demands the brain is treated as a quantum mechanical device.

Frank Jackson[31], in his consideration of the rejection of monistic physicalism reduces the Mary (or qualia) problem to a simple syllogism:

The existence of qualia is incompatible with the claims of (monistic) physicalism

But qualia exist

Therefore, monistic physicalism must be false.

Perhaps the most compelling and succinct disposal of monistic physicalism is depicted (by Smetham) in a sequence of diagrams progressing from: 1) macroscopic apprehension of a color (as yellow wall) in cones of retina and visual cortex, to 2) the visual stimulus reduced to the molecular scale, to (3) the sub-quantal scale which essentially

---

[31]   Jackson: *Journal of Philosophy*, (83), 291.

annihilates the last remnants of any permanent particle-ism. As Smetham puts it[32]:

> We are forced to say that . . . probabilistic vibrations within the quantum potential field are the ultimate source and these vibrations are made into determinate matter through perception of them.

In other words, consciousness has primacy, as opposed to being relegated to a secondary effect of particles. If indeed consciousness is capable of altering macroscopic observations then humans become much more than passive spectators to the cosmic drama. They become actual *participators*, re-shaping every scene with their observations. As participators, humans contribute to the evolutionary unfolding of the universe and give meaning to this unfolding. As Henry Stapp puts it[33]:

> Reinstatement of human freedom by appeal to quantum theory resurrects human responsibility . . . this approach to the mind-body problem creates a quantum mechanical conception of man and his role in nature. He is no longer a passive observer of a cataclysmic initial act of creation, but rather an active participant in the process of creation

In the Appendices which follow I will explore in much more detail how a quantum physicalist model of mind can be made plausible. Basic concepts and definitions will be used in the early steps to progressively approach more complex concepts. At each step it is hoped that the nature of the topics themselves will spur further pursuit, even in spite of the mathematics!

---

[32] Smetham, *op. cit.* 30

[33] Stapp: *Foundations of Physics*, (15), 35.

APPENDIX A

Quantum Aspects of Indeterminacy:
Unlike the Bohr model, electrons don't follow defined orbital paths but instead are referenced to regions or volumes in which they will be more or less probable. The basic allocation of electrons, say for the hydrogen atom, is then confined to "orbitals" or regions of higher probability. For example, in the case of hydrogen the first three of these regions is shown in Fig. 1.

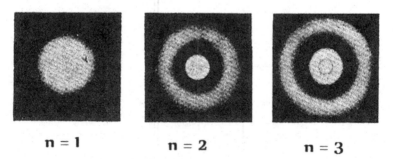

$n = 1$ $n = 2$ $n = 3$

Fig. 1: First Three Hydrogen Atom Orbitals with
Electron Distributions

The Wave-Particle Duality

We look now in somewhat more detail at wave-particle duality as it arises in quantum mechanics. In the particle interpretation, electrons fired from a device such as an electron gun would not all follow the same path since the trajectory of an electron—unlike a missile—can't be predicted from its initial state. We consider here the case of electron diffraction, whereby (based on Fig. 9) electrons are emitted from an electron gun and pass through a slit toward a detector or photographic plate onto which a diffraction pattern appears. This pattern will also coincide with an intensity distribution such as shown.

In effect, the intensity distribution basically describes the probability for an individual particle (electron) to strike each of several areas designated on the photographic film. This discloses a fundamental indeterminacy that has no counterpart in Newtonian mechanics. Now, consider an electron striking at some angle θ, such as indicated in Fig. 2.

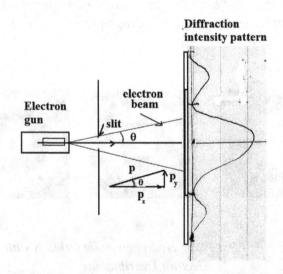

Fig. 2: Showing electron diffraction and intensity pattern.

We have, from the quantities shown:

$p_y/p_x = \tan\theta$ or $\mathbf{p}_y = \mathbf{p}_x\,\theta$ (in limit of small θ)

Therefore, the y-component of momentum can be as large as:

$\mathbf{p}_y = \mathbf{p}_x\,(\lambda/\mathbf{a})$

Where a denotes the slit width. The narrower the dimension of a the broader the diffraction pattern, and the greater Δ p. From Louis de Broglie's matter wave hypothesis (already introduced into the Bohr atom, as we saw, cf. Fig. 7): $\lambda_D = h/p_x$

Therefore:

$p_y = p_x\,(h/p_x\,a) = h/a$ or: $p_y\,a = h$

But 'a' represents indeterminacy in electron position vertically (Δ y), i.e. as it passes through the slit. We can reduce Δp_y only by narrowing the slit width a and vice versa. Thus we get:

$p_y\,a = \Delta p_y\,\Delta y \approx h$

which is one form of *the Heisenberg Indeterminacy Principle* which states that the momentum of a quantum particle and its positions cannot simultaneously be known to the same arbitrary precision. One corollary is that to detect a particle any given detector must interact with it thereby altering the motion of the particle.

A sketch below help to clarify the physical measurements, parameters.

It is important to see from the preceding, how the Heisenberg Indeterminacy Principle arises not just from an ad hoc assumption, but from the limits (or "tolerance thresholds") of explicit quantities (e.g. p, x), when considered in the quantum limit. Hence, the model of the Heisenberg "microscope" provides a useful (although not practical, since it can't actually be constructed) means of deriving the principle based on an observational ansatz.

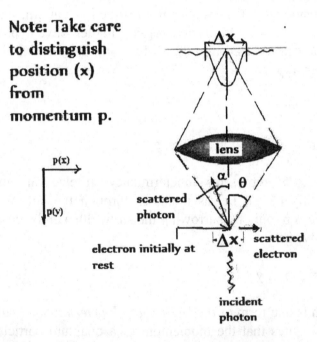

Fig. 3: Sketch of Heisenberg Microscope and key parameter: Conservation of momentum requires $p_y a = h \sin \alpha / \lambda$. *Because of diffraction by the lens opening the electron may be anywhere within the region* Δx

APPENDIX B

On The Pilot Nature of De Broglie Waves

If matter waves, or de Broglie waves, can be piloted then clearly they will have far more theoretical impact than if mere products of random encounters or observations. Hence, de Broglie as well as David Bohm and Brian Hiley later, developed a "pilot wave" theory to accompany the acceptance of B-waves physical reality.

To understand the "clocking" guidance system for these waves, we begin with the basic energy definition for the quantum given some rest frequency, f_o.

Then the energy quantum associated with this frequency is, by Planck's equation:

$$E_o = h f_o$$

Where h is the Planck constant. Then we can also write: $f_o = E_o / h$

In the relativistic limit, for photons: $f_o = m_o c^2 / h$

Now, change to angular frequency ω_0 to make the synchronous mechanism consistent with the proposed by de Broglie and Bohm, Hiley[1]. Then:

$$2\pi f_0 = m_0 c^2 / h$$

Replacing the Planck constant by $\hbar = h / 2\pi$, the Planck constant of action:

$$2\pi f_0 = m_0 c^2 / \hbar$$

Then:

$$\omega_0 = m_0 c^2 / \hbar$$

Which is the "clock frequency" in the rest frame.

There is also an additional condition (known as the "Bohr-Sommerfield" condition) for the clock to remain in phase with the pilot wave:

$$\oint p \, dx = n \, \hbar$$

Now, $p = m_0 c$, so that the integral becomes: $2\pi x (m_0 c) = n \hbar$

And the de Broglie wavelength emergence ($\lambda_D = h / p$) is evident in the equation. In this sense, we have:

$2\pi x = n (h / m_0 c) = n \lambda_D$ or the same expression ($2\pi r = n \lambda_D$) we saw in Chapter VII for the standing waves in an atom.

In Bohm's own development, in his marvelous book, Quantum Theory, the procession of B-waves is actually

---

[1]   Bohm and Hiley: *Foundations of Physics*, (12), No. 10, p. 1001.

enfolded within a "packet" of P-waves. A basic diagram of the arrangement is shown below.

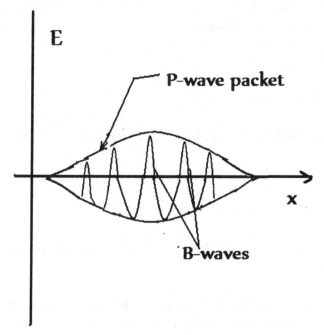

Fig. 4: B-waves enfolded by a P-wave packet.

The axis labeled E is actually the real part of the electric field component, E_z. The width of the p-wave packet is denoted by the spread:

$$\Delta k = \pi / (x - x_0)$$

Where x_0 denotes the center point of the wave packet. In other words, if the center point is at $x_0 = 0$, the packet width is just $\Delta k = \pi / x$. The wavelength, $\lambda = 2\pi / \Delta k$ then is much less than the width of the packet. E.g. if $\Delta k = \pi / x$ then $\lambda =$

Philip A. Stahl

$2\pi / (\pi / x) = 2x$. so if $x = 1$ nm, then $\lambda = 2$ nm and $\Delta k = \pi / x$ $= \pi / (1 \text{ nm}) = \pi$ nm, but π (nm) > 2 nm.

The maximum of the wave packet is approximated closely by the square of the amplitude

$[E_z]^2 =$

$4 \sin^2 \Delta k (x - x_0) / (x - x_0)^2$

We can check the limits of the preceding. Let $x_0 = 0$ then:

$[E_z]^2 = 4 \sin^2 \Delta k \, x / x^2$

And: $[E_z]^2 = 4 \sin^2 \Delta k / x$

Conversely, let $x_0 = x$, then: $[E_z]^2 = 0 = 4 \sin^2 \Delta k (x - x) / (x - x)^2$

Thus, the p-wave packet ceases to exist as a discrete or localized entity and thereby loses its particle properties. But what about mass?

Mass can be derived as a basis for the wave packet spread $\Delta x = (x - x_0)$. Thus, a "particle" is represented as a finite wave packet with wavelength-based spread $\Delta\lambda$, such that, according to the Heisenberg Indeterminacy Principle:

$\Delta x = \Delta k = \Delta (1/\lambda) \sim 1$

Now: $\lambda = \hbar / m \, v\gamma$

Where: $\gamma = (1 - v^2/c^2)^{-\frac{1}{2}}$

Recall we saw the basic clock frequency (in the zero reference frame):

$$\omega_o = m_o c^2 / \hbar$$

Which may now be generalized for relativistic speeds as:

$$\omega = m \gamma c^2 / \hbar$$

And, in terms of the Compton wavelength:

$$\xi = \hbar / mc$$

$$\omega = \gamma (c / \xi)$$

Given a spread in the velocity $\Delta v = \Delta k = \Delta (v\gamma)$ then the Heisenberg Indeterminacy Principle states:

$\Delta x \, \Delta p \approx \hbar$ where $\Delta p = \Delta (m \, v\gamma)$

Therefore: $\Delta x \, \Delta (m \, v\gamma) \approx \hbar$

Or, since the "ultimate" lower limit on Δx is of the order of the Compton wavelength, i.e. $\Delta x \approx \xi$ or $\hbar / m c$, we have:

$$m \approx \hbar / \underline{\Delta x} c$$

Where $\underline{\Delta x}$ denotes a lower limit to Δx. And it can be shown that the quantity $1/\xi$ possesses the additive and inertial properties of mass.

APPENDIX C

More on the mathematical underpinning of traditional quantum mechanics:

The brilliance of the early quantum mechanicians lay in substituting the concise operators (E_{op}, p_{op}) for the corresponding quantities of the original classical Hamiltonian, then multiplying through by the wave function ψ :

$$H_{op}\, \psi = E_{op}\, \psi$$

In this way, a drastically simplified basic quantum mechanical equation could be obtained, which could then be expanded once one substituted the operators, i.e.:

$$p_{op} = -i\, \hbar\, (\partial / \partial x)$$

$$E_{op} = i\, \hbar\, (\partial / \partial t)$$

So, the full wave equation becomes:

$$\boxed{-\hbar / 2m\, (\partial^2 / \partial x^2)\, \psi + V(x)\, \psi = i\, \hbar\, (\partial / \partial t)\, \psi}$$

A more common form of the above equation for less advanced work, say as applied in Calculus Physics courses is the 1-dimensional form of the Schrodinger equation, which is not time-dependent but time-independent.:

$$d^2\psi/dx^2 + 8\pi^2 \, m_e \, /h^2 \, \{W - V(x)\}\psi = 0$$

Where W is *the total energy* of each electron so (W – V) is *the kinetic energy*, i.e.

$$W = V + [m_e \, v^2/2] = V + KE$$

so: $KE = W - V = [m_e \, v^2/2]$, thence:

$$2 \, m_e \, (W - V) = [m_e \, v^2/2],$$

Then:

$$m_e{}^2 v^2/ \, h^2 = 2 \, m_e \, (W - V)/ \, h^2$$

Illustrating some basic properties of the 1-dimensional Schrodinger is straightforward. The best approach is to apply it to a specific case for which some parameters are known. Consider then an electron of charge e, moving in an electric field, E. The electric force F_E acting is: $F_E = e\mathbf{E}$

The potential energy V(x) is obtained from:

$$dV(x)/dx = F_E$$

whence:

$$dV(x) = F_E \, dx$$

Integrating both sides:

$$V(x) = F_E\, x = eE\, x$$

The beauty of this is that the same argument can apply to any equation of the form:

$$d^2\, \psi/dx^2 + F(x)\, \psi = 0$$

where $F(x)$ is some known function.

Another interesting facet of the Schrodinger equation refers to the **superposition** aspect. If we start, say, with two different initial conditions, to obtain two waves:

$$\psi = \psi 1(x)$$

and $\psi = \psi 2(x)$

Then *all solutions* of the given Schrodinger wave equation are of the form:

$$\psi = A\, \psi 1(x) + B\psi 2(x)$$

In the task of understanding quantum mechanics it is useful to see the working from actual examples. As I've learned in teaching the subject, students are apt to get much more out of it if several different examples of quantum systems are explored and solved.

To that end, we now consider a simple QM system set up such as shown in the simple sketch below where we have a beam of electrons of energy kinetic energy W incident on a plane where there is a potential step such that Q is less than W. (E.g. the energy of the step is at energy Q, less than W).:

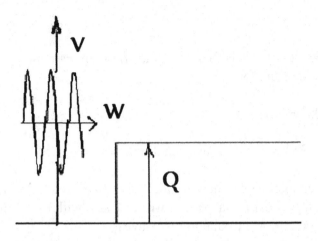

Since there is a sharp change in potential there must be also a sharp change in the electron wavelength, so the wave ought to behave like a light wave incident on a slab of glass where we expect partial transmission and partial reflection.

The amounts transmitted and reflected can be calculated as follows:

If we take the potential energy V(x) to be:

a) $V - Q, x > 0$

b) $V = 0$, (x less than 0)

We suppose the wave function for the respective cases to be:

a) $\psi = [\exp(2\pi i(Kx) + A \exp(-2\pi iKx) \exp(-2\pi ift)]$

b) $\psi = \exp\{2\pi i(K'x - 2\pi ift)\}$ where:

$K^2 = 2mW/h^2$ and $m = m_e$, is the mass of the electron.

Then $K = 1/\lambda$ where λ denotes the wavelength as before, and $K'^2 = 2m(W - Q)/h^2$.

The wave function here represents one electron per unit volume in the incident wave, therefore, $[A]^2$ particles per unit volume occur in the reflected wave and $[B]^2$ in the transmitted wave.

Thus, v particles cross unit area per unit time in the incident wave and v $\|B\|^2$ in the transmitted wave. Since: $v'/v = K'/K$ then the proportion of the beam reflected is: $\|A\|^2$ and the proportion transmitted is: $(K'/K) \|B\|^2$.

The problem then is to calculate the constants A and B. Then we need to know the boundary conditions satisfied at $x = 0$. These are basically that ψ and $d\psi/dx$ should be continuous. Integrating both sides of the Schrodinger equation:

$$d\psi/dx = -8\pi^2 \, m/h^2 \int_0^\infty (W - V) \, \psi \, dx$$

so even if V is discontinuous, its integral must be continuous. So $d\psi/dx$ is continuous, and hence ψ is continuous. Inserting these boundary conditions, since ψ is continuous at $x = 0$ it follows that:

$1 + A = B$ and since $d\psi/dx$ is continuous at $x = 0$ it follows that: $K(1 - A) = K'B$

Solving for A and B:

$A = (K - K')/(K + K')$

$B = 2K/(K + K')$

A most interesting thing to be deduced from the above is that the *sum* of the proportions of the reflected and transmitted waves comes out to unity.

Philip A. Stahl

This is so if: $\|A\|^2 + K' \|B\|^2 / K = 1$

If it wasn't so there'd be something wrong with the wave equation, as it would predict creation or disappearance of the particles at the step. Consider now the case where: $Q > W$.

Here we expect *all particles to undergo reflection*. For $x < 0$ we have the wave function:

$$\psi = [\exp(2\pi i(Kx)) + A \exp(-2\pi iKx] \exp(-2\pi ift)$$

For $x > 0$:

$$\psi = [B \exp(-2\pi c\, x) + C \exp(2\pi cx)] \exp(-2\pi ift)$$

$$c^2 = 2m(Q - W)/h^2$$

For similar reasons that applied in the previous case, to describe total reflection we take the solution that decreases with increasing x and thus set $C = 0$.

Then we obtain:

$$\psi = B \exp(-2\pi c\, x - 2\pi ift), x > 0$$

Putting in the boundary conditions as before we have:

$$1 + A = B$$

$$iK(1 - A) = -cB$$

Eliminating B, i.e. by setting: $iK(1 - A) = -c(1 + A)$

we obtain:

$$A = (iK + c)/(iK - c)$$

The important thing to note here is that:

$$\|A\|^2 = [(iK + c)/ (iK - c)]^2 = 1$$

so the reflected wave has the same amplitude as the incident one, which should be obvious to any reader familiar with the math associated with the complex numbers!

Application: Finding the Probability of a Particle in a Box

Consider one of the simplest quantum models, that for a particle confined to a 1-dimensional box, as shown.

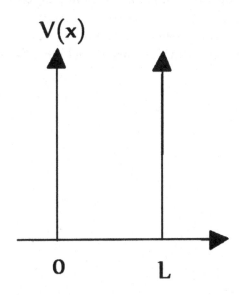

In the above case, the particle is confined to the above 'box' of length L and has a wave function: $\psi = \sqrt{2}/ \sqrt{L}$ [sin $(2\pi x/L)$]. We wish to use quantum mechanics to find the probability the particle is between $x = 0$ and $x = L/4$.

We use for this probability: $P_{ab} = \int_a^b \|\psi\|^2 dx$

Philip A. Stahl

Then: $P_{ab} = \int_{0}^{L/4} (\sqrt{2}/\sqrt{L})^2 \sin^2 (2\pi x/L)\, dx$

Let $\theta = 2\pi x/L$ and use the trig identity: $\sin^2 \theta = \frac{1}{2}(1 - \cos 2\theta)$

$P_{ab} = 2/L \int_{0}^{L/4} \frac{1}{2}[1 - \cos(4\pi x/L)]\, dx$

$P_{ab} = 2/L [\frac{1}{2} \int_{0}^{L/4} dx - \int_{0}^{L/4} \cos(4\pi x/L)]\, dx$

And: $P_{ab} = x/L - 1/2\pi \sin(4\pi x/L)]_{0}^{L/4}$

$P_{ab} = \frac{1}{4} - 0 = 0.25$

Or a 1 in 4 probability of being found in that region.

Similar computations can be made for more complex systems, i.e. such as a particle in a 3-dimensional box of dimensions x, y and z.

APPENDIX D

More Advanced Treatment of the Bohm-Stapp Basis for Nonlocality

In 1952 David Bohm resurrected aspects of the deterministic "pilot wave" theory of Louis de Broglie which were threaded into his own "Stochastic Interpretation of Quantum Mechanics"—and which is now often described as "Bohmian Quantum Mechanics". In 1952, Bohm published two papers on the topic. The first basically worked out the consequences for a one-body system using de Broglie's real matter wave basis.

Again, for clarity, the real matter wave profile is shown below:

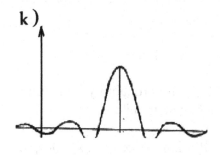

With the field intensity displayed on the vertical axis and the "particle" defined within the central limits of the pilot wavelength spread ($\Delta\lambda$) as described earlier (See Appendices A, B)

Recalling the history here, the fate of de Broglie's pilot wave hypothesis (and the quantum deterministic theory linked to it) was sealed at the Solvay Conference at which Wolfgang Pauli made strong objections on the basis that it didn't provide a consistent account in terms of a many-body system. Thus, the Copenhagen Interpretation (based on the wave function as purely statistical) won the day.

The second paper extended the treatment to the many body system which effectively neutralized many of Pauli's objections to Solvay.

The key insight, for practical purposes, is to look and see how Bohm dealt with a trajectory *in a many-body system*. He begins by writing the N body-wave function:

1) $U(x_1 \ldots x_n) = R(x_1 \ldots x_n) \exp(iS(x_1 \ldots x_n)/\hbar$

to define the momentum of the nth particle as:

2) $p_n = \nabla_n S$

where S is the 'action'

On substituting (2) into the many-bodied Schrodinger equation Bohm obtains the conservation equation in configuration space:

$dP/dt + \Sigma_n (\nabla_n) (P \nabla_n S)/m = 0$

where $P = U^*U$ is the probability density and the modified Hamilton—Jacobi equation is:

$dS/dt + \Sigma_n [\nabla_n S]^2/2m + V(x_1 \ldots x_n) Q(x_1 \ldots x_n) = 0$

From the preceding,. Bohm deduced that each particle would be acted upon not only by a classical potential but also an added quantum potential Q.

$$Q = \{ -\hbar^2 / 2m \} \sum_i [\nabla R_i]^2 / R$$

In this view, novel features of QM are seen to arise from Q

In the orthodox Copenhagen (and most conservative) interpretation of quantum theory, there can be no separation of observed (e.g. spin) states until an observation or measurement is made. Until that instant (of detection) the states are in a superposition. More importantly, the fact of superposition imposes on all quantum phenomena an inescapable 'black box'. In other words, no information other than statistical can be extracted before observation.

Meanwhile, in the Bohmian acausal deterministic setting[1]: "it *is supposed that each experimental result is determined completely by a set of hidden variables, φ. Thus, the result A of measurement of spin in the direction â depends only on φ, while the result C, of measurement of spin in direction ĉ depends only on φ and ĉ*"

This was a brilliant tour-de-force which can be summarized:

$$A = A(\hat{a}, \varphi)$$

$$C = C(\hat{c}, \varphi)$$

where measuring *entanglements* such as: $A = A(\hat{a}, \hat{c}, \varphi)$ and $C = C(\hat{a}, \hat{c}, \varphi)$ are specifically excluded.

---

[1]   Bohm, D. and Hiley, B.J.: 1981, Foundations of Physics, No. 11, No. 7/8, p. 529.

Thus, as the authors note[2]:

"In other words, while nothing is said about the general dynamical laws of the hidden variables, φ, which may be as nonlocally connected as we please, we are requiring that the response of each particular observing instrument to the set φ, depends only on it own state and not the state of any other piece of apparatus that is far away".

This is a critical distinction, because it eliminates the pure objection Einstein had to unlimited nonlocality. Thus, Bohmian quantum physics introduces a measure of locality by tying the action of hidden variables to the particular observing device.

To fix ideas and show differences, in the Aspect experiment four different analyzer orientation 'sets' were obtained. These might be denoted:

(A1, A2)I, (A1, A2)II, (A1, A2,)III, and (A1, A2)IV

Each result is expressed as a mathematical (statistical) quantity known as a 'correlation coefficient'. Aspect's final result (sum) yielded:

$$S = (A1, A2)I + (A1, A2)II + (A1, A2,)III + (A1, A2)IV = 2.70 \pm 0.05$$

What is the significance? In a landmark theoretical achievement in 1964, mathematician John S. Bell formulated a thought experiment based on a design similar to that shown. He made the basic assumption of locality (i.e. that no communication could occur between A1 and A2 at any rate faster than light speed). In what is now widely recognized as a seminal work of mathematical physics, he set out to show that a theory which upheld locality could reproduce the

---

[2]   *Ibid.*

predictions of quantum mechanics. His result predicted that the above sum, S, had to be less than or equal to 2 (S *less than or equal* 2). This is known as the *'Bell Inequality'*.

In the case of Bohm's hidden variables, deterministic model, the above sum came *to less than 2.*

The E-P-R experiment:

This was probably conceived explicitly because Einstein wanted to show quantum theory was incomplete, and hence an unlimited nonlocality could not be accepted—since otherwise anything could occur say at point (x1, y1, z1, t1) 20 million light years from Earth and affect events on Earth, say at point (x2, y2, z2, t2). If that was true, then both locality and determinism went right out the window.

The original form of the experiment invoked *the quantum state of a two particle system* in which position differential (x1 − x2) and momentum sum (p1 + p2) are both determined. Then the wave function is:

$$U(x1, x2) = f(x1 - x2 - a) = \sum_k c_k \exp[ik(x1 - x2 - a)]$$

where $\sum_k$ denotes a summation over the k elements; and f(x1 − x2 − a) is a packlet function sharply peaked at (x1 − x2) = a (for an example of such a functional form) Also c_k is a Fourier coefficient. Thus, in this particular dynamic state, p1 + p2 = 0 and x1 − x2 can be as well-refined as one pleases. (In the normally applied *Heisenberg Indeterminacy Principle*, when nothing is known on the momentum then the position x can be precisely obtained. It's just that both position x and momentum p can't be known to the same exact precision simultaneously)

In the EPR experiment when one measured x1 then one immediately knew: x2 = x1 + a. Alternatively, if p was measured, then one knew immediately that p2 = -p1 since p1 + p2 = 0. In both cases the 1st particle is "disturbed" by measurement and this accounts for the Heisenberg indeterminacy relations applied in 1-d. However, the 2nd particle *is taken not to interact with the 1st at all*—so one can obtain its properties minus the assumption of any disturbance. Still, the Heisenberg principle applies so: $\delta p2 \, \delta x2 \geq \hbar$.

where $\hbar = 6.62 \times 10^{-34}$ J-s and $\delta p2$, $\delta x2$ denote the uncertainties in the 2nd particle momentum and position. The key point here is that given the above conditions and parameters Heisenberg's explanation of the indeterminacy arising from a "disturbance" can no longer be used. It was exactly this which prompted Einstein, Podolsky and Rosen to argue that since both x2 and p2 were measurable to "arbitrary accuracy" *without any disturbance*, then they already existed independently (in particle 2) as localized elements of reality with well-defined values before any measurement took place. Hence, they erroneously concluded that QM is merely a mathematical abstraction which gives only an incomplete picture of reality—and hence QM itself is incomplete.

The key insight for Bohm was in terms of the evolution (time change) of the *probability density*:

$$dP/dt + \Sigma_n \, (\nabla_n) \, (P \, \nabla_n \, S)/m = 0$$

From the preceding, and the modified Hamilton—Jacobi equation (see earlier) Bohm deduced that each particle would be acted upon not only by a classical potential but also an added quantum potential Q.

We now examine this in the context of an experimental underpinning. Since Bohm's deterministic theory includes what he calls "*hidden variables*"—which effectively drive the determinism toward a relative locality—then these must be incorporated. The problem is to invoke an experimental basis which can allow the determinism to be checked.

The original proposal[3] by Rietdjik and Selleri was to show that if a photon is successively transmitted by 2 polarizers (using appropriate settings or orientations) then the very first transmission must influence a hidden variable which co-determines the second one. *"Malus law"* was first formulated by Etienne Louis Malus in 1809 and asserts that the intensity of light transiting an analyzer and polarizer is proportional to $\cos^2(\theta)$ where θ is the angle through which the analyzer is rotated with respect to the polarizer.

One can proceed by first considering a set-up with 2 orthogonally polarized correlated photons (designated 'γ 1' and 'γ 2' in the diagram shown) and these interact with three polarizers denoted A, B and C.

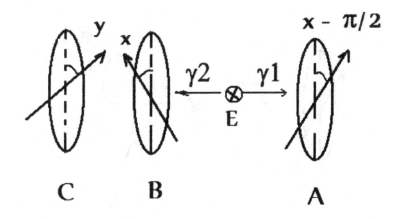

If 'E' is the causal event (e.g. photon departure from location), then by causal determinism one must find:

AE < CE < BE

---

3   Rietjik, C.W. and Selleri, F., op. cit.,

In other words, the interaction event denoted 'AE' (whereupon the designated photon for γ 1 interacts with polarizer A) *occurs before* CE and CE before BE.

By appropriate computations one is led to a theorem:

A deterministic theory with hidden variable φ reproduces Malus' law for a photon (γ2) transmitted by two polarizers C and B, with arbitrarily chosen settings of their axes, only if the hidden variable φ undergoes some change (a redistribution) when γ 2 crosses the first polarizer.

To refine the experiment, one moves the polarizer C from the set up shown above and defines p1,2(x—π /2, y) to be the probability that, in the new setup γ 1 is transmitted by A, and γ2 by B.

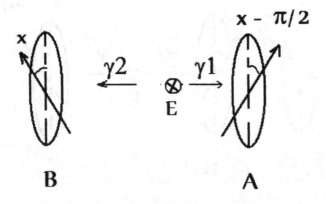

For the setup in the diagram above, the predictions of quantum mechanics allow us to write:

$$P1,2 (x - \pi/2, y) = \tfrac{1}{2}\sin^2(x - \pi/2, y) = \tfrac{1}{2}\cos^2(x - y) = p2(x, y)$$

So long as polarizers A and B of the original setup are orthogonal (e.g. perpendicular to one another) photon γ 2 is transmitted by C if γ 1 is transmitted by A. Thus, in the case of A and C orthogonality, then for each micro-condition of the system (γ1, γ2) for which γ1 is transmitted so also is γ2. This must mean the relevant sets of hidden variables $\varphi_{i,j}$ are identical, viz.:

$$\varphi_i (x - \pi /2) = \varphi_j(x)$$
and
$$\varphi^*_i(x - \pi /2) = \varphi^*_j(x)$$

Therefore, one can deduce that if the hidden variable φ, (implicit in the lower arrangement) experiences no change from the previous interaction (of γ1 and A, via transmission or absorption) then we have:

$$P1,2(x - \pi /2, y) = m (\varphi_i(x - \pi /2) \cap \varphi_j(x))$$

Where /x\ denotes set intersection

As Rietdjik and Selleri note[4] the preceding expressed "*a mutual physical independence of the transmission events at A and B, respectively, in the sense that one of the events does not change the hidden variable φ as it is relevant to the other.*" This is precisely what confers a *relative locality* since the action of φ *is constrained.*

Here is where some difficulties in reconciling results enter. For this basis we return to the initial arrangement. We focus on the polarizers B and C and arrange three separate settings as follows—keeping in mind the x-orientations refer to C and the y-orientations refer to B.

1st setting: x = a and y = b

2nd setting: x = b and y = c

---

4   Ibid.

3rd setting: x = c and y = a

A diagrammatic view is shown in the next graphic.

One can show from assuming no overlap between hidden variable sets: $\varphi_i(x)$ and $\varphi^*_i(x)$, then let p2(x, y) be the probability that the *unpolarized* photon γ2 is transmitted by both polarizer C with axis x, and polarizer B with axis y as:

$p2(x, y) = m(\varphi_i(x) \cap \varphi^*_i(x))$

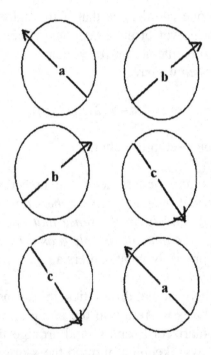

Either one of two propositions must be valid, supporting or refuting a deterministic effect:

1) Transmission across C generates a change in φ and *thereby allows transmission through B*, or

2) *No change transpires with the crossing at C, so none occurs at B* (no influence, so null hypothesis)

Let's look at each in terms of the hidden variable sets: $\varphi_i(x)$, $\varphi_j(y)$. Then in order for $\gamma2$ to transit C we need: $\varphi(-\varphi_i(x)$; and to transit B, we need $\varphi(-\varphi_j(y)$. Then to transit both:

$$\varphi(-\varphi_i(x) \cap \varphi_j(y))$$

Using this one can estimate the probability condition by way of summing all orientations, as applicable to the null hypothesis:

$$p2(a, b) + p2(b, c) + p2(c, a) \geq \tfrac{1}{2}$$

Which, of course, violates Malus' law which predicts:

$$p2(x, y) = \tfrac{1}{2}\cos^2(x - y)$$

Using partial derivatives we can move further on this.

Let $S = p2(a, b) + p2(b, c) + p2(c, a)$

And apply the Malus' law requirement, viz. based *on the orientations for axes x,* y:

$$S = \tfrac{1}{2}[\cos^2(a - b) + \cos^2(b - c) + \cos^2(c - a)]$$

Take the partial:

$$\partial S/\partial a = -\tfrac{1}{2}[\sin 2(a - b) - \sin 2(c - a)]$$

At this point, we review the concepts of max-min theory to do with partial derivatives of functions of several independent variables (say a, b, c etc.)

Consider a function of x alone such that: $F(x) = f(x, a, b, c \ldots)$

which has an extreme value (extremum) at $x = a$. Then if f has a partial derivative with respect to x at $x = a$, that partial derivative must be zero by virtue of the theory for max-min functions $F(x)$ of a single independent variable., viz.

$\partial f / \partial x = 0$ at $x = a$

Similar reasoning allows us to arrive at the necessary conditions for minima say, when one has a function of several independent variables.

The number of simultaneous equations $\partial f / \partial x = 0$ etc. thus obtained is equal to the number of independent variables. In the case of S, we have three independent variables a, b and c representing the different polarizer positions. For minimization we need:

$\partial S / \partial a = 0$, $\partial S / \partial b = 0$ and $\partial S / \partial c = 0$

We see that since: $\partial S / \partial a = -\frac{1}{2} [\sin 2(a - b) - \sin 2(c - a)]$

$\partial S / \partial a = 0$ implies: $(a - b) = (c - a)$

E.g. let $(a - b) = (c - a) = \pi / 2$

Then: $-\frac{1}{2} [\sin 2(\pi/2) - \sin 2(\pi/2)] = -\frac{1}{2} [\sin(\pi) - \sin(\pi)] = 0$

Of course, since we've three polarizer orientations, a, b and c the minima must hold for all, then also we have:

$\partial S / \partial b = 0$ implies: $(a - b) = (b - c)$

And:

$\partial S/\partial c = 0$ implies: $(b - c) = (c - a)$

Further computations disclose that we need:

$(a - b) = (b - c) = (c - a) = 120$ deg

Then:

$S_{min} = \frac{1}{2} [\cos^2(120) + \cos^2(120) + \cos^2(120)]$

Since $\cos (120) = \frac{1}{2}$

$S_{min} = \frac{1}{2} [(\frac{1}{2})^2 + (\frac{1}{2})^2 + (\frac{1}{2})^2] = \frac{1}{4}$

Or: $S_{min} = \frac{1}{2} [(\frac{1}{4}) + (\frac{1}{4}) + (\frac{1}{4})] = \frac{1}{2} [(3/4)] = 3/8$

Since 3/8 is less than ½ this violates the null hypothesis of no influence, and hence *proves that a deterministic hidden variables effect is present*.

This refutes Victor Stenger's claim that the Aspect experiment nullified David Bohm's hidden variables deterministic theory.

Connection to Henry Stapp's Heisenberg Ontology Picture:

It was physicist Henry Stapp that first noted that human free will is likely bound up to quantum mechanical brain states, and the extent to which a superposition of states can occur in association with such states:
As we know, a quantum wave function U is resolved into component states:

$U = U(1) + U(2) + U(3) + U(4) + \ldots U(n)$

which make up what we refer to as a *"superposition of states"*. Thus, the vector sum of all the component wave states

343

are integrated into the single wave state U. Stapp, for his part, has pointedly noted that indeterminacy principle limitations applied to calcium ion capture near synapses shows they (calcium ions) must be represented by a probability function[5]. More specifically, the dimension of the associated calcium ion wavepacket scales many times larger than the calcium ion itself. This nullifies the use of classical trajectories or classical mechanics to trace the path of the ions. But does it nullify determinism or more specifically acausal determinism? This is the question we must address.

In the depiction being formulated here, I assume in line with modern neuroscience, that brain dynamics and function is contingent upon the neuron and its connections to synapses. Thus we want networks with the prescriptions given i.e. quantum units that invoke *Pauli spin operators* as effective gates, junctions, along with connecting these to each other through a multitude of neural sub-networks.

The Pauli spin matrices are as follows:

$\sigma_x =$
$(0, \ldots 1)$
$(1, \ldots 0)$
$\sigma_y =$

$(0 \ldots -i)$
$(i \ldots 0)$
$\sigma_z =$
$(1 \ldots 0)$
$(0 \ldots -1).$

Recall the first diagram in Chapter X showed the two types of concept to be interwoven: biological networks (left

---

5   Stapp, H.: *Op. cit.*, p. 42.

side) and an associated quantum vector superposition in terms of wavefunctions. In that model, a neuron in sub-complex 'A' either fires or not. The 'firing' and 'not firing' can be designated as two different quantum states identified by the numbers 1 and 2. When we combine them together in a vector sum diagram, we obtain the superposition:

$$U (n (A] = U (n1 (A1] + U(n1 (A2)$$

where the wave function (left side) applies to the collective of neurons in 'A', and takes into account all the calcium wavepackets that factored into the process. What if one has 1,000 neurons, each to be described by the states 1 and 2? In principle, one can obtain the vector sum as shown in the above equation for all of the neuronal sub-complex A, and combine it with all the other vector sums for the sub-complexes B, C, D and E in an optimized path. The resulting aggregate vector sum represents the superposition of all subsidiary wave states and possibilities in a single probability density function. This allows the (theoretical) computation *of the density function*, as well as distinct probability amplitudes for the various sub-complexes.

As we've seen, application of the Heisenberg Indeterminacy Principle to Ca^{+2} ions (at body temperature) discloses the associated wave packet dimension increases to many times the size of the ion itself[6]. Any classical Newtonian mechanics is therefore inapplicable and irrelevant. Worse, use of such—say for the ions' trajectory, certainly ensures an erroneous result. Thus we represent the ion uptake superposition as a separate contributor to the aggregate assembly:

$$U (n (A, B \ldots E) = \{U(Ca^{+2}) [n_i (A), n_j(B) \ldots n_m (E)+ \ldots n_m(N)]\}$$

---

[6]   *Ibid.*

wherein all possible states are taken into account.

The total of these taken in concert enables a quantum computer modality to be adopted for a von Neumann-style consciousness. In quantum neural networks it is accepted that the real world brain generation of consciousness is more along the lines of a quantum computer-transducer than a simple collective of switches. As S. Auyang has observed[7], consciousness *"is more than a binary relation between a Cartesian subject and object"*

Because a binary relation doesn't cut it, it leaves the door open to an acausal unfolding of brain processes. So, how would quantum acausal determinism enter?

In terms of the example given in Stapp (book already referenced):

$$[A_n, L (Ca++)] = -i\,\hbar$$

and the neuronal assembly expectation value (neuron firing sequence initiated at nth A neuron) mutually interferes with the wave packet dimensions (L) of the nth Ca^{++} ions. Now, let an assembly of neurons (A_n) then be operated on by a set of hidden variables, e.g. $\varphi\{A_n\}$ such that we obtain a P-wave packet (pilot wave packet comprised of an ensemble of de Broglie waves or B-waves)

$$\varphi\{ A_n \} = \wp \exp [iS/\hbar]$$

where $\wp$ is the vector wave density and S a common phase for the P-waves. Then the assembly A_n moves with a group velocity $v = df/(d(1/\lambda)$ where f is the group frequency and λ the wavelength.

---

[7]   Auyang, S.: 1995, *How is Quantum Field Theory Possible?*, Oxford University Press, p. 112.

A_n must also satisfy:

$$[A_n - (m^2 c^2 / \hbar^2)] A_n = 0$$

where the bracketed quantity is none other than the "clock guidance" feature from the de Broglie pilot wave hypothesis, hence the deterministic underpinning of Bohmian QM.

One solution of the preceding can be shown to be:

$$A_n(b) = \wp \exp[2 \pi (i) [ft - (x/\lambda) + \varphi]$$

where f is frequency, t is time, λ is wavelength and x is position in direction of wave propagation. f is the phase angle. (For generality, one can assume $\varphi = 2 \pi$)

These vector waves would have a superluminal velocity. But to put it in terms more apropos of David Bohm's Stochastic QM concept—we instead say that the waves *interconnect with particles at a higher dimensional level.*

Assume now the total set of one's thoughts contains waves of frequencies ranging from f' (highest) to f, then the quantum potential V_Q can be expressed:

$$V_Q = h(f' - f), \text{ where h is Planck's constant.}$$

Thus, V_Q has units of energy as the other potential functions in physics, e.g. gravitational and electrostatic. On average, the greater the number of possible states, the greater the difference (f' – f) and the greater the quantum potential. In general,

$$V_Q = \{-\hbar^2 / 2m\} [\nabla R]^2 / R$$

Of course, in a real human brain, we have a "many-particle" field (especially since we're looking at neuronal complexes) so that the quantum potential must be taken over a sum such that:

$$V_Q = \{-\hbar^2/2m\} \sum_i [\nabla R_i]^2 / R$$

The velocity of an individual B-wave is expressed by:

$$v(B) = \nabla S/m$$

where m is the mass of the particle associated with the B-wave, and S is a phase function obtained by using: $U = R \exp(iS/\hbar)$

And R, S are real. Thought then occurs with the collapse of the wave function U and the onset of a new phase function S' as a result, such that the B-waves in an original P-wave packet can become dislodged and arrange as a modulated waveform.

But what of a deterministic thought? Is there a particular condition needed—let's call it a sufficient condition for acausal determinism? I believe there well might be and may enter at the following nexus:

Let the associated de Broglie wavelength of a particular Ca^{+2} ion be defined:

$$\lambda_D = \hbar/m\gamma v$$

where γ is the Lorentz factor and m the mass. The angular frequency (ω) can be written:

$$\omega = m\gamma c^2/\hbar$$

and the phase velocity:

$$v(p) = \lambda_D \omega = c^2/v$$

In practice a particle has some finite extension, dx, and in a certain limit:

$$dx *d(1/\lambda_D) \sim 1$$

must be represented as a superposition of waves. In this case also, the interference of observables emerges via:

$$[x, p] = -i \hbar$$

However, if *the hidden variable φ operates*, viz. $\varphi\{A_n\} = \wp \exp [iS/ h]$, it is conceivable that dx may achieve a spread which renders superposition of states no longer applicable, say for a tiny increment or indeterminacy in time, dt. In this case, a deterministic acausal quantum potential may act with energy:

$$dE \approx \hbar/ dt$$

It is this energy that can be available to drive a "deterministic" thought. Clearly also, if superposition of states is what elicits "free will"—then that attribute may conceivably vacate for that interval dt.

The condition on the critical spread to achieve this can be expressed:

$$dx \approx \hbar/ d(m\gamma\ v)$$

so if the velocity v approaches a critical threshold such that $v \rightarrow 0$, we can see dx spread out to elicit deterministic thought.

Hence, the nonlocal de Broglie-Bohm pilot wave thesis conforms with the Stapp Heisenberg Ontology in the limit of $dx *d(1/\lambda_D) \sim 1$.

More Complex Thought:

Complex thought requires *coherence of quantum states* such that:

$$\{s_1, s_2, s_3, s_4 \dots \dots \dots \dots \dots s_n\} \rightarrow \wp$$

Where the bracketed states refer to Goldstone bosons. With coherence, these assemble into a single state or density.

Entanglement and increased entropy of neuronal states is dictated by:

$$ENT(\wp) = -Tr \, \wp \, ln \, \wp$$

Where Tr denotes trace or sum of diagonal elements) of the corresponding density matrix. Since the sum of probabilities for all alternative must yield unity, then:

$$Tr(\wp) = 1$$

The entropy then will be the total aggregate of accessible states:

$$ENT(\wp) = ln \, \wp$$

Conservation of probability requires:

$$\partial P / \partial t = \partial / \partial t \, (Tr(\wp)) = 0$$

Violation of this condition is what entails generation of creative novelty.

At the other extreme there exists the possibility of continuous tendency for quantum entanglement. That is, the waves within the microtubule (associated with a pure quantum coherent state ρ) become 'entangled' with the wave states of the surrounding environment. This leads to a condition called *quantum decoherence*. This is simply the opposite of the orderly wave condition, with information (and energy) now being lost from the wave form in the microtubule:

MICROTUBULE

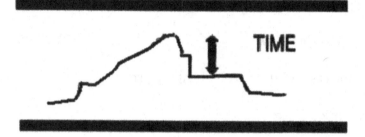

TIME

Decoherence arises from wave entanglement

To get the maximum possible microtubule frequency (10^{24} /s) the information content must be reduced to 1 bit! However, to be more realistic, say that the content is reduced to 10^{10} bits or about 1 bit per neuron. (This may be do-able by a small percentage of contemporary humans). Then the maximum frequency is 10^{14}/s. What we want to know is the energy needed to drive that much information into a coherent state for complex thought or mentation. We can start by recalling that there is an energy equivalent of 0.693kT Joules per bit.[8] Then for the number of bits specified, the energy needed is:

---

[8]   Here, k is the Boltzmann constant: 1.38 x 10^{-23} J/K and T is the temperature (in Kelvin) for which we will take 300K as a

Philip A. Stahl

Energy for all bits = 10^{10} x 0.693 kT = 2.87 x 10^{-11} Joule

The energy produced from the energy-time indeterminacy for the given frequency is:

$$\delta E = h/\delta t = h/10^{-14} = 1.05 \times 10^{-20} \text{ Joule}$$

which is far, far too low. Thus, *we need the quantum potential* to get the extra energy. In meditation, that would be:

$h(\delta f)/2 \approx h(f' - f)$

In the case of $\Delta t \approx 0$, $\Delta f = 1/\Delta t = \infty$, so:

$\varXi = h(\infty)/2 = \infty$

Or, essentially total access to the energy of the Dirac ether.

By way of example, if a Yogi, Christ, Buddha or other adept could get his thought beat cycle to one per tau (at the $\tau = 10^{-43}$ second limit) and *do that for ten minutes* this would yield a total of 6 x $10^{45}\tau$ and yield energy of magnitude:[9]

$$6.3 \times 10^{54} \text{ Joules}$$

which, while not 'infinite' is more than all the physical/active energy in the Milky Way galaxy!

One item of marked interest is the analytical finding that the quantum potential term in the Jacobi equation, i.e.

---

reasonable room temperature (300 K = 27°C or about 75F).
[9]   We have: $\delta E = h/10^{-43}$ s = 1.05 x 10^9 Joule per tau, and total energy over meditation/ mentation period = $\Sigma \, \delta E = (1.05 \times 10^9/\tau) \times 6 \times 10^{45} \, \tau = 6.3 \times 10^{54}$ Joules.

$$(\nabla S)^2 + m_o^2 c^2 = h^2 \,\square\, a/a$$

Can be associated with *a time reversible frictional force* in a manner by which fluctuations in the Dirac Ether can be analogized to the Brownian motion as described by Einstein and Smoluchowski[10]. For example, consider a cubic centimeter of empty space with exposed sub-quantal fluctuations at the scale of the Planck Length ($L_p \approx 10^{-34}$ m). Then time reversibility is implicit at that scale and which can become accessible on the scale of neural action such that: A_n (b) = $\wp \exp[2\,\pi\,(i)\,[ft - (x/\lambda) + \varphi]$

A Note on Quantum Bayesianism:

No topics such as examined above can be complete without considering quantum Bayesianism. This is critical because probability runs as a thread throughout these more detailed discussions, and probability is interpreted (and computed) differently in the Bayesian and Frequency—based contexts.

To fix ideas, the typical quantum physicist has a confirmed frequentist concept of probability. Hence, a probability is determined by the frequency with which event E appears in some ensemble K of events, all of which have been identically prepared in the same system.

For example, consider a system of ten coins, each of which is equally weighted, balanced to yield—for ten separate tosses:

H H T H T H H T T T

Then out of this ensemble of ten fair tosses, T appears as many times as H which is 5, so

---

[10]   Gueret: *Open Questions on Quantum Mechanics Conference.*

$P = E/ K = 5/ 10 = 0.5$

Thus, the objective observer will assign a probability of P = 50% to a single event embodying any such coin toss and this will reflect the observer's belief the event will occur at least half the time.

On the other hand, for the Bayesian the probability is not inherent in a similar system of events but is projected via different agents who may have different beliefs based on pre-supposition. Say Agent X has the pre-supposition a particular series of coin tosses is weighted toward tails to appear, for whatever reason, then his expectation will be: $P(T) = 0.6$ perhaps.

N. David Mermin refers to this as[11]:

a personalist Bayesian view of probability is widely held, though not by many physicists

This implies a definite opposition between physics and other fields which employ Bayesian statistics. In formal quantum mechanics, arrival of states, probabilities is contingent on information, knowledge. For example, knowledge may be obtained using an Aspect-type device such (as depicted below) which acts to disperse the individual atomic "magnets" (net-spin atoms) and send them in pairs (always in pairs) to D1 and D2 simultaneously. The question is, what spin is detected by each detector at the instant of observation?:

D1 $(+\frac{1}{2})$ <-------------[D]------------->$(-\frac{1}{2})$D2

---

[11]   Mermin,: *Physics Today*, (July, 2012), p. 48.

The knowledge or information arrived at is correlations or anti-correlations, for the spin of an atom, say helium, captured at detectors D1 or D2.

If a ½ spin appears simultaneously we have correlation, otherwise anti-correlation.

Prior to the observation (actual detection), neither spin value can be known according to the Heisenberg Uncertainty Principle of Quantum Mechanics. That is, while the atomic magnets are in transit—from device to either detector—there is no definite information concerning which spin is going where. The reason has to do with what is called the superposition of states. To fix ideas, consider the whole atomic magnet in the device, before being ejected. If it's a helium atom, then there'll be one up spin and one down spin and we can write for simplicity:

$$U = \sum_i \{(ups)_i + (downs)_i\}$$

In the orthodox (and most conservative) interpretation of quantum theory, there can be no separation of observed (e.g. spin) state until an observation or measurement is made. Until that instant (of detection) the states are in a superposition, However, quantum Bayesianism asserts that each switch introduces a different probable outcome based *on each observer's belief about the system* and how he makes state assignments.

More profoundly, there's a bifurcation between the world—universe in which an agent or observer lives and her experience of it. According to Mermin this disconcerting aspect arises:

> From a failure to realize that like probabilities, like quantum states, like experience itself . . . . the split belongs to the observer.

Each agent and system experiences its own split. Thereby, an uncontrolled *complementarity of experience* enters with respect to any other observers. If Judy "experiences any observations that are macroscopic (i.e. related to the large scale world of planets, stars etc.), Roy will experience microscopic reality (the world of atoms, electrons and Higgs bosons!) Mermin notes that each split is between an object (the world) and a subject which is really *"an agent's irreducible awareness of his or her own experience."*

Mermin also makes the point, which I tend to agree with, that: *"ambiguities only arise if one fails to acknowledge that the splits reside not in the objective world but at the boundaries between that world and the experiences of the various agents who use quantum mechanics."*

In more technical detail, let operators be in one-to-one correspondence with the closed subspaces of the Hilbert space, $\hat{\mathbf{H}}$. Then if $\mathbf{P}$ is a projection, its range is closed, and any closed subspace is the range of a unique projection. If $\underline{\mathbf{u}}$ is any unit vector, then $\mathbf{P} = [\mathbf{P}\underline{\mathbf{u}}]^2$ is the expected value of the corresponding observable in the state represented by $\underline{\mathbf{u}}$. Since this is $\{0,1\}$—(binary) valued, we can interpret this as *the probability that a measurement of the observable will produce the affirmative answer 1*. In particular, the affirmative answer will have probability 1 if and only if $\mathbf{P}\underline{\mathbf{u}} = \underline{\mathbf{u}}$; that is, $\underline{\mathbf{u}}$ lies in the range of P.

In the Quantum Bayesian view, this is not so. The quantum state assignments are relative to the one who makes them. So if I, as a quantum Bayesian, assert that: $\mathbf{P} = [\mathbf{P}\underline{\mathbf{u}}]^2$ is the expected value of the corresponding observable in the state represented by $\underline{\mathbf{u}} = 0$ and the result is $\{0,0\}$, then $\mathbf{P} = 0$.

According to Mermin[12]:

---

[12] Mermin, *op. cit.*

QBism eliminates the notorious measurement problem . . . . an agent unproblematically changes her probability assignments discontinuously whenever new experiences lead her to change her beliefs. It is just the same for her quantum state assignments. The change in either case is not in the physical system the agent is considering. Rather, it is in the quantum state the agent chooses by which to encapsulate her expectations

The bottom line here seems to be that an active, conscious agent—on altering or adjusting the quantum states to her experimental expectations—can effectively change probability outcomes any time she chooses.

APPENDIX E

Connecting to the Emergent Whole:

Physicist Bernard d'Espagnat has observed:

> . . . every human being would have a possibility of establishing some kind of link to Being. It is then up to him to discover the nature of that link. More precisely, it cannot be excluded that between every particular man and Being itself there exists a relationship that, while ineffable, is still describable in the least appropriate way by the expression 'a call from Being to man . . .
>
> When we think of such calls, we interpret our relationship with Being as embedded in time, whereas, like everything that relates to independent reality or Being, such a relationship should in fact transcend time, at least in some respects.

This encapsulates the basis for higher order mental processes such as mentation.

This is also identified with what Jacob Needleman has called total attention and meditation. In other words, one goes beyond the mere recognition of a higher order reality in what I call the Emergent Nonlocal Ground form or what Bohm calls the holomovement and d'Espagnat simply calls *Being*.

If life is likened to the journey of a ship across a tempestuous sea, mentation is analogous to consciously taking control of the ship and guiding it in a preferred direction as opposed to having its course governed purely by the random forces/currents of the sea[1]. In meditation, the nature of the link is the passive recognition of our implicit relationship, as diverse images enfolded into one Being. The emphasis is on the contemplation of that sense of unity and "Isness". As taught by most of the eastern religions, this in itself is a high form of prayer. Indeed, pairs of universes (at least possible parallel or multiple cosmic cycle wave functions) are mutually annihilated to form a continuous'present when we meditate

In mentation, each person is an active co-creator with Being in explicating its reality in the cosmos. This is accomplished through the conscious direction of non-contingent energy into the world of forms and entropy (cosmos). Recall non-contingent energy is that already present in every cubic centimeter of empty space.

Whether I meditate or mentate I *am* doing something in a real sense. Using quantum potentials in my own brain, I'm altering the space-time field structure in my immediate vicinity. To be sure, this activity isn't primary, but rather secondary. That is, it results from the energy displaced by having meditated/ mentated. Thus, I do not leave the ambient space-time in the same way I found it. If I genuinely

---

[1] Mentation is probably similar to the "modulation of the frequencies of certain process 1 actions that act upon brain-sized patterns of neurological activity" according to Henry Stapp, e.g. Stapp: *Mindful Universe*, 109.

meditated, for example, I would certainly have left more taus as more quantum foam interconnections. Of course, these are at the level of subatomics (Planck Length) so would not be visible to ordinary senses—but the effects (e.g. telekinesis as in the Jahn experiments) would support that space-time volumes had indeed been altered.

In mentation, thought is focused and projected into the cosmos to *create* a thought representation in the outer world. In this way, ISNESS is not diffuse but channeled directly into a specific image held in consciousness.

$$\Xi \to O \mid {\sim}O \to \Sigma_i \, [\psi(\text{'past'}) + \psi \, (\text{'future'})]i = \Xi$$

This image (Ξ) is the thought-form of that which we wish to project into the temporal and localized world of experience and (localized) entropy ($L = R \times t$). Mentation accomplishes this by forcing a partial cancellation between real time waves (offer and echo) that are processed.

Alteration of Temporal Sequences:

Cautionary Point: *This Section is highly speculative!*

The most common contention of physicists today is that the universe is likely a *multiverse*, consisting of innumerable parallel universes. If this is so it may mean that we can't think exclusively on one plane or for one universe when considering consciousness and mental processes.

If these time waves—in the form of offer and echo waves—are able to impact mutually proximate universes, one may have to consider the effects. Think of the following diagram:

Philip A. Stahl

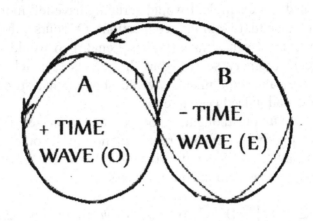

PARALLEL UNIVERSES VIA (+) AND (-) TIME WAVES

Here, A and B denote precisely parallel cosmic cycles, in a multi-cosmic hyper-toroid. They are actually mirror images of each other, since:

$$\psi(O) + \psi(E) = \sqrt{2/\pi} \, \exp(\tau) - \sqrt{2/\pi} \, \exp(-\tau)$$

That is, they are separated by imaginary time. Where or how does an imaginary time separation arising between two parallel universes? In meditation, of course! Therein, remarkable things happen with the meditator's time sense. Evidently, consciousness can alter the intensity and direction of time, e.g.:

$$\tau \rightarrow [-3\tau] \rightarrow 2\tau \rightarrow [-\tau] \rightarrow 3\tau$$

Where each tau (τ) denotes a unit Planck time or 10^{-43} s. The sample above also contains elements of both objective

362

(proper) and subjective time. The first is defined directionally by an 'arrow' of time and so must increase toward states of increasing entropy (or disorder). Thus, we go from τ to 2τ and so on. However, the negative values enclosed in brackets [ ] give a counter-intuitive time sense which is just opposite to increasing entropy, and hence opposite to the objective or proper time sense. This is the appearance of subjective time. It is the emergence of consciousness into the objective or proper time field (the toroidal coordinate φ).

In effect, the negentropy produced by an inverse tau creation generates information. Evidently, it is necessary for there to be a window or channel from the future to the past (in the form of inverted taus) which allows information flow from the future. Contrary to what skeptics may believe, this "retro-causality" is perfectly permissible within the framework of existing laws of physics. Richard Feynman once observed, for example, that a positron (positive electron) behaves exactly like an electron traveling backward in time.

Meanwhile, the concept of *retarded potentials* is well known in electro-magnetic theory. These potentials are defined in terms of:

$$V(r, t_a) = f1(r, T_a) \text{ and } A(r, t_a) = f2(r, t_a)$$

Where t_a is the advanced time: $t_a = t + r/c$

And the $f1$, $f2$ are functions of the electric potential and vector potential, respectively. In the advanced potential case, we ascertain conditions for the future potentials based on the past, and are able to use them in appropriate calculations in the future. In the *retarded potentials* (with $t_a = t - r/c$) we ascertain conditions for past (or present) potentials based on the future, and are able to use them in appropriate calculations in the present.

Energy is also relevant and computable using the Heisenberg energy-time indeterminacy conditions. How much energy, for example, might a brain gain in the case of enhancing negentropy by 2 *taus* (-2τ). Since the tau is bracketed within a quantum (actually sub-quantum) time domain, we can apply the Heisenberg Energy-Time Indeterminacy Principle equation:

$$\Delta E \, \Delta t \geq h/2\pi$$

In this case, the time indeterminacy would be 2 taus where:

$$2\,\tau = 2 \times (10^{-34}) \text{ s}$$

so the calculated energy change ('indeterminacy in energy') is:

$$\Delta E \approx (h/2\pi)/ \Delta t$$

Or:

$$\Delta E \approx 1.05 \times 10^{-34} \text{ J-s}/ (2 \times (10^{-34}) \text{ s}) \approx 0.5 \text{ J}$$

So one half joule is available to increase the informational content, energy and order within the brain. This is roughly equal in energy to that given off by a half-watt bulb (say in a small flashlight) for one second.

It is also useful to estimate how much information—as bits—this amount of energy corresponds to. We already know that one bit has 0.693 kT of energy (in joules) where k is the Boltzmann constant and T is the ambient temperature. Then the number of bits would be:

$$N(\text{bits}) = (0.5 \text{ J})/(0.693kT)$$

Taking $k = 1.38 \times 10^{-23}$ J and T = 300 K (about typical room temperature), one obtains:

$$N(\text{bits}) = (0.5\text{J})/(0.693 \times 1.38 \times 10^{-23} \text{ J/K} \times 300 \text{ K})$$

$$N(\text{bits}) = 1.74 \times 10^{20}$$

or, an amount of bits about 870 million times more than the number of stars in the Milky Way (numbered at 200 billion). If this were divided by the 'tau' we saw earlier, one would obtain:

$$1.74 \times 10^{54} \text{ bits/sec}$$

or very close to the (upper) Bekenstein Bound ($\approx 4 \times 10^{53} \text{ s}^{-1}$) given by Frank Tipler.[2]

Finding Higher Being in a Quantum Nonlocality Sense:

If the above speculations have a basis, and they well may, then it means Being need not be remote from our experience, but within the grasp of a higher-plane consciousness. I mentioned both mentation and meditation and these bear on more recent brain research, in particular by Andrew Newberg, M.D. and his associate Eugene D'Aquili M.D. The authors note among their startling findings:[3]:

> In normal circumstance, the OAA helps create a distinct, accurate sense of our physical orientation to the world. To do its job well....depends on a constant stream of nerve impulses from each of the body's senses. The OAA sorts and processes these impulses virtually simultaneously during every moment of our lives

So, in other words, without the benefit of the OAA **(orientation association area)** brain region, we'd be

---

[2]   Tipler: *The Physics of Immortality,* 408.
[3]   Newberg and D'Aquili: *Why God Won't Go Away: Brain Science and the Biology of Belief,* 5.

essentially discombobulated vegetables, unable to even get out of bed in the morning. We wouldn't know which end is up or down, or right from left, and certainly wouldn't be able to find our way out of a room, far less walk through a downtown of any major city.

The authors' investigation of how the brain's OAA translates an image into a religious reality is also described in detail[4]. This is in connection with a person given an image of Christ and asked to focus on it. Within minutes, neurological measurements, i.e. from PET and SPECT scans[5], showed electrical discharges spiraling down from the right attention area (right OAA) to the limbic system and hypothalamus "triggering the arousal section of the structure".

The authors' test results and measurements revealed the activation of both the left and right association regions as their subjects focused on an image of Christ. As assorted cortical thresholds were crossed, a maximal stimulation (given by spikes in the SPECT scans) produced a neural "flood" that generated feedback to the attention association area.

To make a long story short, the visual attention area of the OAA was seen to begin to deprive the right orientation area (responsible for balance) of the OAA of all neural input not originating with the contemplation of Jesus. In order to compensate, and thereby preserve the neuro-spatial matrix (in which the self could still exist) the right orientation area had to default to the attention area focusing on "Jesus". As the authors describe the situation:[6]:

---

[4] *Op. cit.,* 121-22.

[5] PET = positron emission tomography, SPECT = single photon image tomography.

[6] *Ibid.*

It has no choice but to create a spatial matrix out of nothing but the attention area's single-minded contemplation of Jesus

In other words, we have an extreme example of mentation, probably represented by a density matrix of the form: $\mid \Theta > < \tau \mid$

Newberg and D'Aquili note that as the process of *re-cerebralization* continues, all irrelevant neural inputs are stripped away until the only reality left is Jesus. That reality (actually a pseudo-reality confected by the right attention area) thereby takes over the entire mind. Or, in the words of the authors, *"it is perceived by the mind as the whole depth and breadth of reality."*

This is a profound insight, and fully explains why it is essentially impossible to wean believers away from their objects of worship or devotion based on logic and reason alone. What has happened, in other words, is the subject's whole existence and identity has become bound up with the focus of his brain's OAA—or more specifically—the right attention area's focus which channels nearly all neural inputs to that region.

In the mind of the professed believer, focused on Jesus as his "Savior", there is no possibility of leaving that focus behind because his OAA brain areas are now exclusively dependent on it for him to survive. Take them away, say by surgically removing the right attention areas of the OAA, and the person will die. He'll either commit suicide, unable to ground himself in any continuous or recognizable reality, or go mad.

What is more interesting about the whole OAA dynamic, and hence more relevant to my book, is that it actually has a much broader, more generic basis than mere narrow beliefs on Jesus, or any patriarchal God figures. Indeed, the authors were able to replicate states in which the activation area generated a stable state of absolute unitary being in which *subjective observations were impossible on the one hand, and no subjective self existed to make them on the other.* In the context of my earlier conjectures, one may propose that this absolute unitary being is evolved by virtue of a mode of thought that can access the Dirac Ether, say via meditation, and hence become one with it.

More intriguing are the more complex cognitive functions of the brain Andrew Newberg lays out in his text accompanying a series of lectures on *The Spiritual Brain*. In one lecture, he refers in turn to *the reductive function* and *the holistic function*[7]. The first seeks to break things down in order to better analyze them, and the second seeks to integrate apparently disparate constructs, events. Combined with the causal functioning dynamic it is easy to see that brain configuration, architecture may well dictate whether a person is more reductive or holistic in attributing causes to phenomena in the natural world.

An ardent cognitive reductionist will form some construct [C] which is derived from an original event [E] resolving it into: {a, b, c, d, e} where the bracketed set denotes component sub-events with differing time intervals t1, t2, t3, t4, and t5.

Thus, the reductionist's brain processing for outer events is always via the template:

$$[E] => \{a(t1 +t), b(t2 + t), c(t3 + t), d(t4 + t), e(t5 + t)\}$$

Where, say t = 1 sec, is the consciousness 'delay' interval

The processing is never: $[E] \rightarrow [E]$

---

[7] Newberg: *The Spiritual Brain: Science and Religious Experience*, 22.

Which would imply t = 0 and a = b = c etc. In other words, this would indicate instantaneous real time event processing.

The conclusion here is that the whole constellation of objects, events perceived must be assembled piece by piece by the brain from an architecture embedded in its synapses, neural pathways and neuronal assemblies. The dynamic process of this assembly is governed by Newberg's reductive function which identifies *mind* with the collective operations of the physical brain.

As depicted in the earlier case [E] → [C] means that all our experiences are second hand only, not direct. In other words, they conform to the claim by ultra-reductionist Alex Rosenberg. It is this disconnect that raises profound questions and issues concerning whether a human brain can know anything directly. Consciousness, in this template, arises merely as a kind of epiphenomenon of the material brain so no appeal need be made to emergence, or even quantum mechanics. By the same token, God can't exist other than as an outcome of the brain's processing activity.

On the other hand, if the holistic cognitive function is more dominant, the person is more likely to use a causal model that conforms to it and also more likely to practice meditation and mentation. In this case, mind is more likely to be accepted as a holistic reality which extends beyond the physical bounds of the brain, not only as energy but for communications.

In an interview with Renee Weber, David Bohm suggested this possible connection to meditation[8]:

Perhaps meditation will lead you deep into this ocean of physical and mental energy which is universal.

---

[8]   Weber: *The Holographic Paradigm and Other Paradoxes*, 213.

Newberg, meanwhile, cites MRI studies that compared brain activity in meditators against non-meditators (non-believers) and found much lower frontal lobe activity in the latter. According to Newberg, it appeared the atheists-non-meditators were *struggling with a sense of cognitive dissonance*[9]. They were trying to focus on something they didn't like very much.

An even more startling find, according to Newberg, is that when atheists were given dopamine their perceptions conformed more to those of spiritual practitioners[10]. Newberg reasoned that perhaps the absence of this key neuro-transmitter plays a role in engendering hard core disbelief and radical skepticism-atheism.

Thia is what the authors of *Why God Won't Go Away* call the state of Absolute Unitary Being. In their parlance, it is exactly this state which is the closest one will come to God. As the authors note[11]:

If the brain were not assembled as it is, we would not be able to experience a higher spiritual reality even if it did exist

The authors then go on from this to speculate why the human brain, ostensibly evolved for the purpose of survival, would possess such "an impractical talent". The most they can offer is that the transcendent unitary brain states evolved as by products of the more survival-oriented features[12].

The focus-mandate of the OAA brain total de-afferentiation of the orientation region gives rise to the state known as *Absolute Unitary Being*: otherwise also

---

[9] Newberg: *op. cit.*, 32.

[10] *Ibid.*

[11] Newberg and d'Aquili: *op. cit.*, 123.

[12] *Op. cit.*, 124.

described as the One Mind linking all minds, so that it must transcend all subjective or secondary conceptions of God.

The authors of the OAA research explain[13]:

It is difficult for the rational mind to accept these cryptic pronouncements as fact: The One Mind is uncreated, it is not non-existent, but at the same time cannot be said to exist; it transcends all limits and comparisons, and outside of this One Mind nothing is real

One last insight from the authors unifies my own thesis with that of Henry Stapp, David Bohm, and Bernard d'Espagnat[14]:

In Absolute Unitary Being, nothing is experienced but the pure and complete unity of all things or of No-things. One thing cannot stand apart from another, so individual beings and objects cannot be perceived. The egotistical self cannot exist, because it has no non-self against which to define itself. In the same fashion, God cannot be set apart from this ultimate oneness as an identifiable, personal Being—since to do so would be to conceive of a God who is less than absolutely real

This last statement is extremely important, because the experiments performed which locate *the God site* in the brain's OAA (and also show a real, biological connection), do not allow human rationality to limit it to the personal. Once we do that, it ceases to be real. This means that all the personal God concepts used by most religions are only

---

[13] *Op. cit.,*148.

[14] *Op. cit.* p. 160.

caricatures, since they actually modify the brain's attainment of the Unitary state of being. In other words, one cannot simultaneously have an Absolute Unitary Being and a personal Being, putatively described as the One True God.

As the authors note[15]:

> The perception of an absolute reality, therefore, would demand that God be more than a knowable Being and make it clear that all personifications of God are symbolic attempts to grasp the ungraspable.

The final question for the Atheist is simple: Do the OAA neurobiological experiments of Newberg and D'Aquili *prove a real God exists* as an Absolute Unitary Being? The answer is 'no'. Even Newberg and D'Aquili are non-committal on this, pointing out that they have only found a brain site that elicits a state of unity, or what can be perceived as Absolute Unitary Being. This does not mean an actual Absolute Unitary Being exists *though it could.* However, the possibility or plausibility doesn't amount to an ironclad proof.

As Newberg writes in the book epilog:

> At the heart of our theory is a neurological model that provides a link between mystical experience and observable brain function. In simplest terms: the brain seems to have the built in ability to transcend the perception of an individual self

In other words, the authors appear to have demonstrated a powerful brain state. But, at the same time, they've cautioned that the underlying entity remains open to question. Clearly, if a transcendent Being is behind it, then it makes sense it is analogous to the Bohm *holomovement*.

---

[15]   *Ibid.*

Meanwhile, physicist Henry Stapp has gone so far as to indicate that the ultimate nature of quantum reality hints at a God, viz[16].:

Quantum theory opens the door to, and indeed demands, the making of these later free choices. The situation is concordant with the idea of a powerful God that creates the universe and its laws to get things started, but then bequeaths part of this power to beings created in his own image.

Stapp then goes on to remark that he "sees no way for contemporary science to disprove this religious interpretation of quantum theory[17]." Hopefully, these insights will help make sense of my central thesis: That just as atheism represents a kind of spiritual and philosophical dead end, so does embracing or worshipping a personal God, or investing reality in a verbal-oral symbol.

It is hoped that this book inspires seekers of all denominations and types to instead transcend both limited reductionist thinking, as well as naïve religious thinking. The first encourages over-simplicity via Scientism and committing to a system wildly at odds with reality. The second encourages childish and unquestioning acceptance of personal gods (including unique Saviors), as opposed to embracing a higher order being and reality. Worse, it predisposes people to treat a meaningless verbal symbol G-O-D as if it has abiding significance and objective reality apart from an idea, or concept.

Bernard d'Espagnat may provide the best note on which to end[18]:

---

[16]   Stapp: *Information and the Nature of Reality,* 117.
[17]   *Ibid.*
[18]   d'Espagnat,: *op. cit,.*158.

The archaic notion that is conveyed by the words 'Lord' and 'Almighty' will presumably never recover its full efficiency for lulling the ontological qualms of mankind. For a religious mind, turning towards Being should therefore become a subtler endeavor than the mere acceptance of the heavenly will stated in the Bible, formulated by the priests, and exhibited by miracles

BIBLIOGRAPHY

Alford, Mark, *The Skeptical Inquirer*, May-June, 2011.

Aspect, Alain., Grangier, Phillippe. and Roger, Gerard: *Physical Review Letters*, Volume 47, No. 7, 1981, 460.

Aspect, Alain., Grangier, Phillippe. and Roger, Gerard: *Physical Review Letters*, Volume 49, No. 2, 1982.

Auyang, Sunny.: *How is Quantum Field Theory Possible?*, New York, Oxford University Press, 1995

Ayer, A.J.: *Language, Logic and Truth*, London, Penguin Books, 1983 (reprint).

Baldwin, Dorothy: *Understanding Male Sexual Health*, New York, Hippocrene Books, 1993

Bartlett, Albert: Thoughts on Long-Term Energy Supplies: Scientists and the Silent Lie *in Physics Today*, July (2004), 53-5

Bartlett, Albert: Letter to the Editor *in Physics Today*, November, (2004), 18.

Bar-Yam, Yaneer:, *Dynamics of Complex Systems*, New York, Addison-Wesley, 1997.

Baum, Robert: *Logic*, New York, Harcourt Brace College Publishers, 1996.

Bell, John. S. On The I possible Pilot Wave, in *Foundations of Physics*, 12, October, 1982, 989-999.

Bohm, David. J. and Hiley, Basil.J: The de Broglie Pilot Wave Theory and the Further Development of New Insights Arising Out Of It, in *Foundations of Physics*, 12, April, 1982., 1001-1016.

Bohm, David. J. and Hiley, Basil.J: *The Undivided Universe: An Ontological Interpretation of Quantum Theory*, London, Routledge, 1993.

Bohm, David: *Causality and Chance In Modern Physics*, Philadelphia University of Pennsylvania Press, 1971.

Bohm, David: *Quantum Theory*, New York, Dover Publications, 1951.

Bohm, David in The Enfolding—Unfolding Universe (interview with Ken Wilber) in *The Holographic Paradigm* (Ed. K. Wilber), Boston, New Science Library, 1982, 103-104.

Bohm, David : *Wholeness and the Implicate Order*, Great Britain, Routledge and Kegan Paul, London, U.K.,1980.

Boi, Luciano: *'The Quantum Fluctuation*, Baltimore, Maryland, Johns Hopkins University Press, 2011

Boole, George: *An Investigation of the Laws Of Thought—On Which Are Founded the Mathematical Theories of Logic and Probabilities*, Queen's College, Cork, Ireland, 1854. (Accessible compliments of Project Gutenberg)

Boslaugh, John: *Stephen Hawking's Universe*, New York, Avon Books, 1984.

Bostrom, Nick.: Are You Living in A Computer Simulation?, *in Philosophical Quarterly,* No. 211, (53), 2003, 243-255.

Boyer, Pascal : *Religion Explained: The Evolutionary Origins of Religious Thought'*, New York, Basic Books. 2001.

Bunge, Mario: *Causality and Modern Science*, New York, Dover Publications, 1979.

Burnham, Terry and Phelan, Jay: *Mean Genes*, New York, Basic Books, 2000.

Byrne, James: *GOD*, New York, Continuum Books, 2001.

Campbell, Joseph: *The Power of Myth*, New York, Anchor Books-Doubleday, 1988.

Camus, Albert: *The Plague*, New York, Vintage Books, 1948.

Chalmers, Alan: *Science and its Fabrication*, Minneapolis, University of Minnesota Press, 1990.

Comfort,, Alex: *Reality and Empathy: Physics, Mind and Science in the 21st Century,*

Albany, State University Press of New York, 1984.

Coveney, Peter and Highfield, Roger: *The Arrow Of Time*, New York, Fawcett-Columbine Books, 1990.

Cramer, John G.: The Transactional Interpretation of Quantum Mechanics, in *Reviews of Modern Physics*, Vol. 58, No. 3, 1986, 647-687.

Crossan, John Dominic: *The Historical Jesus: The Life of a Mediterranean Jewish Peasant,* New York, HarperOne Books, 1993.

Cufaro-Petroni, Nicole and Vigier, Phillippe.: *Physics Letters,* Vol. 93A, 1982, 383-386.

Dennett, Daniel: *Darwin's Dangerous Idea: Evolution and the Meaning O f Life*, New York, Simon and Schuster, 1995.

d'Espagnat, Bernard: *In Search of Reality*, New York, Springer-Verlag, 1983.

De Waal, Frans: Has Militant Atheism Become a Religion, in *Salon.com.* March 25, 2013.

Dewart, Leslie: in:*Casta Connubii:The Development of Dogma, in Contraception and Holiness: The Catholic Predicament* (A Symposium), London, U.K., Fontana-Collins, 1964.

Dirac, Paul. A.M.: The *Principles of Quantum Mechanics*, Great Britain, Oxford University Press, 1947.

Donnelly, Mark P., and Diehl, Daniel: *The Big Book of Pain: Torture and Punishment Through History*, Great Britain, The History Press, 2011.

Douglass, James: *JFK And The Unspeakable—Why He Died and Why It Matters*, New York, Touchstone Books, 2010.

Dyson, Freeman: *Infinite in All Directions*, New York, Harper and Row, 1989.

Ehrman, Bart: *Misquoting Jesus: The Story Behind Who Changed The Bible And Why*, New York, HarperCollins, 2005.

Ehrman, Bart: *Forged: Writing in the Name of God—Why the Bible's Authors Are Not Who We Think They Are*, New York, HarperOne Books, 2011.

Einstein, Albert., Podolsky, Boris. and Rosen, Nathan.: Can Quantum-Mechanical Description of Physical Reality be Considered Complete? In *Physical Review*, Vol. 47, 777-780.

Epstein, Greg M.: *Good Without God*, New York, William Morrow Publishers, 2009.

Fernandez, Manny and Cowan, Alison Leigh: When Horror Came to a Connecticut Family, *The New York Times*, August 7, 2007, 1.

Feynman, Richard: *The Feynman Lectures in Physics*, Reading, Massachusetts, Addison—Wesley Publishers, 1965.

Flew, Anthony. *Thinking About Thinking*, London, Fontana-Collins, 1975.

Flew, Anthony.: *A Dictionary of Philosophy*, New York, St. Martin's Press, 1987.

Flynn, Thomas: The Trouble with Christmas, in *Free Inquiry*, Fall, 1993.

French, Marilyn: *Beyond Power: On Women, Men and Morals*, London, Abacus Books, 1985.

Froese, Paul and Bader, Christopher: *America's Four Gods: What We Say About God—and What That Says About Us*, Oxford, U.K., Oxford University Press, 2010.

Fröhlich, Herbert: Long Range Coherence and Energy Storage in Biological Systems in *International Journal of Quantum Chemistry*, Vol. II, 1968.

Gödel, Kurt: *On Formally Undecidable Propositions of Principia Mathematic and Related System*, New York, Dover Publications, 1931.

Goldstein, Sheldon: A Theorist Ignored, in *Science*, (275), March, 1997, 1893-1895

Garay, P. and Levefer, R.: *J. Theoretical Biology*, 417, 1978

Graham, Lloyd.: *Deceptions and Myths of the Bible*, New York, Citadel Press, 2000.

Gray, John: Atheism Wars, *Playboy*, Vol. 60, No. 3, (April, 2013), 49-53.

Gueret, Phillippe: Recent Progress in De Broglie Nonlinear Wave Mechanics, in *Open Questions on Quantum Mechanics Conference., 1983*.

Haisch, Bernard: *The God Theory*, San Francisco, CA, Weiser Books 2006.

Hameroff, Stuart R. *Ultimate Computing: Bio-Molecular Consciousness and Nanotechnology*, Amsterdam, North-Holland Publications, 1987.

Harris, Sam: *The End of Faith*, New York, W.W. Norton Publishing, 2005.

Heinberg, Richard: *The Party's Over: Oil, War and the Fate of Industrial Societies*, New York, New Society Publishers, 2005.

Herbert, Nick.: *Quantum Reality—Beyond the New Physics*, New York, Doubleday, 1985

Hofstadter, Richard.: *Anti-Intellectualism in American Life*, New York, Vintage Books, 1962

Hume, David: *An Enquiry Concerning Human Understanding*, Buffalo, New York, Prometheus, Books, 1988.

Inman, Mason: The True Cost of Fossil Fuels, in *Scientific American*, Vol. 308, No. 4 (April, 2013), 59-61.

Jacoby, Susan: *The Age of American Unreason*, New York, Pantheon Books, 2009.

Jillette, Penn: *I don't know so I'm an atheist libertarian*, at CNN.com, Aug. 17, 2011.

Kafatos, Menos and Nadeau, Robert: *The Conscious Universe: Part and Whole in Modern Physical Theory*, Springer-Verlag, 1990.

Kant, Immanuel: *Critique of Pure Reason*, New York, Cambridge University Press

Kekes, John: *The Roots of Evil*, Ithica, New York, Cornell University Press, 2005

Keltner, Dacher.: *Born to be Good—The Science of a Meaningful Life*, New York, W.W. Norton & Company, 2009.

Koestler, Arthur: *The Ghost in the Machine*, London, Penguin Books, 1967.

Kramer, Heinrich, and Sprenger, James: *The Malleus Maleficarum* (transl. Montague Summers), New York, Dover Publications, 1928.

Kung, Hans. *Infallible? An Inquiry*, New York, Doubleday, 1983.

Kung, Hans: *Theology for the Third Millennium*, New York, Anchor Books, 1988.

Lea, Henry Charles: *The Inquisition of the Middle Ages,* New York, Barnes and Noble, 1954.

Leibniz, Gottfried Wilhelm, *The Principles of Nature and Grace, Based on Reason,* Springer-Verlag, 2004.

Lewis, C.S.: *The Screwtape Letters*, New York, HarperCollins, 2001.

Lewis, C.S.: *Mere Christianity*, San Francisco, HarperSanFranciso, 1952.

Livingstone Smith, David: *Less Than Human: Why We Demean, Enslave and Exterminate Others,* New York, St. Martin's Press, 2011.

Lloyd, Seth.: *Programming the Universe*, New York, Vintage Books, 2007.

Margenau, Henry: *The Miracle of Existence,* Boston, New Science Library, Shambhala Publications, Boston, 1987.

Mermin, N. David.: QBism and Why Quantum Physicists Hate It, in *Physics Today*, (July), 2012, p. 8.

Neilsen, Kai: *Ethics Without God*, Buffalo, New York, New York, Prometheus Books, 1992.

Newberg, Andrew.:*The Spiritual Brain: Science and Religious Experience* (Great Courses Guidebook), Chantilly, Virginia, The Teaching Company, 2012

Newberg, Andrew and D'Aquili, Eugene.: *Why God Won't Go Away: Brain Science and the Biology of Belief,* New York, Ballantine Books, 2002.

Murphy, Ian: *Atheists Who Ruin It for Everyone Else,* Salon. com, Aug. 4, 2012.

Needleman, Jacob: *WHAT is God?* New York, Tarcher Books, 2009.

Newlands, Samuel: Natural Disasters and the Wrath of God in *The Wall Street Journal,* April 7, 2010, A15

Ornstein, Robert: *The Evolution of Consciousness*, New York, Prentice-Hall, 1991.

Padmanabhan, T: *Universe Before Planck Time—A Quantum Gravity Model* in Physical Review D, 28, No. 4, 1983.

Pagels, Elaine.: *The Gnostic Gospels,* New York, Vintage-Random House, 1979.

Pagels, Heinz: *The Cosmic Code*, New York, Bantam, 1982.

Parsons, Paul: A Warped View of Time Travel, in *Science*, Oct.11, 1996, Vol. 274, 202-203

Paul, Gregory S.:2009, *The Big Religion Questions Finally Solved*, Free Inquiry, 29: 24-33.

Paulos, John Allen: *Irreligion*, New York, Hill and Wang Books, 2008.

Penrose, Roger: *The Emperor's New Mind: Concerning Computers, Minds and the Laws of Physics*, New York, Penguin Books, 1990.

Penrose, Roger: *Shadows of the Mind*, New York, Oxford University Press, 1994.

Perlmutter, Saul: *Supernovae, Dark Energy and the Accelerating Universe* in Physics Today, April, 2003, 53-57.

Persinger, Michael: *The Neuropsychological Bases of God Beliefs*, New York, Praeger Publishers, 1987.

Philipse, Herman: Reason and Religion, in *Free Inquiry* (Feb./Mar. 2007), 37-38.

Pickens, T. Boone, Oil Futures Near $140 Amid fears of Shortage, *The Financial Times* May 21, 2010,

Prigogine, Ilya and Stenger, Isabelle: *Order Out of Chaos*, New York, Bantam, 1984.

Putnam, Hillary: *Boston Studies in the Philosophy of Science 5*, Dordrecht-Holland, 1968.

Radon, Dean: *The Conscious Universe*, New York, Harper, 1997.

Rand, Ayn: *The Virtue of Selfishness*, New York, Signet Books, 1961.

Rosenberg, Alex: *The Atheist's Guide to Reality—Enjoying Life Without Illusions*, New York, W.W. Norton, 2012.

Rucker, Rud*y: Geometry, Relativity and the Fourth Dimension*, New York, Dover Publications, 1977

Rucker, Rudy: *Infinity and the Mind*, New York, Dover Publications, 2004

Sagan, Carl: *The Dragons of Eden: Speculations on the Evolution of Human Intelligence*, New York, Coronet Books, 1977.

Sagan, Carl and Druyan, Ann: *Is It Possible to be Pro-Life and Pro-Choice?*, in *PARADE*, April 22, 1990.

Schlegel, Richard: *Superposition and Interaction: Coherence in Physics*, Chicago, University of Chicago Press, 1980.

Sheiman, Bruce: *An Atheist Defends Religion—Why Humanity Is Better Off With Religion Than Without It*, New York, Alpha Publications, 2009.

Shermer, Michael: *The Science of Good and Evil*, New York, Henry Holt & Company, 2004

Shermer, Michael, Quantum Quackery, in *Scientific American*, January 2005

Smetham, Graham: On 'Known to be False' Materialist Philosophies of Mind, in *Philosophy Now*, No. 93, 28. (Nov./Dec. 2012), 28-30.

Smith, George: *The Case Against God*, Buffalo, New York, Prometheus Books.

Soames, Scott: *Understanding Truth*, New York., Oxford University Press, 1998.

Solomon, Andrew: *The Noonday Demon: An Atlas of Depression*, New York, Scribner-Touchstone Books, 2002.

Squires, Euan: *Conscious Mind in the Physical World*, Bristol, Great Britain, Adam Hilger, 1990

Stahl, Philip, A.: *The Atheist's Handbook to Modern Materialism*, Chapel Hill, N. Carolina, Professional Press, 2000.

Stahl, Philip, A.: *Atheism: A Beginner's Handbook*, Bloomington, Indiana, iUniverse, 2007.

Stahl, Philip A.: *Dialectical Atheism: Demonstrations of Atheist Argument in Action,* Rayleigh, N.C., Lulu.com Publishers, 2010.

Stahl, Philip A.: Mind Viruses and Memes in *Colorado Springs Independent*, May 9-15, 2002, 5

Stahl, Philip A.: Science and God, in *The Barbados Nation*, September 27, 1978, 14.

Stapp, Henry: *Mind, Matter and Quantum Mechanics*, New York, Springer-Verlag, 1993.

Stapp, Henry: Consciousness and Values in the Quantum Universe, in *Foundations of Physics*, Vol. 15, No. 1, 1985, 35-47.

Stapp, Henry: *Mindful Universe—Quantum Mechanics and the Participating Observer*, Berlin, Springer-Verlag, 2011.

Stapp, Henry: Mind and Values in the Quantum Universe, in *Information and the Nature of Reality* (Eds. Paul Davies and Neils Henrik Gregerson), New York, Cambridge

University Press, 2011, 104-119.

Stapp, Henry: *Physical Review Letters*, Vol. 49, No. 20, 1982, 1470-76.

Stedman, Chris, Toxic Atheism Drives People Apart, in Salon.com,. Oct. 21, 2012.

Stenger, Victor.: *God—The Failed Hypothesis*, Amherst, New York, Prometheus Books, 2007.

Stenger, Victor: *God and the Folly of Faith*, Amherst, New York, Prometheus Books, 2012.

Stenger, Victor: *Physics and Psychics*, Amherst, New York, Prometheus Books, 1990.

Stiglitz, Joseph: *The Price of Inequality: How Today's Divided Society Threatens Our Future*, New York, W.W. Norton, 2012.

Talbot, Michael: *The Holographic Universe,* New York, Harper Collins, 1991.

Tarozzi, G.: Experimental Tests of the Properties of the Quantum Mechanical Wave Function, in *Lettere al Nuovo Cimento,* (42), No. 8, 1, 1985

Teilhard de Chardin, Pierre *The Future of Man,* Great Britain, Collins Books, 1970.

Teilhard de Chardin, Pierre: *The Divine Milieu,* New York, Harper Torchbooks, 1957.

Tertzakian, Peter: *A Thousand Barrels A Second,* New York, McGraw-Hill, 2007.

Tipler, Frank J.: *The Physics of Immortality,* New York, Anchor Books, 1994.

Tipler, Frank.: Extraterrestrial Beings Do Not Exist, in *Frontiers of Modern Physics* (Ed. Tony Rothman), New York, Dover Publications, Inc., 1985.

Tipler, Frank: *The Physics of Christianity,* New York, Doubleday, 2007.

von Mises, Richard: *Probability, Statistics and Truth,* New York, Dover Publications, 1957

Watts, Alan: *Behold The Spirit,* New York, Vintage Books, 1971.

Weber, Renee: The Physicist and The Mystic (interview), in *The Holographic Paradigm* (Ed. K. Wilber), Boston, New Science Library, 1982, 213-15.

Weinberg, Steven: *The Quantum Theory of Fields,* Cambridge, UK, Cambridge University Press, 1996, 167-177.

Whittrow, G.J.: *The Nature of Time*, Pelican Books, Great Britain, 1972.

Wilber, Ken: Psychologia Perennis *in Journal of Transpersonal Psychology 2.* 1975

Wildiers, Norbert Max: *An Introduction to Teilhard de Chardin, London,* Fontana Collins & Sons, Ltd., 1967

INDEX